P9-DDC-328

SWEET SPOT

SWEET SPOT

An Ice Cream Binge Across America

AMY ETTINGER

DUTTON

An imprint of Penguin Random House LLC
375 Hudson Street
New York, New York 10014

LIBRARY OF CONGRESS CATALOGING-IN-PUBLICATION DATA

Names: Ettinger, Amy, author.
Title: Sweet spot : an ice cream binge across America / Amy Ettinger.
Description: New York, New York : Dutton, [2016]
Identifiers: LCCN 2016049802 (print) | LCCN 2016055151 (ebook) |
ISBN 9781101984192 (hardback) | ISBN 9781101984208 (ebook)
Subjects: LCSH: Ice cream, ices, etc.—United States—History. | Ice cream, ices, etc.—Social aspects—United States. | Ettinger, Amy—Travel—United States. | United States—Social life and customs. | BISAC: COOKING / Essays. | HISTORY / United States / General.
Classification: LCC TX795 .E87 2016 (print) | LCC TX795 (ebook) |
DDC 641.86/2—dc23
LC record available at https://lccn.loc.gov/2016049802

Printed in the United States of America
1 3 5 7 9 10 8 6 4 2

BOOK DESIGN BY CASSANDRA GARRUZZO

To Julianna and Dan

CONTENTS

SWEET SPOT

Introduction

THE FOOD FIGHTERS

Family dinners in my house were a death match. My older brothers stabbed food off my plate and tore into the artichoke heart while I was still working my way through the rubbery outer leaves. I was given the tiny wings off a Cornish hen for protein during the Shabbat meal—and if I dared complain about the paltry portion, my mom might open up another can of soggy green beans and dump them into a bowl with their juices.

I was vulnerable but also learned to be ferocious, a girl who compensated for her youngest-child status with a pouf of extremely curly hair that added an extra half foot to my tiny frame. That's because everything had to be larger than life to get noticed in my family. When you are the youngest and also a girl, you learn to shout in a house where everyone is playing a different Beethoven concerto on separate instruments in their own rooms with the doors and windows flung wide-open.

And so I embraced a fierce persona and became a person

who had to holler and scream just to register at all. I was the identified patient, waving the red flag of family dysfunction. Compensation—seeking redress for slights, making up for my lowly family position—became an obsession. But what were my options? How to make up for such indignities? There is so much scheming in any given childhood, and I was outmaneuvered at every turn by my brothers. At the same time, there just was not much money to go around—not quite enough to satisfy our needs, let alone our insatiable appetites.

But there was one saving grace: Ice cream truly was a cheap thrill for my family. Dad would buy these immense tubs of generic-brand ice cream, the kind that came in gallon buckets with long, looping plastic handles; you could barely cram such a thing into the icebox, forcing the frozen peas and bags of broccoli into all kinds of contortions.

Ice cream didn't necessarily make misery go away, but it somehow made that misery taste so exquisite. What was better than crying in my room over a boy who didn't like me, with Abba's "The Winner Takes It All" oozing from the radio as I attacked a container of Jamoca Almond Fudge with a giant spoon?

Ice cream had the ability to add the words *So what?* to life's dire circumstances. So what if Dad screamed at his superiors and lost his seventeenth job? So what if he spent the day hunting for treasure with a beeping, stupendously dorky-looking bounty-hunter metal detector, which he'd swing back and forth on top of some sandy lawn or beachhead, seeking the million-dollar buried booty that would allow him to buy clothes that actually fit his kids? So what if he insisted that his two sons and little daughter trail right behind him on these woebegone adventures, lest he stumble upon Captain Kidd's buried treasure in the sandboxes of Pioneer Park and need their help carrying the sacks of gold doubloons that would allow them to buy a Silicon Valley McMansion?

Dad attempted to make up for his poor abilities as a provider by making oversize sundaes. Each one of them delivered a wallop of sweetness that could knock the sour things out of our lives for a few moments. His balm in those days was the Manhattan cocktail, that heady concoction of rye whiskey, vermouth, and grenadine, but he spared a few of those precious maraschino cherries to place atop his marvelous ice cream creations.

Ice cream snobs would laugh at these sundaes now, but they oozed with pleasure and sent me soaring. I would close my eyes and let the sugar surge through me, along with the sticky syrup. Perhaps that's why I expect so much of my ice cream now. What could compete with such blissful memories? There was something about those enormous tubs, the brilliant, almost iridescent color of those cherries, thanks to the glories of bright red artificial food coloring and the cataracts of Hershey's syrup that my father dumped on the ice cream. When I tucked into my sundae, I was eating a metaphor: heaps of vanilla-flavored hope and comfort rising from a jet-black lakelet of swirling chaos.

The enjoyment I got from those sundaes was far greater than anything I experienced later on even at the finest restaurants. The best work of Mario Batali, the finest examples of ethnic fusion, were pathetic comedowns compared to that cherry-vanilla-chocolate explosion. Part of it had to do with the fact that it was good eating. But it also had to do with the fact that sundaes had become not just a food but a place in my mind where the whole family remained together.

Ice cream is not just a snack but a circumstance and a time of year—frozen forever in memory. Unstructured summers when I whiled away the hours watching *As the World Turns* and jumping through the sprinkler were marked by trips with Mom to Fosters Freeze. Mom couldn't bake—even a dump-and-stir Betty Crocker mix was too much for her. We didn't own a single cake pan, pie tin, or baking dish. Every year on my birthday she bought me a Baskin-Robbins ice cream cake that she served on a musical rotating dish (she even outsourced the singing of "Happy Birthday").

The author enjoying her annual ice cream birthday cake at her childhood home in Cupertino, California.

Mom was a feminist who wanted to work full-time and never bake for her kids. Grandma didn't bake either, except for a dreaded

Passover candy with honey and nuts that could break one's teeth. In fact it did. A neighbor once broke a molar on it. But none of that mattered on long summer afternoons, when I could always grab hold of Mom's hand and walk her down to the Fosters Freeze.

School was out. No girls were excluding me from the Recess Club. Ice cream was a permanent recess. As long as my ice cream cone lasted, Alice Cooper's dream had come true; school was out forever. Mom, her attention always diverted to the eldest, the cello-playing genius, or the glad-handing middle child, was mine alone. The sweetest, saddest thing about these moments was their evanescence; the high and the comfort went away all too soon, which only raised the value and the urgency of the next big fix.

ICE CREAM CAKE BY THE OCEAN

¾ cup (1½ sticks) butter
1½ cups water
2 cups sugar
1 teaspoon vanilla extract
Pinch of salt
2 eggs, beaten
½ cup unsweetened cocoa
2 teaspoons baking soda
2 cups all-purpose flour
1 quart vanilla bean ice cream
2 8-ounce containers Cool Whip

- Preheat the oven to 350°F. Grease a 10-by-15-inch non-stick pan.
- Cut the butter into 4 pieces. Boil the water. Remove the water from the heat, immediately add the butter, and stir until it melts. Add the sugar, vanilla, and salt. Allow the mixture to cool until it is warm, and then mix in the eggs.
- In a separate bowl, combine the cocoa, baking soda, and flour. Stir in the butter-egg mixture, making sure there are no dry clumps. Spread the batter evenly in the prepared pan.
- Bake for 30 to 35 minutes. Insert a fork to test doneness; the fork should come out clean. (Be careful not to overbake! The cake should be tender.) Remove from the oven. Allow the cake to cool for at least 1 hour.

- Cut the cake in half widthwise; you should have two evenly sized stackable pieces.
- Place the cake halves on two separate plates, in your freezer, for 1 hour. Slather the ice cream on top of one of the pieces, making sure the ice cream goes all the way to the edges. Stick the other cake half on top of the ice cream layer, and slather the top and sides of the cake with the Cool Whip (and don't try to substitute whipped cream, because it won't freeze as well). Freeze your ice cream cake for at least 4 hours before serving. This treat will keep for several days. In fact, the flavor vastly improves if you let it sit for 24 hours or so before eating.

1.

CONSUME MASS QUANTITIES

I keep between fifteen and thirty dollars' worth of ice cream in my freezer at all times. Let me be clear: This ice cream is not for guests, and most of it will never be consumed by anyone. These pints are my emergency backup system in case the nearby San Lorenzo River jumps the levee and floods the city of Santa Cruz or a new crack opens along the Loma Prieta segment of the San Andreas Fault. I prefer my ice cream fresh, and I detest the little ice hairs that form when a carton has been left in the back of the icebox too long. But when I've spent a long day chaperoning twenty kids on a four-hour kindergarten field trip to some buggy swamp, museum, or waste-reclamation center, I'm not above scraping tiny icicles off the top and letting a bowl of Old Tyme Vanilla sit out for five minutes until it thaws to an acceptable degree. Then I will devour it in less than two minutes. On any given day I have so many containers of ice cream stacked in my freezer, I can't find the bread, broccoli, unshelled soybeans, or other staples my family needs to survive. If we're low on freezer space, I sometimes shove these lowly vegetables in the trash without telling anyone. I've allowed the ice cream to dominate; pints and quarts are stacked vertically and shoved into crevices horizontally. Each time I open the freezer doors, a quart of vanilla tumbles to the floor, landing on my foot.

An ice cream maker, left over from my stash of wedding gifts, occupies a third of my freezer. It has traveled across the country with me *twice.* My husband wishes I would haul it out of there and put it in the cabinet. That is out of the question. In order to make ice cream, the machine must be kept frozen for at least twenty-four hours. On any given night, I could wake up with a craving for rum raisin ice cream, the incapacitating kind, soaked with boozy flavor. Most store-bought rum raisin is ersatz; you could eat seven gallons of the stuff and not feel the slightest buzz. My homemade version could knock you out cold in a single scoop. I like to think of it as a twenty-first-century "remedy"—like the drug-filled concoctions at unscrupulous Victorian-era pharmacy soda fountains. My rum-soaked concoction once sent my husband careening into our living room furniture.

I also make a vanilla that's more of a frozen custard, an eggier version with real Tahitian vanilla and a dense consistency, very different from the whipped-cream confections you will find in most ice creams. I have taste-tested dozens of store-bought pints and can proudly say that mine is the perfect topping for vodka-crusted apple pie.

Here are a few more facts I'm only vaguely ashamed to admit: I live within walking distance of three high-end supermarkets that carry half a dozen artisanal brands and several locally made pints. I visit one of the shops at least daily, checking on the supply of my favorite flavors. I have also "liked" the local ice cream parlors on Facebook just to track their daily flavors on my news feeds. One local creamery has four different scoop shops but, in a nod to Santa Cruz's laid-back style, has an online listing for flavors in just one of those shops. As a result I must set aside ten to fifteen minutes after dinner on summer nights just to call around and see which has the dark chocolate salted caramel.

I understand the hypocrisy of my choices. While I limit my daughter's consumption of sugar to one dessert a day or less, including juice drinks, I have always thought that the one and only benefit of being an adult is that I can choose what I put in my mouth. If I must walk an extra thirty minutes a day or suffer through a Jillian Michaels video twice a week to offset my high calorie intake, so be it. I am neither proud nor ashamed of the amount of time and energy I spend on my preoccupation with ice cream.

After all, I share an obsession with millions of other Americans. Every man, woman, and child in this nation consumes, on average, almost twenty-two pounds of ice cream per year.[1] That works out to be roughly 26,400 calories' worth of ice cream. If I'm in some way responsible for helping make this country the world leader[2] in consumption of frozen treats larded with mouthwatering butterfat, I happily accept that honor.

Our collective obsession with ice cream goes all the way back to our founding fathers. If my ice cream consumption seems outrageous, consider George Washington, who spent two hundred dollars on ice cream during the summer of 1790.

That's the equivalent of about three thousand bucks today, if you factor in inflation.[3] Thomas Jefferson, whose Declaration of Independence is one of the greatest pieces of persuasive and declarative writings in history, also wrote the first American ice cream recipe, a French-inspired vanilla dessert that called for two bottles of cream, six egg yolks, and half a pound of sugar. Jefferson even had an icehouse built at Monticello, in large part because he wanted to keep his treats from turning into a puddle of goo.[4]

"Man and woman eating giant ice cream cone." *The New York Public Library Digital Collections. 1935–1945.*

My almost daily ice cream consumption has warped my mind and reset my taste buds. Part of the problem is that I eat so much of it—and ice cream is more like a drug than any other food. Researchers have studied the brains of addicts like me and have found that the more ice cream you eat, the more you have to eat it to regain that "high." Eat too much high-fat or high-sugar food and it's harder to feel that pleasure reward activate in your brain. "This down-regulation pattern is seen with frequent drug use, where the more an individual uses the drug, the less reward they receive from using it," according to Dr. Kyle Burger, coauthor of the study conducted by the Oregon Research Institute, which focuses on human behavior in relation to health issues, including obesity. "Repeated, overconsumption of high-fat or high-sugar foods may alter how the brain responds to those foods in a way that perpetuates further intake."[5] This high-fat drug has been in my bloodstream for as long as I can remember.

But I've become more fussy about my fixes as the years have passed.

I can remember eating generic Rocky Road with the jagged little nuts, the sticky and cloying chocolate, and those slippery, well-chilled little indestructible marshmallows that squeaked between my teeth like cheese curds. It makes no sense now, but I loved every bite. I was easy to please. Most anything could transport me, even my father's squat and staticky black-and-white TV set, in front of which I'd find myself swept away by *Space: 1999,* a television program featuring Barbara Bain and Martin Landau clinging to the moon as it hurtles through outer space, having gone off its orbital rails thanks to exploding nuclear waste.

How did I grow up into an ice cream snob?

It isn't just my fault. Part of the problem is social conditioning and changing standards. To be more specific, my taste buds and my brain were forever altered by the introduction of "gourmet" Ben & Jerry's flavors in the 1980s.

One winter afternoon I had a chance to talk with one of the

men who blew up my taste buds—Jerry Greenfield, the Jerry in Ben & Jerry's.

"The universe of Ben & Jerry's flavors opened a whole other universe," he told me during a phone chat while he was on vacation in Austin, Texas. Jerry gives all the credit for the ice cream renaissance to his cohort, Ben Cohen. In fact, Jerry tells me that his partner will be remembered as the greatest ice cream flavor creator ever. I can't help it—I laugh with enthusiasm and giddiness to be talking this kind of history with one of modern ice cream's founding fathers.

"You can laugh if you want, but it's true," he admonished.

His scolding surprised me. He was just a bit more prickly than I imagined he'd be. "But . . . don't you think people will remember you the same way?" I asked him. He was quiet, as if taken aback at the reminder of his own legacy in the ice cream world.

"I never created a flavor," he admitted. "I was making ice cream to Ben's specifications and taste."

During all my college evenings spent eating Phish Food and watching *Friends,* I imagined Jerry to be a bit more creative, free-spirited, and mellow, the type of person who would allow you to weep on his shoulder after a bad breakup. But there's the difference between the product and the person who creates the product. It was the tubs of sugar and fat that brought me comfort, not the man himself.

Jerry said he grew up eating supermarket brands like Breyers, which was considered a classy choice in the 1950s and 1960s because of its "all natural" ingredients. Before Ben & Jerry's, the ice cream scene was much more staid, consistent, and predictable—and brands like Breyers exemplified comforting, unchallenging food choices and convenience at a time when most Americans lived in daily fear of nuclear incineration at the hands of the Soviet Union. Without Breyers and other brands setting the tone, people like Ben and Jerry would have had no context for their acts of insurrection.

Breyers dates back to 1866, when William Breyer started the business by making ice cream in his kitchen and delivering it by horse-drawn wagon in Philadelphia. Bassetts Ice Cream—launched in 1861—actually predates Breyers as America's oldest ice cream company. But Bassetts, which still sells its spectacular eggless Philadelphia-style flavors at the Reading Terminal Market and select retail spots, never had the distribution success that Breyers enjoyed, and Breyers became the bestselling American ice cream for generations.

West Coast dwellers have enjoyed the similarly named Dreyer's. The brand, founded in 1928 by Joseph Edy and William Dreyer, was originally named Edy's, a name that stuck until 1948, when Dreyer built a large ice cream factory in Oakland and changed the company name. Dreyer's still markets its ice cream as Edy's on the East Coast, but the name change has caused confusion in other parts of the country. In the 1980s, the Breyers and Dreyer's companies had a bitter war over shelf space in Southern California's supermarket cases after Breyers, based on the East Coast, started selling its merchandise out west.

It's not surprising the two businesses competed with each other so much. Sometimes I feel like I've spent half my life trying to tell these brands apart in the supermarket freezer section. No question about it: Breyers and Dreyer's are, truly, the Tweedledee and Tweedledum of mass-produced ice cream. And if you aren't confusing the brands, you will spend your time struggling with their varying strategies regarding punctuation. Breyers does not carry a possessive, while Dreyer's, for some nefarious reason, has an apostrophe after the *r*.

When I am buying ice cream, the last thing I want to feel is confused. Perhaps out of hurt pride or a wish for revenge, Breyers, in vintage 1980s commercials, accused Dreyer's of using less-than-natural ingredients, including corn syrup. In a rather lame effort to avoid mix-ups, Breyers used to have advertisements proclaiming that its name was "Breyers with a B."[6]

If you wanted more variety, you needed to go to a scoop shop, like Baskin-Robbins, which offered its famous thirty-one flavors. Then, in 1960, Reuben Mattus, a Bronx-based street peddler of homemade ice creams, decided to add some intrigue and complication to this rather boring ice cream landscape. After pushing his wares in a horse-drawn wagon on hot, dirty avenues for years, he decided to rebrand. He and his wife, Rose, came up with the exotic-sounding, and utterly meaningless, name of Häagen-Dazs and started charging premium prices for the faux-Danish product. The umlaut hanging over that first *a* added a frisson of Scandinavian freshness and wholesomeness, conjuring up images of pristine fjords, bottomless gorges, and waves crashing against the Baltic coast, never mind the fact that Danes don't use umlauts.[7] It was, in other words, an utterly noncontextual and arguably bonkers marketing maneuver. But it worked. Mattus gained notice. Suddenly people were willing to pay more for the high-butterfat, low-air ice cream. Mattus had three flavors at first: vanilla, chocolate, and coffee.

"When I came out with Häagen-Dazs, the quality of ice cream

had deteriorated to the point that it was just sweet and cold," Mattus told *The New York Times.* "Ice cream had become cheaper and cheaper, so I just went the opposite way."[8] A few pseudo-Nordic copycats hit the ice cream scene not long after. Richard Smith created a shell corporation in Sweden and started Frusen Glädjé out of a plant in Utica, New York.

My mom often walked around the house repeating the tag lines of Frusen Glädjé commercials: "If you don't feel guilty, it wasn't that good" and "Who ate all the Frusen Glädjé?" (The name means "Frozen Joy" in Swedish.) Häagen-Dazs sued unsuccessfully in 1980 to stop Frusen Glädjé from using a Scandinavian-themed name to market their product. Häagen-Dazs accused them of "umlaut infringement," according to *The New York Times;* the plaintiffs pointed out that both Häagen-Dazs and Frusen Glädjé carried an umlaut over the first *a*'s in their names. That ploy didn't work; Frusen Glädjé prevailed. But Häagen-Dazs ultimately won our bellies.[9] Who ate all the Frusen Glädjé? I guess we all did. After the Frusen Glädjé license was sold off, initially to Kraft, and then to Unilever, the brand vanished from the marketplace completely.[10]

Ice cream imitators come and go, but true innovators are rare. One of the few entrepreneurs who truly deserves the term *innovator and pioneer* is Steve Herrell. Herrell's claim to fame: inventor of ice cream with chunks of Heath English Toffee Bar mixed into it. Herrell, like so many who go into the ice cream business, was determined to work for himself. He experimented with adding inclusions to ice cream, like Oreo cookies and Heath Bars, and called them mix-ins.

Then came Ben and Jerry. The two schlubby hippies gave me hope that there was more to life than bad synth pop, scrunchies, and *Falcon Crest.* Suddenly I could eat ice cream with pretzels in it! I woke up one day to find that thirty-one flavors were no longer enough.

"When I think of the ice cream titans, I think of Steve Herrell, Reuben Mattus, and Ben," said Jerry.

Then I asked him the question that has haunted me for the past thirty years. How did Ben and Jerry think to add cookie dough to ice cream?

It turns out that the creation of one of the greatest culinary inventions in the late twentieth century was pure happenstance.

"We were baking cookies on the side," said Jerry. "The guy who was making cookies turned to the guy who was making ice cream and wondered what would happen if he put raw cookie dough in."

This real-life scenario reminded me of the old absurdist commercials for Reese's Peanut Butter Cups, featuring a young actress named Diane Franklin, who went on to star in *The Last American Virgin.* Franklin is walking down the street holding a tub of peanut butter and runs straight into a man holding a bar of chocolate, causing mutual outrage. "Hey, you got your chocolate in my peanut butter!" she complains. "You got your peanut butter in my chocolate," he counters.

Once the cookie-dough-flavored Pandora's box was opened, Gen Xers were not going back to the bizarrely cheap and curiously cylindrical Thrifty Ice Cream scoops from Rite Aid. The more ice cream I eat, the more discerning I become. As an adult faced with childcare headaches and lingering student loans, I want my treats to be picture-perfect pleasure-delivery systems. I'm willing to pay extra, to travel more, for the perfect scoop that will transport me back to the simpler times of childhood—when I was able to find comfort in the cold sweetness of a cone.

Ben & Jerry's changed the landscape of American ice cream and continues to have an impact, even after the company's sale to Unilever. After all, Jerry said Ben & Jerry's was never meant to be an "artisanal brand." It's never been about "delicate flavors" . . . "Ben has a somewhat more traditional sense of ice cream being cookies and candies and those types of inclusions," Jerry told me. It's one thing to mix in crunchy treats that get lumped into the "junk food" category. It is quite another to have olive oil–infused ice cream, something Ben & Jerry's never tried. But Jerry added that Ben's "traditional" culinary tastes are his only nod to conventional thinking.

"He's one of the most untraditional people I know," he said.

That quirkiness continues to set Ben & Jerry's apart, even if the flavors, these days, are nothing shocking. Part of it has to do with the scale of the operation. Widespread distribution is a game changer when it comes to flavors, said Jerry. When you are marketing all across the country, you have to find a middle ground for the American palate.

"You can be a lot more creative in an ice cream shop," said Jerry. "You can make weird and interesting flavors. You can be as experimental and creative as you want to be if you're only making five gallons."

As for Ben & Jerry's, they had no choice but to appeal to the broadest customer base, with just enough marketing edge that they could cater to liberal ice cream tasters without making red-state ice cream lovers run for the hills. Could it be that the hippies who were so radical in the seventies have, somehow, become the status quo—the new vanilla of the ice cream world? If this is true, then Ben & Jerry's at least deserves credit for opening the door for all those tatted-up, finicky microcelebrity chefs in small shops who are pushing our taste bud limits almost to the breaking point, coming up with some of the most insane flavors ever to appear in an American ice cream shop.

In doing so, Ben & Jerry's helped pave the way for the artisanal ice cream wars that are breaking out in every state of the union today.

2.

IT'S ALL ABOUT THE BASE

I walked down to the Mission Hill Creamery, my neighborhood ice cream shop, to gain a better understanding of America's current obsession with artisanal ice cream. The owner, Dave Kumec, is in a long-standing cold war with another ice cream maker in Santa Cruz.

Kumec looks a bit like Clark Kent with his glasses and wiry frame. Also, he has a history of dressing up in skintight superhero costumes for Halloween, while delivering free scoops to the masses of kids who trick-or-treat at the shop each year. But the way Kumec sees it, that's just the beginning of the freebies.

Kumec explained to me how crazy things have gotten in my small town, where he is working fourteen-plus-hour days and enduring car accidents, family resentments, and carpal tunnel syndrome to build a frozen empire. He told me he makes ice cream for free. Kumec hasn't given himself a paycheck since he opened the Mission Hill Creamery. Some of his signature flavors—like pistachio—cost more to make than he can possibly charge for them. "I want to be the best even if it's not lucrative," he said.

The pistachio flavor is on the menu of the Mission Hill Creamery every Friday, and when I tell him it's my family's favorite, he winces—as if our pleasure is a reminder of his own deprivation.

I get some kind of perverse enjoyment when I hear about the sacrifice that's gone into producing it. Something that good shouldn't be easy or painless to make.

Each week the pistachio flavor flares the amygdala center in my brain. The scoop is like whipped and frozen nut butter, with just a hint of salt. A kid's scoop is dense and flavorful enough to set off the pleasure center in my brain—the cavewoman instinct that makes me crave the perfect combination of nut protein and fats to get me through the long winter. There are tiny chopped pistachios mixed in—the smell reminds me of the roasted-nut candy counters they used to have at department stores where you could buy your peanuts, cashews, and filberts roasted to order on the spot, enrobed in white, dark, or milk chocolate, and sold by the pound as bridge mix.

Kumec tried to explain the logic behind continuing to sell the weekly loss leader.

He learned to make pistachio gelato with Bronte pistachios, which grow in volcanic soil in Sicily northwest of Mount Etna. The farmers of the region claim that they harvest the pistachios only every two years. The nuts sell for seventy-eight dollars a pound in the United States. The paste that's a key part of the recipe is priced at a hundred dollars a pound—roughly the street value of Jamaican cannabis.

"I'd need to sell the pints for thirteen to fourteen dollars at the supermarket—at that price we're sort of breaking even," said Kumec.

The cost of pistachios has forced Kumec to discontinue the flavor on several occasions. He announced these decisions in agonized Facebook postings: "This year (this week), the price of pistachios and hazelnuts have doubled again. Unfortunately, unless the price comes back down, it doesn't make sense to make our famous pistachio ice cream, even on Fridays. So, until further notice, we will no longer be able to offer Pistachio ice cream. We still have a little bit of pistachios and some hazelnuts. We will make a few more batches. Yes, we are sad!"

Reading the news about the pistachio flavor put me into hoarder mode—I was tempted to run out and fill my freezer. Other ice cream makers in town don't seem to notice or care about the nut price hike. They just go on cranking out the pistachio pints, using Santa Barbara–grown nuts. Not Kumec. "I can't compromise and put something in half as good."

But Kumec is a businessman, and a year after discontinuing the flavor he caved to pressure from the public and brought back California Pistachio. He wasn't as happy with its flavor, but he didn't feel he could compete without having a pistachio on the menu. I tasted it and had to admit it had a chalky texture that hinted of concession.

As a writer married to a writer, I'm intimately familiar with the psyche of a tortured artist. When Kumec talked about the process of ice cream making, I felt like I'd met a kindred spirit.

The stakes are high for Kumec to succeed. He's not an artist—he's a businessman who has traded in a high-profile tech career and invested everything in his creamery. He's able to avoid homelessness because of the financial support of his wife—who works in the city's fire department.

Kumec said he isn't running a nonprofit. He's willing to "live poor" if it means he will rise above what he considers the mediocrity of the small-town competition, which seems to infuriate him. It's in his face—literally. His main artisanal ice cream rival is the Penny Ice Creamery, which opened its doors six weeks after Kumec started his business in 2010. The Penny Ice Creamery made headlines because it is one of the few ice cream shops in California that makes its own base—the egg-dairy-sugar mixture that's the main ingredient in all ice cream products. The base is mixed with attention-grabbing ingredients to create flavors like Whiskey Custard, Black Sesame, and Juniper Lime.

By every indication, the competition is winning. The owners of the Penny Ice Creamery, Kendra Baker and Zachary Davis, also opened a full-service restaurant, Assembly, directly across the street from Kumec's storefront. Kumec glanced over at Assembly as he talked to me, a nervous twitch that looks like a long-ingrained habit, as if he must keep his eyes on it to stop Baker and Davis from encroaching on even more of his territory.

Kumec's strategy involves trying to beat the competition through his wholesale distribution—which he hopes to double in a year. He even hired Chef Chris, a bearded, tattooed competitive CrossFitter who does not eat ice cream.

I finally worked up the nerve to ask Dave for a behind-the-scenes tour. As the day approached, the excitement was almost too much for me to bear; as a kid, I imagined Oompa Loompas dressed in tiny parkas and beanies to stay warm as they created new flavors. On a rainy winter day I met Chef Chris and Dave in the back of the store to watch them work. I thought, at the very least, that the scene behind the doors would be like the inside of an ice cream freezer at a supermarket—with pints or bins of different flavors just waiting to be sampled. Imagine my surprise when I walked into a place that looked so clean, brightly lit, and aseptic that it resembled an urgent care facility, which in a sense it was for ice cream zombies like me. The kitchen had stainless steel counters, a sink, and an ice cream maker. To my disappointment there was no ice cream in sight. The room wasn't even cold. I started sweating through my rain parka. The environment seemed, in fact, hostile to ice cream's survival. Though I didn't say anything about my shock, it was profound; truly, the veil of Maya had been pierced, and I wondered if it would ever be repaired.

But, as I soon found out, the jolting surprises were just getting started.

On the whiteboard was a list of all the flavors that needed to be produced that day—along with a bucket list of future flavors and potential names. Kumec likes to crowdsource flavor names; for instance, a tasty vanilla-with-chocolate-chunk mix is named after a customer who suggested the treat. Other names, like Laurel Street Construction—a twist on the traditional Rocky Road, referring to a steep and traffic-heavy street near downtown Santa Cruz—are works in progress.

The next surprise took place while Dave and Chris were showing me a specialty flavor in progress—dark chocolate made with blueberry compote. This was a special order they were making to woo a client, Driscoll's, a berry-growing giant in Watsonville, not far from Santa Cruz. I could tell Dave was ambivalent about this creation, which he made with the help of a gleaming twenty-three-thousand-dollar Emery Thompson machine, the standard high-end freezer-mixer combo you will find in artisanal ice cream places all over the United States. "I think it would work better with milk chocolate," Dave said. "But you know what they say—the customer is always right."

I was very surprised that Dave, this visionary and maverick, would ever compromise with anyone for any reason. But a far bigger surprise came when Chef Chris grabbed hold of two big containers full of a milky liquid and prepared to add it to the machine. Wait, I wondered. What is that stuff, anyway? Why wasn't he cracking open a bunch of newly laid cage-free eggs and boiling cartons of fresh-squeezed milk? "This is a good time to talk about the base," Dave said.

The what? I thought.

"We buy our base from Straus. It's the best in the area."

I'd simply assumed that Kumec and all other artisanal ice cream makers everywhere made the creamy base that serves as the body of the ice cream—that one-of-a-kind amalgam of egg, butterfat, milk, sugar, and flavoring that makes a good ice cream coat your tongue and melt slowly in the sun. When you look up any ice cream recipe, you'll find that 99 percent of the ingredients are for the custard base—and everything else is just flavoring or nut and fruit texture. Vanilla ice cream is the most popular flavor on the planet. If you eliminated the need to make, mix, and prepare ingredients for the base from an ice cream recipe, all you would need to do was add vanilla, put it all in an ice cream maker, and harden it in a freezer.

But Kumec explained to me that his particular "base" came premade, prepasteurized, and prepackaged from Straus Family Creamery, a highly prestigious dairy in Northern California.

My dismayed facial expressions must have given me away.

Kumec tried to alleviate my concerns with what sounded a bit too much like a well-rehearsed, prepared speech, reminding me of a rainy summer day on the Olympic Peninsula in Washington, when we had nowhere to stay, and my daughter wanted me to rent a cottage for 350 dollars a night. Annoyed, I patiently told her it looked like an army barracks and was way out of our price range. Her response was, "I don't mind."

"Straus provides us with the same product with every order," Kumec explained. "We have more control over the product because the base is the same every time."

I was not sure how to react. Part of me wondered if I was making too much of this. Did the backstory of an ice cream make any difference if it tasted wonderful? Still, it felt like a betrayal. It was like the moment at my daughter's school when I fell all over myself praising another mother's class picnic chicken salad, only to find out she'd purchased a small bucket of the stuff from Costco. Not only that, but this revelation called into question everything else I thought I knew about my sense of good taste.

Chef Chris noticed my discomfort.

"Was Picasso less of an artist because he didn't make his own paint?" he asked.

He had a valid point, but when I brought up the argument that creating your own base allowed for more control—strongly implying that *control* meant shortcuts—Kumec let loose with a laugh. "I can't tell you how many different arguments I've heard. Compare our products. I think you'll find that ours is more delicious and more consistent."

Immediately my thoughts turned to his archrival, the Penny Ice Creamery. Their pasteurizer and lack of a prebought base was their big selling point. Didn't it drive him crazy, knowing they had a piece of machinery he lacked?

"The Penny Creamery has its own pasteurizer," Kumec said. "Personally, I don't think it makes better ice cream." I nodded in agreement forcefully, my journalistic impartiality forgotten. Here's the thing: I have always *wanted* to like the Penny Ice Creamery's ice cream more than I actually do. As a mouthfeel obsessive, I find it a touch too icy, and sometimes flavorless. Even though Baker creates highly adventurous-sounding flavors, including Black Sesame, Brown Butter Spiced Pumpkin Seed, and Whiskey Custard, the ice cream—to my palate, at least—needs a bolder flavor punch.

Kumec and other base-buying ice cream makers are hemmed in by superstrict regulations. Kumec clearly understands the rules—and knows that ignoring them can have disastrous results. In 2011, the Illinois Department of Public Health cracked down on Chicago-based artisanal ice cream maker Kris Williams Swanberg. Swanberg closed her ice cream business after being offered the difficult choice of either switching to premade ice cream mix or buying a pasteurizer and getting a dairy license. Although her ice cream samples had bacterial levels that were deemed safe, the results were not enough to appease state officials, and her business closed. Things seemed to have turned out okay for Swanberg, a filmmaker married to Joe Swanberg, who directed *Happy Christmas* and starred in the indie horror film *You're Next.* The pair are the only husband-and-wife team to have separate feature films premiere at the Sundance Film Festival. Still, I could not help but wonder what culinary heights she might have reached if only she'd found a way to keep her ice cream business going.

Pasteurization is a process that involves using heat to destroy microorganisms that can sicken consumers and make food, wine, and beer taste horrible. With his keen understanding of germ theory, the French microbiologist Louis Pasteur helped rescue the wine industry from financial ruin in the 1860s. By puzzling out the connection between microbes and spoiling, he figured out what was fouling all those bottles and making customers gag. His solution was simple: To stop these critters from ruining their products, winemakers could heat their grape juice to a temperature of 120 to 140 degrees Fahrenheit. Later, Pasteur applied this same principle to the brewing process. These days, winemakers have little use for pasteurization because it wreaks havoc with the flavor of wine. A German chemist named Franz von Soxhlet first advocated pasteurizing bottled milk in 1886. The practice caught on in Europe in the late nineteenth century. Dairies in the United States started pasteurizing in the early twentieth century. Chicago was the first American city that made milk pasteurization mandatory.

Most milk is heated for just fifteen seconds at 161 degrees Fahrenheit. But ice cream base, with its higher fat content and egg yolks, must be pasteurized for a longer period of time—either for thirty minutes at 155 degrees Fahrenheit or twenty-five seconds at 175 degrees Fahrenheit. That's why artisanal ice cream makers can't get away with just using pasteurized milk or cream. The whole mix needs to be pasteurized (requiring an expensive pasteurizer or buying premade mix). Each state gets to oversee these regulations. In California, any ice cream shop that sells more than a thousand gallons of ice cream per year needs its own "clean room."

The laws about pasteurization in the United States hearken back to the early twentieth century, when people died from milk-borne illnesses—including listeria, salmonella, and E. coli. Flipping through some musty old newspaper clippings about ice cream in the 1920s, I could not believe how many headlines screamed about kids taking ill from frozen dairy treats. The majority of public health professionals and healthcare providers consider pasteurization to be one of the most effective food-safety interventions in history.

I asked Kumec if he wished he could make his own base, and he looked wistful. "Ice cream base is my artistic canvas," said Kumec. "But what can you do? I wasn't born with a silver spoon in my mouth."

While I was speaking with him, I wondered if a sense of being the persecuted underdog pervaded Kumec's psychology. He works ten to fourteen hours a day, six or seven days a week, roughly the same work hours as a flight-deck control officer on an aircraft carrier. He personally delivers ice cream to stores all around the Bay Area—in a hundred-mile radius that reaches from Monterey to San Francisco. I've been at coffee shops around town and seen him dressed in a Mission Creamery T-shirt, jeans, sneakers, and a Giants baseball cap, making deliveries.

This is grunt work he doesn't get paid for, and part of his whatever-it-takes business mentality.

To make matters worse, the long hours seem to have impacted his concentration. He has a bad habit of getting in accidents, having totaled two delivery trucks trying to get his wholesale business going.

"I work harder than any of the other ice cream makers in town," he told me. On any given day his workload might include scouring the local farmers' market for fruit, spending five to six hours preparing the fruit, filling pints with a spatula, or scooping ice cream himself on busy weekday afternoons. He looked jittery about trying to impress Driscoll's, the berry-growing giant that commissioned the chocolate-fruit flavor. Carefully he checked the machine one last time to make sure it was cleaned and ready to go. He was surprised when brown sludge—remnants from an earlier batch of chocolate—escaped the hatch. He motioned to Chris to get the remnants cleaned up.

Dave gave the go-ahead to begin ice cream making, and Chris grabbed the gallons of Straus.

After he emptied the two gallons of ready-made base, he discussed with Dave the best speed for the new flavor. American ice cream often contains 50 percent air. Chris said that when he first started making ice cream a few years back, his rookie mistake was that he would whip too much air into the product. The result was fluffy ice cream.

All the Mission Hill recipes are kept in a black three-ring binder—with proprietary information on whipping speed. Dave picked the binder up and thumbed through it. Of course, I was dying to have a peep. "I'm not going to share these with you," Dave said.

Once again I thought, helplessly, of Willy Wonka and his supersecrecy, and how he closed his whole factory down to avoid the spies of his archenemy, Slugworth. In Kumec's shop, the supersecret recipes include information on how long each flavor should be whipped—chocolate, for instance, must be beaten longer than vanilla because of the higher fat content—and how long the Emery Thompson has remained idle. Dave and Chris set the speed and then the timer for seven minutes. "You really have to listen to the machine," Dave said. "When it starts to sound like laundry, then you know the ice cream is ready."

While the Emery Thompson whirled and spun Dave's dark chocolate and Straus's base, Dave stirred up the tub of bobbing blueberries. He grabbed the empty tubs, ready for filling. Seven minutes later, Chef Chris turned off the machine.

He waited a moment, and then, when Dave gave him the okay, he opened the hatch of the machine that allows a driblet of chocolate ice cream to slide down the metal shoot. It was gloppy and left a smeary residue.

"It's not ready," Dave said, starting the Emery Thompson up again.

After a few more minutes, he gave it another try. This time the core sample was firmer—it looked a little like chocolate cream cheese—and Kumec declared it done.

Chris opened the hatch and allowed the chocolate mixture to fill up a third of the bucket. Then he added a layer of blueberry compote, opened the hatch, and filled another third. After the last layer of blueberry mix was added, Dave took it to the counter near where I was standing, grabbed a white metal spatula, and swirled the blueberry and chocolate together in three gentle strokes. "Get a couple of tasting spoons," he told Chris.

He presented me with a metal spoon. This was more what I imagined the kitchen of an ice cream shop to be like—constant access to the fresh product. I dug my spoon into the large tub and stuck it in my mouth. The ice cream felt like soft-serve. The blueberry mix had been swirled in so that just a slight taste of the berry was infused with the chocolate. Chris transferred the tub to the batch freezer, where it would harden to the perfect consistency that Mission Hill is known for.

There were still half a dozen flavors to make that day—and it was already four P.M. Dave left the rest of the day's ice cream production to Chris and went to go pay bills. His day, in many ways, was just beginning.

Creating ice cream the way he does is laborious—but Kumec's goal, in all this strenuous work, is not to transport ice cream out of the realm of kids and hand it over to a bunch of suburban sophisticates. His process is more like the opposite—trying to disarm sophisticated adults and turn them into children again.

"Sometimes we have older people who come in, and one person will take a lick and then look at the other person, and then they get the look of being two years old again."

Bringing people to that childlike state is the reason he opened his business and the reason he continues despite the long hours and the financial hardships.

It's also the reason he has a gimlet eye for flavors that are so wild and edgy, they might leave kindergarteners in a state of confusion. He insists that a visit to the Penny Creamery is more of an "adult experience." Flavors like Celery and Black Sesame are interesting for the palate, but they don't transport us back to our youth.

"I don't put creativity over the emotional experience," said Kumec.

But other people apparently do. The Penny has three storefronts (not including Assembly). Lines on a weekday afternoon are usually out the door.

Days later, I was still reeling from Kumec's revelation about his ice cream base. I still felt ambivalent—convinced of the superior quality of the product, but still feeling let down, maybe even duped, by all the American creameries who don't sweat and struggle to put their own bases together. For months I'd been telling people that Mission Hill is the greatest ice cream around, but the truth is that the Penny Creamery is creating a product from scratch. The only way to get more authentic is if they sat there with a stool and a pail and milked the cows themselves.

In other words, I needed to give them another try, even though purchasing a cone from them is my definition of heartbreak—expectation followed by disappointment, ending in a feeling of subdued helplessness.

On a weekday afternoon I took my daughter to sample the flavors at Penny. We lined up to taste the oatmeal cookie flavor and a cherry vanilla concoction.

It was better than I remembered—with a less icy mouthfeel. The flavor was intensified by the knowledge that the base was made painstakingly from scratch but not good enough to entice me to purchase even a kid's scoop.

I decided to talk to Baker to understand her need to create her own base and to see if she suffers the same torments that plague Kumec. But I was suddenly transported back to the dynamics of junior high. What if Kumec saw me talking to Baker and felt betrayed? What if he barred me from his ice cream shop? Suppose I never got to taste his astoundingly wonderful pistachio ice cream so long as I lived? I needed to take the risk.

I arranged a meeting with Baker at Assembly—her fancy full-service restaurant across the street from Mission Hill. She chose the risky time of eleven A.M.—Kumec's shop doesn't open until noon—and I parked on a side street and snuck (yes, I'm not ashamed to admit it) into the restaurant.

Baker was huddled at a corner table with her restaurant manager and business partner. The trio was silently typing away on their MacBooks—like a mini writers' grotto.

At exactly eleven A.M. she rose to greet me. I noticed she was nine months pregnant. She smiled, but her greeting was a bit icy—as if she'd spent a little too much time around her own product.

Baker was a pastry chef at Los Gatos restaurant Manresa and Bar Tartine in San Francisco and developed her ideas for ice cream flavors while working on other chefs' menus. She teamed up with Zach Davis and launched the Penny with a forty-thousand-dollar investment by the owners, as well as sixty thousand dollars from investors, all of whom were family or friends. A critical component of the business start-up was a 250,000-dollar Small Business Administration 7(a) loan with a

90 percent guarantee under the American Recovery and Reinvestment Act.

You can see Baker and Davis thanking President Obama in a YouTube video.[11] It's gotten more than a hundred thousand hits. In 2011, it got the attention of Vice President Joe Biden, who called up the shop and uttered the exuberant—but easily misconstrued—line, "I'm coming for ice cream." That year they attended the State of the Union address and reception as guests of Michelle Obama.

I asked Baker if the competition locally has made it tough for her. "No one does what the Penny does," she replied.

In fact, because of the strict pasteurization laws and the high cost of the equipment, very few ice cream makers in the country make their own base.

"When we were developing this business plan, we wanted to have complete control over our recipes and what went into our product. Taking a base that's premade for you—it's not going to give you the same texture that you need," Baker said. "Why have I been honing these skills if I'm going to buy ninety-nine percent of the product and just add flavor to it?"

She doesn't seem plagued by the money woes that have haunted Kumec. "We do tremendously high volume for such a little shop." Even in the winter months the storefront has a line out the door.

"The Penny is always profiting," she said. In fact, it does so well that the partners invested their profits from the Penny to open the Picnic Basket and Assembly.

Baker said she enjoys pushing the limits of what the customer expects in flavors. Each store sells nine flavors—and some are always the same. "We always have chocolate sorbet—it's become a cult classic. We have people emailing us about it from all over the world." The case also includes a fruit sorbet, an alcohol-flavored ice cream (the Whiskey Custard is my favorite), and vanilla (which sells two to one over any other flavor). The other six flavors allow Baker to go wild with the flavor palate.

She sells the more out-there flavors in downtown Santa Cruz—and keeps things relatively tame at her storefront near more conservative Capitola. "Each location has its own demographic."

The menu for the main ice cream shop downtown can seem like something a mad scientist concocted, with a few crowd-pleasers: Brown Butter Spiced Pumpkin Seed, Ginger Pluot, Honey Yogurt Walnut Jam, Black Pepper Quince, Cookies n' Cream, Black Sesame, Raspberry Sorbet, Tahitian Vanilla Bean, and Dark Chocolate Sorbet. Her favorite is the fig leaf. The store forgoes an "organic" label because it often uses foraged items like candy cap mushrooms that don't fit under those strict regulations.

Baker has no desire to move into the wholesale market, not wanting to give up control of the product. Her reason, ironically, is concern about consistency. "You can't control the freezing temperatures in the ice cream case. Customers opening and closing the freezer doors in a grocery store is terrible for the consistency of the product."

She insisted that the strength of her product is the freshness—the antithesis of what you find in a grocery store freezer case. "We sell everything within two weeks of spinning it."

The ice cream chefs at the Penny are pasteurizing all day to keep up with the demand. Baker creates different bases for each flavor. "The process for that is you have to bring up the base to a minimum of one hundred fifty-five degrees with an airspace temperature of five degrees above that. We have to hold it for thirty minutes, after which you draw your product and pull it down to below forty degrees. Our production cycle is actually a two-day process. There is a cooling and an aging period, because ice cream is actually enhanced when it is allowed to sit for about twenty-four hours. The next day you spin it and then it goes through a hardening period where it needs to go into a deep freezer. After that we can start to temper it, which is a softening of the ice cream, before we actually serve it."

Officials from the California Department of Food and Agriculture visit the Penny Ice Creamery at least quarterly, and the inspections are no joke—penalties for tampering with pasteurization records are punishable with prison time.

After half an hour of talking, Baker shows a rare moment of insecurity. "You like our product, right?"

I am an honest person. But I was in a tough spot—needing her cooperation to explain the mysteries of her ice cream making process.

I hesitated before I assured her that I do in fact enjoy her ice cream—but admitted to enjoying Mission Hill, as well. My husband, Dan, chose a sundae at the Penny Ice Creamery to celebrate his forty-sixth birthday. The marshmallow topping on the sundae can cover any imperfections in the ice cream.

Baker seemed reassured by my explanation. "We've made a niche in this community. People love our product and what it's about. They love the uniqueness of our flavors."

She said there was enough room in the marketplace for multiple artisanal ice cream makers, even in a small town like Santa Cruz. But she has no doubt in her mind that her product is superior—like a mom of a kid who's been accepted to Harvard and can't stop bragging to the state-school parents.

To be fair, I decided I needed to further investigate the issue of the ice cream base. Does Straus really deliver a more consistent product? Does using a homemade base really give an ice cream chef more control over her product? And what about the cost and the risk involved in doing it all yourself? In December 2014, Snoqualmie Ice Cream, which does make its own base, did a voluntary recall of *all* ice cream, gelato, custard, and sorbet for all flavors and container sizes produced on or after January 1, 2014, until December 15, 2014, because these products had the potential to be contaminated with *Listeria monocytogenes.*

I began to wonder if I needed to get over the idea that made from scratch was best. After all, some of the most popular artisanal ice cream places in California, and a few of the brands I love best, use the Straus base. The Bi-Rite Creamery in San Francisco has long been considered one of the city's best places to get a scoop. I have stood in twenty-minute lines down Eighteenth Street in the Mission and braved raving street lunatics to get a double scoop of their famous Salted Caramel. Humphry Slocombe also uses Straus. Popular ice cream makers that I assumed concocted their own base—Big Gay Ice Cream in New York City—turned out to be prepackaged baseheads themselves, getting their supply from Ronnybrook Farms in upstate New York. Even Salt & Straw, which made a name for itself with its wacky bone-marrow flavor and now has a cult following in Los Angeles and Portland, has a dairy make their proprietary recipe. The dairy for the Portland shop is located in Eugene, Oregon, where a former opera singer serenades the cows. America's oldest ice cream company, Bassetts, in Philadelphia, has a supplier in Pennsylvania. McConnell's Ice Cream in Santa Barbara has been making ice cream from its dairy since 1948.

But there is a smattering of ice cream spots across the country that pasteurize in their shops, including Lottie's Creamery in Walnut Creek, California. I asked the owner of Lottie's, Deb Phillips, if she was happy with her choice to make her base from scratch.

"It's like when you talk to a mom of a teen and they say they would do it all differently. If I had to go back and do it again, I don't know that I would have started off making my own base." But she said that creating the base allows her to control how much sugar is in each flavor. For instance, she makes a sweet cream base—the standard base for vanilla, coffee, and mint—but she modifies that base by pasteurizing it without the sugar; she calls this her "alt sugar" base. Once it comes out of the pasteurizer, she adds sweeteners like brown sugar, honey, malt powder, and molasses.

A short list of ice cream shops across the country make their own base, including a cluster in New York City—OddFellows, Van Leeuwen, and the beloved Ample Hills.

I met Ample Hills owner Brian Smith in Brooklyn during one of the hottest days of the summer. Smith showed me around his kitchen, where his pasteurizers are always in use. Smith said he sees it as "cheating" when mom-and-pop ice cream stores use bagged mix. "Making our own base allows us to be more creative," said Smith. It's also what sets his store apart from the competition.

"If we went the other route, I don't think we would have sold nearly as much ice cream," said Smith.

Smith is a former audiobook director and screenwriter of TV sci-fi movies. He's used his past profession in his current one, giving his creations riffs on bad B-movie names, like It Came from Gowanus. The Brooklyn canal near the ice cream shop was a Superfund site and its dark swampiness evokes images of an irradiated Loch Ness monster. Smith peddled the two things I love most in the world—ice cream and nerdy escape—and found a way to link them together.

It helped that Disney chairman and CEO Bob Iger is an ice cream fan and reportedly was one of the first people to order Ample Hills on the Internet. Ample Hills cashed in as an official licensee of *Star Wars: The Force Awakens,* with two limited-edition ice cream flavors: the Dark Side and the Light Side. The Light Side has bright marshmallow ice cream with homemade crispie clusters, as well as a smattering of homemade cocoa crispies. The Dark Side is an ultradark chocolate ice cream with espresso fudge brownies, cocoa crispies, and white chocolate pearls.

How did Smith go from writing schmaltzy sci-fi to becoming an ice cream Jedi master?

Up until a week before he opened his shop, he'd never made ice cream with a commercial ice cream maker before. He studied at Penn State's Ice Cream Short Course and experimented on his family and friends. But, he admits, he'd done very little "hard labor" as a writer and was unprepared for the grueling physical labor and the long days. As soon as he opened his store, things changed.

"I was lifting fifty pounds of sugar up and down the steps," said Smith. "I was afraid I was going to gain thirty pounds—but I lost twenty-five."

He said he misses writing, and in fact still has the natural competitiveness of a writer, which has served him well in the ice cream business. When I was arranging my interview and told him about my book, he emailed: "I would love to have thought of that and written it!"

Smith admits he does not have a sophisticated palate. His ice cream includes cereal bits, cookies, and a good dose of sugar. "We're more aligned with Ben & Jerry's than some of the other places out there." But he's trying to improve on our childhood memories.

"Everything we make has got to be better than what I remember from childhood." The samples I had were sweet to me (especially compared to the more subtle flavors of nearby OddFellows), but the consistency of the homemade base was a league above the iciness of my hometown Penny Creamery. And sweet seems to sell.

Smith got rave reviews from *The New York Times* and experienced success not unlike Steve Herrell did. "In the first four days we sold out of all the ice cream and we had to close the door for nine days."

His simple base recipe is tweaked depending on what he

decides to add to it. The Munchies, for instance, has salted pretzels in the base, which infuses the cream before the rest of the snacks are mixed in at the end. He also has a Bananamon, which has a pound of fresh peeled bananas per quart and more cream than many of his other flavors. You can't adjust cream and sugar ratios in that specific way with a premade mix.

Was ice cream that was created with homemade base better or worse than the kind created with a premade base? It depends—both on the brand and on each individual flavor, and I found the inconsistency at many artisanal ice cream shops maddening.

I realized that there was only one way for me to understand why the issue of premade versus homemade bases was such an emotional touching point for me, and to figure out why making their own base is liberating for some ice cream makers but such a headache and a stumbling block for others. Does making your own base mean sacrificing reliability and health safety for personal freedom? To get my mind around this topic, I had no choice but to jump right into the fray and figure out how to make an ice cream base myself.

I'm a cooking control freak. I like the idea of knowing exactly where each ingredient comes from. But what I really demand from food is consistency (because I can't demand it from the rest of my life). There is nothing worse than going to your favorite neighborhood bistro, ordering a dish you've enjoyed half a dozen times, and having it served differently than in times past. Professional chefs should be able to make food the same way every time.

My search for the perfect artisanal ice cream left me confident that I could make a better base and a better product than 99 percent of what I'd sampled. If I could control every ingredient—adding and subtracting the sugar-cream ratio to the taste I wanted (and learn the techniques for keeping that ice cream at a perfect consistency)—I was confident that I would always get the ice cream I craved.

My next stop on this frozen journey would be to explore the world of DIY ice cream.

3.

COOL SCHOOL

I was at the world's most famous ice cream making class, at Penn State University, facing the unappetizing and unanswerable question: Should I spit out or gulp down?

A few dozen of my classmates and I were eager to break into the ice cream samples that white-coated helpers kept setting out in front of us in small scooping cups. But first there was the issue of whether to swallow it or expel it into a disposable white cup sitting in front of each of us. We were sitting in a sleek brick-and-glass building called the Sensory Evaluation Center, a wing of the Food Science Building. The thirty of us had traveled from the far corners of the world just to learn the secrets of ice cream making. Now we were ready to stuff ourselves with fresh ice cream from the university's on-site creamery, only to find out that gorging, or even swallowing, was frowned upon.

"I encourage you all to spit," said Dr. Kerry E. Kaylegian, an international cheese and dairy product judge. "If you taste too many samples, and eat a lot of ice cream or any product, you get really full, and a signal goes to your brain and says, 'I've had enough.' You sort of lose a bit of your objectivity."

I was taken aback by her suggestion, even though I knew we were there to refine our palates, not satisfy our hunger. Spitting out ice cream seemed wasteful, shameful, not to mention disgusting. Besides, this seemed like cruel and unusual punishment; I had traveled more than two thousand miles in the midst of a light blizzard just to visit one of the most famous creameries in the country, only to be told *not* to eat the ice cream.

Kaylegian's short stature, combined with her blunt talk about the mechanisms of pleasure, brought to mind Dr. Ruth Westheimer, the diminutive 1980s icon who answered America's most disturbing and embarrassing sex questions with open-mouthed gusto. Kaylegian gave me equally startling advice about ice cream eating. But how could I spit my beloved dessert as if it were a wad of stale gum? I'd faced a similar dilemma while wine tasting in Napa; as a lightweight I needed to spit out the occasional weak Cabernet into a designated sipper's spittoon just to keep from passing out. Ice cream tasters must face the spit-or-swallow question simply because our brains can't process all that delicious fat at once. Then Kaylegian shared a bit of information that made the dilemma even more painful than I'd realized: The last two samples would be chocolate.

On top of my indecisiveness about what to do with my samples, I was feeling intimidated, out of my league; after all, some of the students in the three-day course were already running their own mom-and-pop ice cream shops. On the other hand, the fact that they were there at Penn State suggested that they were dissatisfied with their ice creams. Some were having all kinds of tsuris with their product. They were churning out ice cream that was too melty, too clumpy, and too filled with fruit seeds.

On the first day, my classmate Dan from Boston had announced he was creating a product that would outsell Häagen-Dazs. "Don't roll your eyes," he said, when he caught me doing just that. "You don't know what we're doing."

I found out that this was his second time enrolling in the Penn State course, which made me wonder what he'd missed the first time around. The course is not easy; it is designed to give students an exacting sense of ice cream making as well as the business climate for ice cream entrepreneurs. These days it's hard to find a high-level ice cream maven who has not passed through the program or is not, at the very least, intimately familiar with the short course. It would be hard to overstate the program's influence, which has been rising steadily since it opened its doors to farmers more than 150 years ago.

The course started out as a way for dairymen and their families to make the most of their milk, converting it into yogurt, buttermilk, and ice cream. Now the program is considered a sort of finishing school for everyone from experimental pop-up ice cream shops to massive conglomerates. While certain rival ice cream making schools have available bookings up to the last minute, Penn State's short course and its short-short course (Ice Cream 101) sell out year after year, often months in advance. Never mind that it's not easy to get to State College, Pennsylvania, which is situated in a valley three hours' driving distance from Philadelphia. When a budding ice cream entrepreneur named Wilbur A. Tharp decided to take the short course in 1923, only a "spur" rail line connected Bellefonte, Pennsylvania, with State College. The rail infrastructure was so threadbare that the train had to do the final stretch into State College backward. "There were no facilities there for a turnaround," Tharp recalled. To avoid this situation, Tharp had to take two trains and a primitive bus called a "jitney" just to get to the ice cream school. On the plus side, the entire course cost just 127 dollars, which also included room and board.

Tharp took a version of the short course that was anything but short; it lasted eight grueling weeks, six days a week, eight hours per day. But the annoying rail journey and the academic slog were worthwhile for Tharp, who ran Tharp's Ice Cream in Shamokin, Pennsylvania. His son, Bruce, went on to earn a PhD in food science from Penn State, wrote one of the leading encyclopedias of ice cream, *Tharp & Young on Ice Cream,* and at one point gave a presentation about "ice cream sensory evaluation" at the Smithsonian Institution.

On the long, ice-slicked road to State College in a rented car, I hoped my journey would pay off as much as it did for the Tharps. As I gawked at snowdrifts on the side of the road, it occurred to me that this frightening journey was by design; the short course is offered only in wintertime, which suited the farmers who first enrolled in the class. That was the best time for them to get away. These days, the winter schedule still makes a lot of sense because ice cream production doesn't ramp up until the spring, when the producers get ready for the summer. For these reasons, generations of short coursers have had the odd experience of learning about ice cream while watching gobs of snow fall from the sky, making the campus look as if it were slathered in vanilla bean ice cream. It's a long-standing tradition for short coursers to leave as early as possible on the last day of class to avoid a storm blowing in.

The course syllabus reminded us to pack warm, comfortable clothes. The first morning I walked to class, the temperature was around eighteen degrees. It was easy to spot the students from warm climates; they came unprepared in leather bomber jackets that were great for LA but completely inappropriate for the middle of Pennsylvania in winter. Even their jet lag seemed the most pronounced.

I could barely feel my toes, and yet I still couldn't wait to be eating ice cream. But I soon found out that the short course would cover the seamy and appalling side of ice cream making and not just the delicious aspects. Part of the craft of ice cream making is learning just how badly you can screw up and how awful the consequences of those screwups can be. In the sensory lab, Kaylegian guided us through an Ice Cream Chamber of Horrors. Ice cream can be flavorless, gummy, greasy, and, worst of all, rancid. "The best way to describe rancid is to imagine baby vomit," she said. Poorly made ice cream can be too salty or too sweet or can take on that unpleasant soupy flavor that too many egg yolks can impart.

Kaylegian explained that our sense of flavor comes in large part from our nose. This explains, in part, why Ben & Jerry's flavors are so sweet, brash, and bold; Ben Cohen had sinus problems and couldn't taste a lot of flavor. By the way, that same sensory defect drove Cohen to ask his partner to make the ice cream full of chunky treats; Cohen's failure to smell properly made him put a premium on textures and mouthfeel.[12] It is easy for food tasters to give themselves a similar sensory handicap;

all you've got to do is pinch your nostrils shut. Kaylegian described an experiment done at the sensory lab where testers are given different flavors of jelly beans and then asked to squeeze their noses, obliterating their sniff capabilities before popping each one in their mouth. "You can't tell whether you've got the cinnamon, cherry, or hot pepper one until you open up your nose," said Kaylegian. "I've seen that done with apple and onions as well."

As Kaylegian spoke, a perky young teacher's assistant set three samples of vanilla in front of me. I was gleeful, even though I knew full well that some of these samples would have "defects." Kaylegian was teaching us how to judge ice cream. "All of our sense of touch with ice cream is going to be done in our mouth. Is it cold, is it icy, when we bite on it do we hear ice crystals? How does it melt in our mouth? Is it melting quickly? Is it melting slowly? Does it coat our mouth? Is it very high in fat? Does it dissipate really quickly?"

My younger Thrifty Ice Cream– and Dairy Belle–loving self would have laughed out loud at all these ways of qualifying ice cream's quality. In a similar sense, my little-girl self would argue that bad ice cream must be better than no ice cream at all. Then again, I'd never had anyone question my old value system, instruct me to devise my own standards for a perfect ice cream, or ask me to square the quality of one ice cream with that of another.

Kaylegian told us to think about some questions. "How does this [sample] compare to the ideal? How does vanilla ice cream taste? What should it taste like?" I had been given three samples of vanilla, marked A, B, and C, set out in small disposable cups with lids. Not all vanilla is the same, apparently. As I dipped my spoon into A, I noticed a frustrating hardness. It took a while for the ice cream to melt on my spoon. Then I placed it in my mouth and swallowed and felt its fluffy texture on the roof of my mouth. My spoon couldn't penetrate sample B at all; it was like trying to eat a piece of shale. It had less air pumped into it, so it was as dense as a brick. Sample C had 120 percent air pumped into it and melted quickly on my tongue. My delight surprised me; I'd once dismissed airy ice cream as second-class and cheap.

When we finished the three samples, another three were placed in front of us, and I had the sense of being at an ice cream shop with an open bar. Sample E tasted like sadness. There was no joy in that mouthful of watery and insipid ice milk mush that settled unpleasantly on my tongue, leaving the flimsiest coating on my palate. It was almost unbearable. After such an ordeal, I needed a physical and psychic break, but the samples kept coming. One by one, unflappable and cheery TAs set them down before me, seemingly unaware of my emotional and physical distress.

Now I was beginning to regret my decision to ignore the teacher's advice and swallow every bite. The ice creams and the instructions kept coming. It wasn't enough for me to just shovel the samples in my mouth; the teacher instructed me to put the ice cream directly onto my back molars. "See if there's any crunchiness."

My classmates were getting flushed from all the eating. Their enthusiasm was flagging. When the tenth ice cream sample was set before me, it was all I could do to repress a groan. The ice cream had a milk chocolate flavor and a heft that allowed the sample to sit perkily on my spoon. As soon as it hit my tongue, I was transported back to the early 1980s, when I would go to the San Francisco Giants games at Candlestick Park with my father and brothers and get a chocolate malted. My teeth were always chattering at the stadium. I would sit there, pulling my legs up so I could tuck them under my sweatshirt, feeling the cold wind whipping up from the bay. And yet I wanted to chill myself even more by grabbing a small disposable wooden spoon and diving into a cup of chocolate ice cream.

The Penn State sample tasted exactly like that ballpark chocolate. One of my classmates made an icky-yuck face. Too sticky! Too cloying! Yes, the sweetness was a little excessive, but my emotions could not have cared less. That is one large and undeniable flaw of sensory evaluation systems for food; they completely disregard the subjective and emotional component of ice cream eating, the same sort of thing that makes certain nostalgic adults long for even the most god-awful frozen childhood treats, from Otter Pops to Good Humor Fat Frog ice cream pops. In that moment, all I wanted to do was relive my girlhood with that ballpark chocolate scoop. Wasn't that my true purpose here, to conjure, or perhaps re-create, the same flavors that set off those deep, dark, fudge-covered memories?

I'd made my own ice cream before enrolling in the Ice Cream Short Course, but the results ranged from sublime to disgusting to traumatic, not just for myself but for all my loved ones. As an independent thinker, I find it very hard to obey commands or follow instructions, and so I ignored the emphatic warnings in the recipes: Never, *ever* try to make homemade ice cream unless you've allowed the mixing bowl to chill in the freezer for at least twenty-four hours. What was the worst that could happen if I rushed along the process just a little bit? For an agonizing hour, I had to watch the ice cream maker's dasher slosh its way through a miserable mess of evaporated milk, fat-free milk, peppermint extract, green food coloring, and egg substitute. The mixture looked a lot like the split pea soup that the pop-eyed, head-swiveling Linda Blair spewed across a room in *The Exorcist.* I'd convinced my husband, Dan, to let me use a fifty-dollar gift certificate on the contraption, promising delicious soft-serves and gelatos. Now I couldn't bear to let the unfrozen ice cream go to waste, so I forced it on my family. Dan braced himself as I poured the green substance into a sundae glass. He took one small taste of the glop and started to gag. "I told you we should have gotten a cake pan," he said.

Dan urged me to put the ice cream maker up on the shelf where it belonged, freeing up the freezer for important things. But I wasn't ready to stop trying, and I hoped the short course would at least minimize the chance of future disasters.

At least I wasn't alone in my failures.

No one is immune from colossal ice cream screwups, not even Dr. Bob Roberts, professor of food science at Penn State, who was charged with trying to teach us how to avoid the gloppiness of bad ice cream in a very short time span.

Roberts, who grew up in Vermont, had a wonky quality that reminded me of Bill Gates. But he also had a disarming down-to-earth and self-effacing aspect. He loves to pepper his presentations with bad dairy puns. "If you can't find the slide, don't have a cow," he advised us at one point. And he readily acknowledges his own ice cream disasters. Even though he earned a master's degree in dairy science from South Dakota State University and holds a doctorate in food science from the University of Minnesota, he once screwed up a batch of ice cream he tried to make on the spot for a roomful of hungry local elementary school kids, including his own child. The problem? He dunked a bowl full of liquid ice cream into supercold brine but somehow forgot to turn on the spade that was supposed to churn up the mixture; the result was a bunch of ice cream slush. Undaunted, Roberts took it right back to the ice cream lab and served his colleagues milk shakes. The kids were left with only the taste of disappointment.

But for me, at least, his confession made me feel even less confident than before; if Roberts could fail in front of a class of elementary school students, what hope was there for the rest of us? After all, so much can go wrong when you make ice cream. Poorly made dairy treats can kill you or leave you in such gastric distress that you'll wish for death. In the late nineteenth century, as ice cream became increasingly popular thanks to the easy availability of ice and hand-cranked ice cream freezers, "ice cream poisoning" became common. As *The Medical News* charged in 1893, "the mystery of ice cream poisoning is a reproach to the professions of science and chemistry."[13] Historians are still arguing about whether President Zachary Taylor died after gorging on an "ice milk and frozen cherry surprise" during a Fourth of July party.[14] You would think that modern-day technology, including home refrigeration, would have put a stop to this sort of thing. Sadly, ice cream–borne illnesses plague us to this day. These ailments are more than just a good reason to exercise extreme caution before you pile drive that vanilla scoop into your face; the very presence of these illnesses has helped bring about a paranoia and hypervigilance that can make it very difficult for entrepreneurs to jump into the ice cream game without relying on mass-manufactured prebought ice cream mixes. The risk is no joke. Even the biggest and most well-established ice cream manufacturers and their loyal customers are not immune. In April 2015, Blue Bell Ice Cream, which has been churning frozen treats for more than a hundred years, recalled all of its ice cream and shut down operations for months after the CDC linked listeria-contaminated Blue Bell products to ten illnesses, including three deaths in Kansas.[15]

Common sense tells us that bacteria thrive in sultry subtropical weather, but ice cream turns that rule on its head. Listeria, the ice cream plague, thrives in cold environments. The bacteria can live for years in drains and machinery where food is made. It can worm its way into ice cream even after it is pasteurized, and can hang on for dear life even in drastically cold conditions. Even worse, the bacteria is insidious; people who have consumed contaminated food can take between three and seventy days to show symptoms, which range from flu-like fever to gastric distress. According to the *Food Poison Journal* (yes, there is such a thing), 89.2 percent of listeria patients end up in the hospital; no other pathogenic bacterial infection does a better job of knocking people off their feet and putting them into the infirmary.[16] Pregnant women are twenty times more likely to get listeriosis, which is particularly ironic given how much ice cream they like to eat.[17]

Strangely, the Blue Bell ice cream news, which made repeated national headlines, didn't affect Texans' appetite for their beloved dairy treat. The day that Blue Bell started redistributing its ice cream in Houston, customers still lined up at Houston supermarkets at five thirty A.M. to get first crack at the best flavors.[18]

When reading the scary news about Blue Bell, I took comfort in the notion that home chefs can impose more hygiene controls than a gigantic creamery can. But making your ice cream at home doesn't necessarily guarantee its safety. Homemade ice cream accounted for 2,594 illnesses between 1990 and 2009, mostly from contaminated eggs or spoiled milk. Because of all this, the FDA considers ice cream a "potentially hazardous food item."

To try to save us from our own inability to properly heat eggs (and, I suppose, refrain from using spoiled milk), the government has strict guidelines about pasteurizing ice cream base.

But some adventurous ice cream makers accuse state and federal governments of overreach and paranoia that restricts the creativity of food artisans. A few of my classmates whispered their shock and outrage when Roberts announced that the outlook for people who wished to concoct their own bases was bleak. Our state and federal laws make it almost impossible. The Penny Creamery in Santa Cruz is a dramatic exception. Having an on-site pasteurizer is ridiculously expensive. Co-owner Kendra Baker had been greatly aided by a small business loan—a highly publicized initiative of the Obama administration—and the publicity of making a homemade base. If you want to make your own base, you can invest in a pasteurizer, which can cost upward of fifteen thousand dollars—and you had better hope that the state health department or agriculture department will allow you to make your own ice cream base. Or you can buy a premade mix and have it shipped. Truly, it is the path of least resistance—and many commercial ice cream makers would rather take the easy route.

Dr. Roberts was gently pushing us all to consider the latter option.

"What about Philadelphia-style ice cream, made with already pasteurized milk and no eggs?" my classmate asked. Roberts explained that even without eggs an ice cream mix needs to be pasteurized, according to the law.

Roberts tried to be diplomatic.

"This is an area where there's often angst," said Roberts.

If you are able to get the equipment and the permits, making a base is a basic process. Roberts couldn't resist a little wordplay: "If it works, it's a piece of cake." If you manage not to sicken anyone, though, there's the very real possibility that your ice cream will turn into inedible gloop, even if you have studied ice cream making for most of your life. And that's when people will turn on you, he said.

How could I ensure that this didn't happen? For one thing, I would have to ramp up my list of ingredients. Despite what I'd learned by reading cookbooks, you need more than just milk, cream, sugar, eggs, and flavoring to make ice cream. At the Penn State short course, I found out about the confusingly named but essential concept of milk solids-not-fat—or MSNF. Milk is made up of about 87 percent water. The rest is milk fat and solids (not fat). One of the most common sources of MSNF is skim milk powder. Basically, you need to add it to your ice cream mix before freezing so that there isn't too much water from milk, which will turn your ice cream into an impenetrable block of ice.

This was news to me. Anyone who has gagged on a glass of reconstituted powdered milk will be pleased to know that this material has another purpose, aside from torturing children at breakfast time during backcountry camping trips. For one, it can improve the texture of ice cream.

Roberts's explanation made sense to me, and yet I couldn't help resisting the use of an ultramodern, space-age ingredient in my ice cream mix. But it turns out that I was wrong about the ultramodern aspect of milk powder, which has been around for ages. In fact, milk powder predates the invention of ice cream by a few hundred years. Marco Polo wrote about thirteenth-century Mongol soldiers preparing and using milk powder. He found them "drying milk in the sun, pulverizing it into powder, and placing it in sacks to be carried on their excursions into the territory of their enemies," wrote Richard Newell Hart in a 1914 book about leavening agents.[19] But it took a long while for milk powder to enter the mainstream. In the early nineteenth century, convenient tablets made out of dried concentrated milk became available. By 1910, the French had puzzled out a way to freeze milk into a "snow powder" and then separate "the soft, greasy milk solids" from the snow using centrifugal action.[20] By the turn of the twentieth century, food producers were using new technology including spray dryers to preserve milk. It is now possible to get powders made out of full-fat or skim milk, buttermilk, and even cheese.[21]

All this is good news for the home chef, considering that adding skim milk powder to ice cream can make it smoother and helps with the horrors that sometimes happen in the home freezer. But my classmates couldn't hide both their skepticism and their initial shock that they needed to add powder to their ice cream mix. Several hands shot up in the air, and a number of students reiterated the fact that they regularly made delicious ice cream at home without the need for chalky additions.

We were urged to reconsider our powder-phobic views. Almost any ice cream tastes good when it's straight out of the ice cream maker. But all too often, the quality deteriorates as soon as you store the ice cream in the freezer, especially if your family includes the kind of people who love to open and close the freezer door constantly. Roberts told us that ice cream makers' biggest enemies were "heat shock" and "freezer abuse." This cruel dairy product maltreatment happens in many forms. It happens before we even bring a pint home with us from the store; countless shoppers open and close the freezers, letting warmer air in, especially when they rummage around, looking for that one pint of cool mint buried beneath a stack of Bananas Foster ice cream pints, leaving the freezer door wide-open all the while. It also happens when an impatient spouse—including, notably, my husband—takes out a granite-hard pint and decides, unwisely, to heat it up in the microwave to get it more scoopable, and then puts the rest of the pint back in the freezer, ruining the remaining pint for a fleeting moment of cheap thrills.

"What's going on in ice cream freezers?" asked Roberts. "I'd be happy to wax poetically about this for days."

Stabilizers help offset some of these indignities, but they are a contentious issue, especially among "artisanal" ice cream makers. I had spoken to at least one who had begged me not to publicize that she used guar gum in her ice cream.

The Penn State Berkey Creamery uses the seaweed extract

called carrageenan in its ice cream. If you dare to Google it, you'll find plenty of cranks. You'll see articles with titles like "The Chemical Hiding in Your Organic Food!" Here's my theory: Carrageenan gets such bad press because the name sounds too much like *carcinogen.* If they changed it to something healthy sounding, like nori, people would mix it into their ice cream bases with no hesitation.

Whatever the reason for our prejudice, there was no doubt that my classmates thought stabilizers were far worse than skim milk powder. But the truth is they play an important role in keeping ice crystals small; you want lots of small crystals in ice cream. Large ones give it that chunky feel that can result in an unpleasant, rasping crunch.

And yet ice cream, at least in theory, can sit in a store freezer for months (if not years) and remain edible. The biggest shock of my Penn State education came when Roberts announced that there is *no expiration date on ice cream.* I am someone who maniacally checks expiration dates. I will not use eggs or milk that's expired, even if the products seem perfectly fine and pass the dastardly sniff test. So how could something that was made from both milk *and* eggs not have an expiration date? Roberts explained that a properly made, dutifully pasteurized product doesn't really need one. Shelf life, however, is another matter. The longer an ice cream stays on a shelf, the more its defects show. Stabilizers can help preserve it, but no amount of add-ins, chemicals, or hacks can correct against human error. Impatience is the enemy of great ice cream. How many times have I gotten fidgety, sick of waiting, and poured a semicool mix into my ice cream machine, then watched in misery as the paddle flailed around in the soupy mess, which resembled a glass of Ensure? As I found out in the short course, a proper ice cream mix must be given time to mature.

"If you're making ice cream mix at home or you're making ice cream mix in your shop, you don't want to just make the mix and immediately go to your freezer," said Roberts. "You want to give it some time so the mix has a chance to age. There are a number of things that are happening there. You are allowing fat to crystalize; you're allowing proteins to hydrate; you're allowing your mix to come together."

His advice was a correction against wishful thinking. How many times had I poured lukewarm mix into my ice cream maker thinking it would freeze anyway?

All in all there are ten different steps in ice cream making that don't even include recipe formulation: ingredient selection, weighing, mixing/blending, pasteurizing, homogenizing, cooling, aging, freezing, packaging, and hardening. There are so many potential pitfalls in ice cream making—and the course highlighted them all.

In an effort to try to help us (or perhaps because he knew ice cream mastery would remain out of our reach), Roberts shared the Berkey Creamery's "secret formula," which I will now reveal to you:

14.1% butterfat
10.5% milk solids-not-fat
12.96% cane sugar
3.7% dry corn syrup solids

.26% stabilizer/emulsifier blend
41% total solids at 80% overrun
For chocolate add 3.5% cocoa powder (22/24% cocoa fat)

The slide was on the screen for only a minute, but I took a picture, in hopes that I might one day unravel its meaning.

The last day at Penn State, we were led down into the bowels of the building, where mix manufacturers showed off their products and machine makers like Emery Thompson, Stoelting, and Carpigiani peddled their fancy machines. Students were not allowed to operate these burly pieces of heavy equipment. It was like trying to buy a Harley-Davidson without being given the keys. When we were able to start the thing up on our own, would we even be able to control it?

We were, however, given sample after sample to feast on. Imagine an on-demand all-you-can-eat ice cream bar, where everyone is wearing hairnets and earpieces. The salesmen had mikes and we had ear sets so that we could hear their spiel over the hum of the machines. I ate ice cream bars, sorbets made in a fancy countertop contraption called a Pacojet, and custard that was squeezed straight from the machine. After three hours of eating, I was given a certificate of completion. I had learned so much that something cramped inside my mind—it felt a lot like an ice cream headache. But the intensive ice cream making course had one glaring flaw: During the entire three-day experience, I never had a chance to make any ice cream.

It was up to me to take what I learned and apply it in a practical setting. But the course gave me no muscle memory of making real ice cream. I began to have terrible anxiety dreams. In one memorable nightmare, I was at a dinner with my entire family, including my brothers, nieces, and mom. We'd just finished a meal of roast chicken and asparagus. I announced that I had made a kugel-flavored ice cream. Kugel is a traditionally Jewish noodle-based casserole made with cottage cheese, sour cream, sugar, cinnamon, milk, eggs, noodles, and cornflakes. No one but my mother seems to know how to make it properly. I was just about to serve up my frozen soul-food confection when it occurred to me that my ice cream was terrible. "It's not ready," I moaned. "It's just not ready!"

I woke up in a sweat, feeling trepidation but also inspiration. Kugel ice cream would be amazing, if I could only figure out how to make it. I also daydreamed about creating a Passover ice cream with chocolate-covered matzo. Where would these dreams lead? I took comfort that the famous *bum-bum-ba-dah-DUM* riff from the Rolling Stones' "Satisfaction" came to Keith Richards in his sleep. He woke up and moaned the riff into a tape recorder, rolled right over, and went back to bed.[22] I doubted my ice cream would garner the same kind of worldwide recognition or lucrative success. But at least I could try.

Over the next few weeks, I kept passing a farm stand with pasteurized eggs, and not buying them. They were nine dollars to the carton. I felt guilty—both at the expense and at the idea that I was cheating by skipping the pasteurizing. Wasn't I dodging the whole fear issue? How would I be able to sustain a seventy-five-cents-per-egg habit? Instead of throwing money away on those fancy eggs, I decided to invest in a thirty-dollar instant-read thermometer that would keep me from poisoning my friends but also stop me from scorching every batch. Now I didn't have to worry about either getting sued by my sickened loved ones or making eggs Benedict by accident.

At last, I was ready for the experiment to begin. Salted caramel ice cream has become all the rage—but what about butterscotch? It's always been a flavor I associate with my dad, who stuffed his linty pockets with hard butterscotch candies wrapped in translucent paper twisted at both ends. Dad wasn't much of a conversationalist, but he had other ways of communicating. He often fidgeted with the paper when he was bored or nervous, and the crinkling was an almost Pavlovian signal; every time I heard that plastic rattling, I salivated for a treat.

My father-in-law, Victor, had just passed away, and I was thinking about my own dad. It would be a nice tribute to both men if I could somehow concoct a flavor that referenced both of them and their oversize personalities. It made me wonder how many recipes are developed out of pure nostalgia, sadness, or some tenuous need to connect to our childhoods. I was planning on debuting this flavor during Dan's forty-ninth birthday party, with his co-workers, family, and friends. I was setting the ice cream bar high, I realized. But that would make success all the sweeter, or failure all the more bitter.

None of the recipes I found for butterscotch ice cream included MSNFs, aka skim milk powder. I'd have to devise my own.

I took an old *Sunset* magazine recipe and adapted it, using all my hard-won ice cream knowledge. I consulted an online butterfat calculator and began to play with the numbers until I came up with something around 15 percent—right in line with superpremium brands.[23]

During my first attempt, the milk powder clumped and the eggs threatened to scramble. But somehow, through whisking and manically checking the temperature of the base, I was able to create a product that churned decently in the ice cream maker and hardened into a scoopable form after a few hours in the freezer.

My family devoured it the next day.

Was it a tad too sweet? I tossed and turned at night. The nagging feeling that perhaps I could improve the flavor profile led me to try to play with the recipe. A few days later, I tried making the Victor with a third less sugar. Was I a bit plumped up by early success? Perhaps. But ice cream making has a way of fluffing up your ego and making you think you will soon outsell Häagen-Dazs.

I decided to experiment with the formula on a weekday, when Dan had the day off from work. I started making the butterscotch sauce that would be whisked into the cream base.

I had a sinking feeling as soon as I saw the runniness of the butterscotch mixture. I debated about starting over, but I needed to see if my tweak would work.

I warmed the milk, cream, sugar, and egg mixture to 165 degrees and added the butterscotch mix. Then the long, agonizing wait began.

I poured the mix into the machine. I shuffled back and forth with my fist against my face, watching the churning and chewing my gum neurotically. I suddenly hated the sound of the ice cream maker: *gar-gnar-gnar-gnar-gnar.* It was like a wretched piece of failing medical equipment. Or a generator on a motor home in the middle of the night in a crowded RV park.

I started talking to the ice cream maker, in the bitter, negative tones of an abusive old-world parent whose American teen has earned mediocre marks in math and will never go on to become a doctor.

"Ooh, I hate you!" I said to the machine. "You did not become what you are supposed to become."

Dan, who has known me for almost two decades, was observing me with alarm.

"You have become an ice cream psychotic, and not in the best sense of the word," said Dan. He drew me a picture to illustrate.

Dan White

Dan thought he knew what went wrong; I'd named the ice cream after his father, only to mess with the original formula.

"My dad did not like people messing with him," Dan explained. "Stick to the original recipe."

Unfortunately, that turned out to be harder than I'd thought. I'd fussed with it so much that batch after batch came out weak and soggy.

In the midst of this eggy, gooey mess, the date of Dan's birthday party neared. What could possibly go wrong? I clearly have the temperament that allows me to perform well under duress in front of an audience.

I wanted the party to be a grand performance highlighting my skills as an ice cream magician. I wasn't trying to lure back repeat customers. But I was to realize that there was something worse than being judged by strangers: being judged by the people you will have to see again, sometimes on a daily basis. About a week before the party, I started testing recipes while trying to recapture the initial success of the salted butterscotch. I tried a vanilla without eggs. It turned out as hard as a rock. In order to get it out of my gallon container and pour it down the drain I had to run hot water over it for three minutes, and even then one-third plopped out in a giant milky ice cube too large to fit down the drain. Another batch of the Victor came out weak and waterlogged.

I spent part of every day shopping for cream and milk. Five days before the party, I stood in my kitchen at six thirty A.M. pouring what I hoped would be chocolate ice cream into my Cuisinart ice cream maker. It whirred away, drowning out my family's bleary breakfast conversation. "It needs to harden in the freezer for at least four hours," I said by way of explanation to my tired family. The machine was so loud, I'm not sure anybody heard me.

I'd learned at Penn State that hardening was essential to make ice cream into a scoopable treat. That's because super-fresh ice cream has a texture that falls somewhere between soft-serve and milk shake when it first comes out of a machine. Professional ice cream makers have something called a blast freezer, which goes to minus forty degrees and accomplishes the hardening in a speedy way. The average home freezer is set at about zero degrees Fahrenheit. Already the ice cream odds were stacked against me.

Thirty minutes later, the mix fluffed up, doubling in size and threatening to spill over the top of the machine. I felt more hope than I had in days, as I put the mix into a quart container to freeze.

In the meantime, I decided to try making marshmallows. But after I'd poured the water, corn syrup, and sugar into the pan, my thermometer broke. I panicked, burning my index finger in the candy mix to try to gauge whether it had hit 250 degrees Fahrenheit and was ready to be poured into the gelatin mix. I dumped it in anyway, whipping everything together until tiny white peaks began to form. I tried to coax the sticky stuff onto a pan coated with confectioners' sugar. It was supposed to fill the entire pan to the brim, but instead it took up a mere quarter, without the promised loft. It was like the matzo of marshmallows.

The days before the party were spent in an ice cream frenzy. I wrote a timeline for base making. There was also the logistical challenge of having only one ice cream maker and needing to leave enough time to let it refreeze before making a new batch. I charted out a rough schedule and then accidently threw it out.

I tested my recipes. I was feeling pretty confident. I had mixes chilling in the fridge. I made homemade marshmallows, using a new thermometer. I roasted almonds and pecans. But I focused too much on the add-ins. The day before the party, I was hours late churning my first flavor. I whipped up a perfect-looking batch of the Victor at four P.M. I still had two other flavors to make in twenty-four hours, and the ice cream in the freezer needed to harden. I was hopelessly in the weeds, with no chance of really recovering.

At eight P.M., I decided to try to make the batch of butter pecan I should have made hours before. It whirled around in the still warm ice cream maker, refusing to whip or churn or harden in any way. "It looks like scrambled eggs before they are cooked," said my daughter, Julianna.

Dan looked alarmed when he saw me. "You look so utterly depleted, as if you were van Gogh slaving away on some picture of haystacks or Michelangelo plucking plaster out of his shaggy eyebrows after lying on scaffolding all day long," he said.

In that moment I envied those tortured artists. They at least knew that if they succeeded, their work would be around for centuries. I was lucky if mine would last four minutes.

I decided I would cut my losses and try making a batch of Arnie's Ballpark Chocolate the next day. I would goose it up and turn it into a Rocky Road, my dad's ice cream of choice.

I slept fitfully, dreaming about failed ice cream.

At seven A.M. on Dan's birthday, I was up churning the

chocolate. I couldn't decide whether to put in the homemade marshmallows and almonds right before freezing or give the guests the freedom to add them as toppings.

"I like your friends, but I don't really trust them to put in the right proportions," I told Dan. The idea of setting out bowls of marshmallows and having guests add too many or too few made my heart want to break. What if they put chocolate and marshmallows on the Victor? We can't always handle the freedoms we're given in life. I decided to do the add-ins myself.

And, yes, perhaps I was being a control freak. But my guests were not paying me, and as a result they did not, in fact, get to put anything they wanted on their ice cream. There is a social contract in an ice cream store. Hand over a few dollars and you have the right to ask for whatever toppings you see on a menu. There's a different etiquette involved when you are giving someone a treat in your own home. This was my chance to manipulate taste on the most basic level—by determining the exact proportions.

I turned off the ice cream maker and poured the shaved chocolate, almonds, and marshmallows into the mix. The marshmallows floated to the top of the still gooey ice cream, which looked and smelled like chocolate milk. My mad creation did not inspire confidence. All my insecurities about having people in my home, allowing them to see my most private self, were brimming to the surface like those overinflated gobs of gelatin and sugar. I was so distraught that I scooped the risen marshmallows out by the spoonful and threw them straight into the trash.

"We may only have one usable quart," I told Dan.

"But we have twenty people coming," he said.

I debated going out to our local store and buying a pint or two of my favorite vanilla, softening it up, and adding the buttered pecans. But I had traveled thousands of miles to attend the best ice cream class in the world and I was supposed to be showcasing my skills. It felt like the ultimate act of cheating—a disloyalty to myself.

I decided to compromise on the quality—and instead of using a properly proportioned base filled with the correct amount of MSNF, I'd whip up my old standby vanilla custard on the spot in the ice cream maker and flavor it with butter pecans. It would give the ice cream maker a chance to freeze, and provide a spectacle at the party.

I made the mix and let it age for a few hours as we started setting up for the party. I checked the Ballpark Chocolate and was relieved to see it was hardening to a scoopable consistency.

As the guests arrived, I started the machine and churned the custard base. I started taking orders: People wanted to try the Victor, then the Rocky Road. The butter pecan became only a milk-shake consistency, but I served it and people ate every bite.

"You should have your own pushcart and go up and down the boardwalk this summer selling your ice cream," said my friend Liza.

"But it's impossible to get a license for that with homemade ice cream," I said. "I would need a separate kitchen, a pasteurizer."

"It would be great publicity," another friend said. "It could become a national story—imagine the headlines: 'How I Made Ice Cream and Wound Up in the Can.'"

I was relieved that people liked my flavors, but I knew that my hesitation about starting my own ice cream business wasn't just because of the regulations. I didn't have it in me to be a full-time ice cream maker.

Ice cream making, I had learned, required the same reliance on repetition, but with an additional crazy-making factor—the chemistry of freezing. Not enough sugar, too many solids, too much milk, can ruin ice cream. If the mix is too warm, your ice cream will fail. If your freezing unit is too warm, your ice cream will never reach the correct consistency. You can try to put a gloopy mess in the freezer and pray that it turns out in time to feed twenty friends, but it will never be edible and you will run to the store in humiliating shame to pick up a pint of vanilla.

During my two straight weeks of ice cream making, I was experimenting with recipes, cooking the base, churning the ice cream, transferring it to containers, and planning the next flavor.

How did people do it? Every day, for years?

More than ever I wanted to find out how the country's best ice cream makers manage to keep their businesses and families together for generations without going entirely insane in the process. Did they have better mental health, a stronger work ethic, or another secret that allowed them to survive in the business? I would need to travel across the country to America's heartland to find out.

THE VICTOR: SALTED BUTTERSCOTCH ICE CREAM

1 cup firmly packed brown sugar
2 tablespoons butter
1½ cups whipping cream (½ cup of this goes into the butterscotch mixture)
1 tablespoon vanilla
1 heaping teaspoon coarse sea salt
6 large egg yolks
1 cup whole milk
½ cup dried nonfat skim milk

- Heat the brown sugar and butter in a quart pan over medium heat. When the butter and sugar are melted, whisk in ½ cup of the whipping cream. Remove from the heat and add the vanilla and salt. In a separate bowl, beat the egg yolks. Heat the remaining 1 cup whipping cream, the milk, and the skim milk powder to 110°F. Whisk so that the milk powder dissolves completely. Add a teaspoon of the milk mixture to the egg mixture to temper the eggs.
- Add the entire egg mixture to the saucepan with the rest of the milk mixture and heat until the base reaches 165°F, 5 to 10 minutes. Remove from the heat.
- Pour through a fine strainer into a bowl or Pyrex measuring cup. Whisk in the butterscotch mixture. Cool and then put in the fridge for at least 2 hours, or cover and chill overnight. Overnight yields the best results.

- Freeze the mixture in an ice cream maker according to the manufacturer's instructions. Most ice cream makers sound like a dryer with clothes rattling around inside when the ice cream is ready. Harden in the freezer for at least 4 hours.

Disclaimer: Do not even think about making even one tiny change or substitution to this recipe, or complete ice cream chaos could ensue.

ARNIE'S BALLPARK CHOCOLATE

For the chocolate paste:

⅓ cup of cocoa powder (22% to 24%)
¼ cup sugar
⅓ cup boiling water

For the ice cream:

1⅔ cups cream
1⅔ cups whole milk
¾ cup sugar
½ cup skim milk powder
3 egg yolks

Mix-ins:

½ cup marshmallows
3 ounces shredded milk chocolate
⅓ cup roasted almonds

- To make the chocolate paste, dissolve the cocoa powder and ¼ cup sugar in the boiling water and let cool. Stir the cream and milk in a saucepan over medium heat. Whisk in the sugar and skim milk powder and continue stirring until the mixture is smooth and the temperature reaches 110°F. In a separate bowl, beat the egg yolks. Temper the egg yolks with a teaspoon of the warm milk mixture, then carefully add the egg yolks to the milk mixture.
- Heat the custard until it reaches 165°F. Pour the mixture through a metal strainer into a Pyrex measuring cup.

- Add the cocoa mixture and stir while the milk mixture is warm so that the cocoa is easily incorporated.
- Cool on the counter and transfer to the refrigerator. Let the mixture chill overnight.
- Add the mixture to an ice cream maker and process according to the manufacturer's instructions. When the ice cream is ready, turn off the machine and incorporate the mix-ins: marshmallows (homemade or store-bought), shredded milk chocolate, and roasted almonds. Transfer to an airtight container and let harden in the freezer for at least 4 hours. If you'd rather, add the toppings to the ice cream after it's frozen.

4.

WHAT MADE MILWAUKEE FAMOUS

The law caught up with me at the Southwest Airlines boarding gate at the Milwaukee airport. I was headed back to California, but there was no chance of getting on the plane without first submitting to a public round of DNA testing and fingerprinting.

Two hundred sets of eyes—those of my fellow passengers—watched as the policewoman escorted me to the stairwell. She pulled out a black ink fingerprinting pad and long cotton swabs. A beefy sheriff blocked the exit.

"The people on my flight must think I've done something very bad," I whispered to the policewoman. "No one will sit with me."

I hadn't wanted to come to Milwaukee, which is one of the most dangerous cities in America. The year I visited, murders had increased by 76 percent and people were fleeing the city to escape the crime spree.[24] Aside from its violent reputation, the city is known for its comfort food—fried cheesy curds, brats, beer, and frozen custard. Sure, you can get a so-called frozen custard in New York City or St. Louis, but no place else has the highest concentration of shops devoted to the decadent specialty or a higher standard of quality. Frozen custard has more egg in it than regular ice cream or soft-serve. It has much less air in it than ice cream, making it both rich and dense.

I'd had real frozen custard once—on a road trip from New York City through Wisconsin back to California in 2007. Dan and I had stopped at Michael's in Madison. It was eighty degrees, we'd driven more than eight hundred miles, and we circled around the capitol building for thirty minutes before finally finding the stand. We were licking our vanilla cones, the custard dripping down our knuckles, when a group of bicyclists wearing RIGHT TO LIFE T-shirts pulled up, distracting and annoying me, while flouting the unwritten rule to never mix politics and ice cream.

To get a fair sampling of frozen custard, hopefully without interference from right-wing agitators, I needed to travel to Wisconsin again. There are few regional delicacies left in the United States, and most involve artery-clogging, gut-busting comfort foods. These treats force you to get on a plane or car and go to the source. To eat a genuine steamed cheeseburger, you must travel to Meriden, Connecticut. To experience the phenomenon that is clam pizza, there is no getting around a trip to New Haven.

The same principle holds true for frozen custard, which is cruelly nontransportable and best served fresh at about twenty degrees Fahrenheit. You could have it shipped overnight to your home, but it would never have the correct consistency. Frozen custard, by requiring us to make an effort (including a trip halfway across the country), flouts our age of technology and convenience. NASA paid a mechanical engineer 125,000 dollars to hack a 3-D printer so it can beam food to astronauts, including decent pizza.[25] But no one has figured out how to "beam" custard across state lines just yet, so I said farewell to Dan and Julianna and packed a few essentials and my yoga mat; I was determined to offset the thousands of calories I was about to consume with a few downward-facing dogs. If nothing else, I would mindfully binge eat.

I boarded a direct flight for Cream City, which gets its nickname from the frozen-custard-colored brick made from lime and sulfur-infused clay and used in buildings around the city. My itinerary was simple: I'd sample as much frozen custard as I could and try to figure out why the regional specialty cannot be re-created outside of the Midwest. In the process, I hoped to learn why ice cream lovers were willing to travel two thousand miles to a medium-size city with an outsize reputation for danger and crime, all for the sake of a cone.

Federal standards for frozen custard state that the treat must contain at least 10 percent butterfat and 1.4 percent egg yolk. As I made my way through Milwaukee in a rented car, I thought that it made no sense that such a treat was available in only one region of the United States. But I was hoping to discover if there was something about Wisconsin—a mystery ingredient or process—that made it the best place to find frozen custard.

During my first stopover in my Milwaukee tour, I posed the question to Tom Linscott, owner of Gilles, the oldest frozen custard stand in the city.

Linscott's dad bought the place from Paul Gilles in 1977, and it has been in the family for three generations. He now runs the shop with his son, Willy, who has a clean-cut, preppy look, his well-groomed brown hair tucked under a baseball cap.

"Why can't I find a good scoop of frozen custard at my neighborhood mall or in the little shopping center down the street?" I asked Tom.

"It's all about the cows," he said with unmistakable regional pride. He went on to explain his theory that because of the lush landscape, Wisconsin cows produced milk that was better for creating frozen custard.

"You can't replicate the frozen custard formula in California," he added.

I wasn't sure of the dairy science behind Tom's theory, but every guy is entitled to his nebulous regional opinions. I'd lived in Manhattan long enough to hear how the bagels and pizza there are superior because of "something in the water."

And I'd talked to enough ice cream makers and dairy hands to believe there might be a link between what a cow eats, its emotional state, and the milk products it produces. Why else would people sing opera to their cows, like they do in Eugene, Oregon?

Although it was only one P.M., I was eagerly listening to Tom's theory while devouring a vanilla cone. The consistency was exactly what I'd remembered during my blissful custard moments in Wisconsin, which the pro-lifers had so rudely interrupted all those years ago. It was smooth and rich, like a saltwater taffy that had been melted and dunked in liquid nitrogen.

It was firm without the unyielding hardness of scooped and packed ice cream. It had the perfect amount of sweetness, and the eggs gave it a heft without adding an egg taste. "I still have custard for breakfast," said Tom, who has a bulky affableness I associate with the Midwest. He reminded me of a leaner John Goodman, the actor who played Roseanne Barr's long-suffering husband.

Tom started working at Gilles when he was fifteen. He's worked twelve- to fourteen-hour days for more than three and a half decades. "It's a lifestyle," said Tom. "I took a week of vacation seven years ago."

Willy said he didn't see his dad much at home as a kid because of the long hours he spent at the custard shop. The father and son have connected much more since Willy came back after graduating and trying his hand in the business world. The corporate life had little appeal. "The clock was frozen in the office," said Willy. "Here time moves so quickly." Willy has committed himself to custard for the long haul. "I'm here 'til I'm six feet under," said Willy.

While we were talking, Willy looked up and started waving to a man driving out of the parking lot—a clench-jawed, bespectacled fellow who looks a bit like Bill Gates but with scaled-down spectacles, a slimmer face, and a bit of an updo. "That was Bud Selig, who just came in for his hot dog," said Willy. Miller Park is just down the road from Gilles, and Bud Selig, who was commissioner of baseball for two decades, is a frequent customer.

Willy explained that the eighty-degree temperature was perfect custard-eating weather. When the temperatures soar above ninety degrees, people don't feel like eating much of anything—not even frozen custard. "We joke that the customers are like vampires. You're looking out the window, waiting for the sun to set."

If these fussy custard customers adhered to strict temperature standards, all the frozen custard stands would go out of business. The weather is almost never ideal in Milwaukee, where temps can dip to twenty below in winter. Still, the custard shop stays open year-round, even when business is understandably sluggish. "We lose about two-thirds of our volume in the winter," Tom said. When he first started at the store in the 1970s, it used to stay closed four months out of the year. Because of payroll issues including health insurance and the need to deliver steady paychecks to employees, regardless of the season and the fickle public, that business model is now impossible, and the team slogs through a slow, long winter every year.

Using a special recipe (all the custard shops in Milwaukee have their own proprietary blend), a company called Classic Mix creates the mix for Gilles custard and the other frozen custard places around town. Gilles uses 13 percent butterfat. Their vanilla custard is made with cold-processed twofold bourbon vanilla extract.

Tom Linscott is a humble man, but he can't resist the urge to brag about how this formula is a crowd-pleaser. "In a blind taste test we've won, hands down, with our vanilla."

After a too-long hiatus from frozen custard, I could not resist my urge to eat that Gilles cone in a frantic rush; something about it defied my efforts to slow down. I finished the cone within minutes of sitting down with the Linscotts. I felt no guilt about the speed of my custard eating, just the satisfaction of eating a perfect meal, keeping hunger at bay, with a wish to perhaps jump into a DeLorean, go back ten minutes in time, and do it all again.

I also had the delighted expectation of even better frozen custard. I had carefully researched the frozen custard stands on Yelp. Although there are more than half a dozen custard shops in Milwaukee, there is little dispute about the top three options: Gilles, Leon's, and Kopp's.

Immediately after my chat with the Linscotts, I headed to another front-runner, Leon's, to sample the product. Leon's is a flashback to the fifties in the middle of a blighted area of South Milwaukee bordered by hospitals and strip malls. It used to be a drive-in, and many Americans think of it as the inspiration for Arnold's in *Happy Days.* Of course, fans of Gilles and Kopp's claim those stands were the basis of the fictional hangout. The truth is that none of them were. The real Arnold's, according to *Happy Days* co-creator Tom Miller, was based on a restaurant called the Milky-Way, which was later remodeled into Kopp's.[26] But Leon's is remarkably photogenic and oozes a vibe of happier days, a reminder that things used to be good and can be once again if you stop long enough for a double or triple scoop.

The customers were already lined up for their scoops. Through the glass I saw metal machines pushing out flavors in long cylinders. I ordered what everyone on Yelp said to order, the butter pecan, even though my mouth was still coated with the vanilla I'd had at Gilles. As soon as I tasted my Leon's scoop, my brain let go of any travel tension, focusing instead on the slight saltiness of

The exterior of Leon's Frozen Custard hasn't changed much since the 1950s.

the pecan and the juxtaposition that is frozen custard—it's both smooth and firm, and it reminds me of being held long ago by a nice babysitter, who comforted me after my brother Steve side tackled me. There is just enough substance to get through a few hours to the next life crisis. It was as if the concoction was insulating me for the worst Milwaukee had to offer.

As I gave myself over to the custard-eating experience, I noticed that the crowd around me was mostly silent. Roy Orbison's "Oh, Pretty Woman" blasted from the speakers, but the chatter died out. Those in line were quiet with anticipation, and those with cones in their hands were too enraptured to speak. There are no seats at Leon's, but I didn't even notice that I was standing until I was done eating.

I had a tentative appointment to talk to Ron Schneider, the owner of Leon's, but when someone told me I'd just missed him, I was too blissed-out to care. I tried my best to savor the cone, but once again it thwarted my efforts. I felt a slight embarrassment that I couldn't overcome my childhood conditioning. I am the youngest in a family of three children, which has led me to eat a treat too fast, fearing that someone larger and stronger will wrest it from my hands.

The clock seems to run faster when there's frozen custard in front of you. Since it's softer than ice cream, it feels always on the verge of melting onto the sidewalk—and the pressure to eat it quickly only increases the urge to gobble it. I felt like I was in a competitive eating game, and it was time to slow down. I needed to put some distance between myself and temptation.

I drove through the city of Milwaukee, which had a long history of enjoying comfort foods, like ice cream, even before modern refrigeration. Milwaukee's raw, bitter, miserable winters made local residents stomp their boots and bundle up by the fireplace, but it also allowed that city to become a champion of two refreshing comfort foods: beer and ice cream. Extreme low temperatures led to an annual bumper crop of lake ice, an essential raw material in ice cream making long before the use of mechanical refrigeration. Ice harvesters would drive their horses and ice plows onto the frozen water. Vintage photographs show workers bundled up against the cold, standing near yawning gaps in the frozen lake, poking at perfectly cut parallelogram-shaped blocks of ice floating in the water, looking as delicate as windowpanes.

"Harvesting Ice on the Milwaukee River," Sumner Matteson, circa 1900. *Courtesy of the Milwaukee Public Museum.*

Commercial ice harvesting on ponds, lakes, and rivers made it possible for nearby residents to store food in "ice boxes." It also allowed dairymen and vegetable growers to expand their markets by placing their goods on insulated refrigerator cars. But these grunt workers also deserve some credit for the beers that made the city famous. By the late nineteenth century, brewery owners were hogging up most of America's harvested ice; by one estimate, they were using three million tons of the stuff per year.[27] The large-scale ice trade also made it possible for commercial creameries and cheese makers to prosper in Milwaukee. This primitive method was so popular that midwesterners kept using ice blocks as a coolant even during the early years of mechanical refrigeration, which was considered too expensive, unwieldy, and even dangerous at first; in those days, artificial refrigeration depended on clunky pipes that were always breaking down, and pressurized ammonia that could make people sick and spoil food if it leaked out.[28]

Those traditionalists felt that good old-fashioned lake ice was better than any fancy new technology. But ice harvesters were vulnerable to temperature fluctuation; the winter of 1877–1878 was so warm that the Chicago and Milwaukee "ice crop" was a complete disaster that year. Besides, some of that "natural" ice was quite disgusting. Quality and purity standards could be loosey-goosey in those times, with stinky swamp ice sometimes showing up in people's drinks. Back in 1855, a Milwaukee-based doctor protested about ice businesses selling ice that reeked with pollution. He said that if water was not potable, then it stood to reason that it should not be used as ice and mixed into people's drinks. After all, no one should be forced into "drinking what was so difficult to inhale."[29]

Lake harvesters first made it possible to make commercial ice creams and store the product indefinitely in insulated "ice houses." But in the end, the new technology won out; by the 1920s and 1930s, the ice industry was considered too cumbersome, too unreliable, and too dangerous to be sustainable. It soon became a ghost of its former self, and once-popular terms such as "ice box" and "ice house" soon turned into anachronisms.[30]

I was looking forward to exploring the beer, cheese, and custard choices with reckless abandon with my friends Heidi and Luke. I drove to the sleepy village of Shorewood, where I was staying with them and their daughter, Symone. The GPS in my phone led me along Highway 43. I passed by European-looking churches lining the leafy freeway—hints at a culture and sophistication I had yet to experience in the city.

I exited through a grungy-looking part of the city. Trash littered the sidewalks. The windows of every apartment building had bars across them. As I drove, the statistics I'd read before coming to the city swirled in my head. More than 28 percent of the city's population lives below the poverty line, and I was getting a clear visual of what their homes and neighborhoods looked like. As I traveled along Capitol Drive, the scene changed without warning. The old cream-colored buildings were tall and clean, the lawns neatly clipped. It looked like a midwestern version of Princeton, New Jersey.

Although both Heidi and Luke had spent their formative years in Wisconsin, neither one had tried Gilles or Leon's. I couldn't believe it. It was like being a native San Franciscan and never seeing the Golden Gate Bridge. Heidi's grandfather, however, is a lifelong custard lover. Heidi's mom, Dawn, remembers her dad driving her into the city once a week as a kid to visit Leon's. Now in his seventies, he checks Kopp's flavor of the day and makes his decision on whether to make the long pilgrimage based on that. He switched allegiances to Kopp's because of proximity. Heidi's strange relationship to frozen custard was a lingering teenage rebellion I devoted myself to curing.

Heidi and I took long walks along the bluffs of Lake Michigan in a halfhearted attempt to burn off some of the custard I was consuming maniacally. I was oohing and aahing over the mansions, which were considered a steal by California standards. Perhaps I could get a summerhouse in this neighborhood one day. Meanwhile, I had a much more immediate goal: "You have to try Leon's," I told Heidi. "I'll meet you there at lunch tomorrow."

We met as planned, and she kvelled over her butter pecan just as I knew she would. Introducing Heidi to the delicacy of her city felt like leading a woman to a place where it was acceptable, and even encouraged, to put on as many pounds as possible; take, for example, a Nigerian fattening room, where ladies go to round up a little bit for the sake of beauty.[31] Certain pleasure-loving, gourmandizing midwesterners do not have the same hang-ups and body issues that you find on the coasts. (Or if they do, they do an incredible job of ignoring them.) They enjoy their treats, and their idea of beauty seems to be different from that of the rest of America—as if the Great Lakes insulate them from America's grim obsession with thinness. Walking down the streets of Milwaukee, you can imagine it's still cool for ladies to be as plump as a partridge.

It took two more trips to Leon's to track down Ron Schneider, the elusive owner. I was heading toward Leon's for the third time in as many days. At the front window, the manager told me to go around the back.

I followed a slippery metal staircase with a wobbly banister, which led to the back door of the building. The rear of the shop was much less photogenic than the storefront—in fact, it resembled my garage, a hoarder's paradise with piles of boxes stacked almost to the ceiling. I waited while Schneider finished his phone call, trying to keep my curious hands from rummaging through the boxes. I walked in on a middle-aged man with short silver hair and black-framed glasses. When he heard me coming, he hung up the phone. There was no denying that Ron Schneider bore an uncanny resemblance to Peter Graves in the 1960s *Mission: Impossible.* He shook my hand and quickly began to explain why Leon's frozen custard is the best there is.

"Our frozen custard has the best texture, the best flavor, and is the most satisfying.

"People who say Kopp's is the best have only eaten at Kopp's."

I wasn't put off by his bragging. It seemed like the kind of bluster you earn from surviving four decades in the business. Ron's dad, Leon, opened his eponymous store in 1942. He borrowed three hundred dollars from his mom. "He didn't know it, but it was all the money she had," Ron told me.

Leon had debts to pay off, but just as he was getting the business up and running, he was drafted into World War II. He put a friend, Bob Palmer, in charge of the store while he was stationed in Grass Valley, California. (He was never sent overseas because he had flat feet and the army never got him the correct boots.) Leon and his wife spent their leave driving from California to Wisconsin and back.

When Leon was discharged in 1944, he took over full-time operation of the business. Leon's was on Route 41—at that time it was a direct stopping spot on the way to Chicago. "We still have plenty of people who drive up from Chicago for our custard," said Ron.

Ron's mom insisted on working the cash register, just so she could spend time with her husband, Leon. Ron needed to start earning some money and began working with his dad at fourteen years old, when a cone was just fifteen cents. He knew early on that he was destined to take over the shop.

"If you want to be in control of your life, you have to be your own boss," said Ron.

According to Ron there are three things you need to be successful in the frozen custard business: the proper machine, a good mix, and the knowledge of how to make and serve it fresh. The first requirement, the machine, is what separates Leon's and Kopp's from the rest of the competition. According to Ron, other places that say they serve frozen custard are often using a soft-serve machine, which just doesn't do a good enough job of pressing out all the air. Aside from its failure at the art of air compression, the soft-serve machine has created a nationwide ignorance about the dessert.

"Most people outside of Milwaukee have never had real frozen custard. They've just had soft-serve. They don't know the difference."

When Leon's opened in 1942, it had custard-making machines, affectionately known as "iron lungs." These clanking and wheezing machines were large and cylindrical and resembled the large tank-like metallic respiratory devices used to treat patients during the polio epidemics of the 1940s and 1950s. As custard makers, they were loud and broke down frequently. They also took up a huge amount of square footage.

Then the endlessly self-promoting mass-produced ice cream cake maven Tom Carvel replaced the hulking machines with streamlined ones that he used to pump out custard. Carvel is famous for his awkward commercials, in which he speaks with a grave and gravelly voice about the Carvel Hug Me the Bear and Fudgie the Whale, among other ice cream cakes. For many years, legends have been circulating about Carvel's "inventing" frozen custard—a story that Carvel himself helped to perpetuate. But two brothers have a much more convincing claim to the "inventor" title: Archie and Elton Kohr, who began selling their concoctions at Coney Island in 1919. During their debut weekend at the boardwalk, they offered up their cones at a nickel apiece—and claimed they sold more than eighteen thousand. Frozen custard was showcased at Chicago's World's Fair in 1933, and it immediately became popular in the Midwest.

But Carvel was among the first to cash in on the custard craze and revolutionize its production. Carvel opened his first shop in Hartsdale, New York, in 1936. He was a tireless tinkerer who developed the frozen custard machines. While Leon Schneider was in California during World War II, Carvel was in Fort Bragg serving as a "refrigeration consultant and concessionaire."

Carvel, through experimentation and many small adjustments, cobbled together a working frozen custard machine. He started off by selling the machine to store owners, who had so much trouble operating it that many of them defaulted on the loans he had given them. These businessmen were, understandably, frustrated, finding themselves struggling to make a profit by operating expensive machines that were supposed to churn out premium vanilla but gave them churning headaches instead.

Aside from this, Carvel, with his oversize personality, did not always get along with his underlings; Leon Schneider was, at one time, the Wisconsin franchise owner for Carvel, but he had a falling-out with Tom Carvel, which says more about the eccentric Greek than about Leon.

"Everyone who had dealings with Tom Carvel eventually wound up having a falling-out with him," said Ron.

In spite of this private cantankerousness, Thomas Carvel nurtured a public image as a gently bumbling old grandpa who just couldn't suppress his boyish enthusiasm for ice cream. Carvel loved to tell the story about starting off in the business as a green twenty-six-year-old in 1934. The former test-driver for Studebaker automobiles was selling ice cream out of a banged-up old truck with help from a fifteen-dollar loan, courtesy of his fiancée. Suddenly, one of his tires blew out on a busy highway, leaving him stranded in Hartsdale, New York, on Memorial Day. "I was so broke that wonderful day . . . that I had to telephone friends to send me a tire," Carvel told a reporter in 1954.[32] While he was lingering, a nearby potter took pity on him and told him to stay where he was and try to sell some ice cream. "By the time my tire arrived, I was sold out," Carvel claimed. By 1985, Carvel's ice cream business was an empire of 865 franchise stores selling 300 million dollars' worth of goods a year.

There was something studied and calculated about Carvel's goofy persona. This wacky grandpa figure had no kids of his own.

Carvel, a Greek immigrant, performed his own halting and gravelly voice-overs for the awesomely mawkish and gloriously cheesy Carvel ice cream cake commercials, which became a cultural touchstone for latchkey children all over the Northeast. The commercials were so out there, they are almost impossible to mock, with their images of ice cream cakes floating through outer space like *Star Wars* spaceships while quavering synthesizer music plays in the background. His Cookie Puss ice cream cake—featuring a hominoid creature with cookies for eyes—and his Easter Bunny special were so unintentionally creepy looking that they brought to mind the installation art of Mike Kelley, who used stuffed animals to sinister effect in his artworks. Today, those commercials have a cult following, thanks to the loopy testimonials of the Beastie Boys, the comedian and actor Patton Oswalt, and many others.

A mannered populism was part of Carvel's marketing strategy. He talked about how much he loathed highfalutin ice cream brands, the sort of stuff that gets the "artisanal" label these days. "Don't make a Rembrandt of it," he used to scold his cake decorators if they tried to show off their lofty artistic ambitions.[33] Carvel, for all his "take me as I am" persona, could be quite calculating. Some considered him an unapologetic control freak. Even from the beginning, he had a fearsome reputation "as a tough businessman who rode herd on his franchisees, refusing to let them start dealer organizations and forcing them to buy everything from cones to napkins from Carvel at prices they considered inflated," *The New York Times* reported.[34]

Carvel shot back at the complainers, insisting he had to be controlling for the sake of America's children. "Sure they call me strict . . . ," he groused. "But poison one child, and 50 years of business goes down the drain."[35] He also insisted that his oversight stopped his franchisees from cheating customers. In an earlier lawsuit, Carvel prevailed and never apologized. "You can't run a business unless you're a tyrant," he once remarked.[36]

Leon sold the Carvel machines around the Midwest in the 1950s and started making replacement parts for them. "We needed them anyway," said Schneider.

Leon's and Kopp's still use the Carvel machine, even though the machines—once considered streamlined—are bulky, loud, and difficult to repair. Schneider believes these Carvel-designed machines are the key to why his custard is so delicious. For this reason, he blames "idiot environmentalists" for pushing for government regulations and jeopardizing his custard's amazing taste and consistency. I was startled to realize that the production of frozen custard is doing more than just occluding American arteries. It is also doing its small part to put new holes in the ozone layer. The machines basically run on Freon, also known as R-12, which has been banned for more than twenty years. Schneider is not convinced that the environmental concerns warrant a change to his business. "We have found that R-12 makes the best frozen custard."

I was struck again by the cruelty of frozen custard production. It's not just that you have to go to Wisconsin to get the stuff. If I was hearing Schneider correctly, at some point you won't be able to get it at all. Somehow, my fear about the end of true frozen custard had trumped all environmental concerns.

"Eventually the R-12 will be gone because it will be used up. I'll worry about that then." Schneider's son, Steven, has worked in the family business for twenty-five years. Ron also has two daughters, who are not involved in the business. So, it will most likely be left to Steven to find a suitable refrigerant replacement.

Schneider said he's experimented with other refrigerants, but they "don't get the product cold enough."

I used to work for the Sierra Club, and I consider myself an environmentalist. My family owns only one car, I separate my recyclables, and I buy organic, locally sourced ingredients. But the idea of a frozen custard–free future seemed so unutterably bleak that I called the federal Environmental Protection Agency (EPA) in part because of my professional curiosity, in part because I was concerned: What if frozen custard is truly doomed because there is no reliable substitute refrigerant?

My request to find out more about rules regarding refrigerants in frozen custard machines bounced around the Midwest regional office before being forwarded to Washington, DC. It took another two months to get a wonky response from Enesta Jones, a spokesperson for the EPA. "Because CFCs and HCFCs deplete the stratospheric ozone layer, they are being phased out globally," she told me. Some of these chemical compounds were phased out of production in 1996, while others will be illegal to produce after 2030. However, recycled CFCs, like the ones Ron swears by, can still be used indefinitely.

I found her response incomprehensible. I'd failed high school chemistry—although it was an Advanced Placement class, so I always argued the F should be bumped up to a D—and her response, with all its murky abbreviations, reminded me why scientists and policy makers are so vilified, even when they are in the right. Despite my lefty California leanings, I sided with the frozen custard makers and worried about their plight. Frozen custard was tangible. It makes me happy. The numbers and letters of the EPA and its rusty canisters reminded me of scolding high school teachers.

I was coming to fear that Leon's custard-making days just might be over once its source of containers of outdated refrigerant runs out. In fact this stuff is so hard to find that Leon's has to buy it on that international repository of archaic material culture—eBay.

As long as there are crusty canisters on eBay for sale, Leon's is safe. Until that well runs dry, the rumbling, locomotive-like custard machines will keep on vibrating night and day.

Leon's machines make a sound similar to what commuters hear in a busy subway station, and they get louder when they are close to running out of mix. The machines introduce very little air into the custard, which is why it has such a smooth, dense consistency. Leon's custard is 10 percent butterfat and 20 percent "overrun," an ice cream industry term for air pumped into each batch of product, making it "light" on the tongue on the one hand, but also using air to puff out each batch so that you wind up with more volume for less cost. Most American ice cream is at least 50 percent overrun.

Frozen custard is best eaten fresh from the machine. If custard sits around, it begins to soften, and if you put it in the freezer, it hardens to the more generic consistency of ice cream. But if you need to take a pint home, it will keep for a quarter of an hour. Just forget trying to save some for the next day. "You can buy a pint and let it sit out for ten to fifteen minutes," Schneider said. "But then you have to eat the whole thing. If you refreeze, it ruins the texture."

That ephemeral quality adds a certain urgency; custard, by its very nature, commands you to eat it all *right now.* "You can go to a gas station to buy ice cream," said Schneider. "If you want good frozen custard, you have to come here."

Despite the fact that the days of ozone-depleting R-12 are

numbered, I found it fascinating that new custard places keep opening up around the city, giving Milwaukeeans an almost unlimited number of choices when it comes to the dessert. Schneider keeps helping out the competition. Like his dad, Schneider has boosted fledgling frozen custard makers, making it possible for them to open their doors. He had a hand in helping out Culver's, the now very popular chain with almost six hundred stores in more than twenty-four states. Schneider believes that custard competition is healthy because it ensures that all the stores are doing a good job. "You can't sell bad frozen custard twice," he said. "If you don't sell good stuff, they won't come back. And that hurts all the other frozen custard shops."

But mentors sometimes lose control over their disciples. Ron sold Craig Culver a frozen custard maker in the mid-1980s and trained him to use it. In the end, Culver decided to replace the machine. In Ron's opinion, there's too much butterfat in the Culver's recipe, but tens of thousands of Americans apparently disagree. Then again, Culver's heavily promotes its hot food menu, which actually gets top billing over custard on the company's website. Leon's only hot food items are a hot dog, a chili dog, and a sloppy joe—convenience foods that remind me of the childhood fare my mom used to serve and evoke involuntary shudders every time I think of them. The benefit of those dishes, as dear Mom could attest, is they don't require any vigilance. Making them badly is almost impossible.

In contrast, no one at Leon's was working the hot food line while I was spending time in the shop. "Ninety percent of what we sell is frozen custard," said Schneider.

Kopp's has three locations in Milwaukee, but Schneider says

Kopp's is too busy making money off of butter burgers, a Wisconsin delicacy that includes a heavily buttered bun. Such foods distract from the frozen custard. Schneider said the business his family helped get started makes a frozen custard that isn't even close to the flavor and consistency of Leon's.

It's well-known in Milwaukee that Leon helped Elsa Kopp start her own business in 1950. "Elsa's husband was sick and she needed a way to support the family," said Schneider. Elsa was working at Militzer's Bakery when she befriended Leon. "My father scouted out a location for her to set up a store and made sure she had frozen custard mix."

The Midwest can be a harsh, unforgiving place, and Schneider's story reminded me that people who live there have learned to help one another out through some of the worst that life has to offer.

Elsa, who died in 2003 at the age of ninety-two, was a marketing genius who came up with the idea of a frozen custard flavor of the day, introducing anticipation and surprise to the custard scene. Instead of the usual vanilla, chocolate, strawberry, and a couple of other wild-card flavors, Elsa introduced a rotating list with hundreds of options. By the 1960s, Elsa was experimenting with different flavorings to create buzz. "In the earliest days of frozen custard, it was considered heresy to tamper with the purity of the vanilla custard experience," Kopp once told the *Milwaukee Journal Sentinel.*[37]

Old-timers used to call on the phone to find out the day's flavors. These days you can check the flavor forecast online or set up an email app that will ping you when Pink Ribbon or Snickers Chunky Cheesecake is being mixed and served.[38] Flavors of the day have included Grasshopper Fudge, Maple Syrup and Pancakes, Rum and Coca-Cola, and Bienenstichkuchen, a German dessert, also known as Bee Sting Cake.

When Elsa ran Kopp's, it was usually open until at least midnight and often stayed open until one A.M. I was struck again by the ingrained Midwest work ethic, which kept employees working long hours and instilled a loyalty to the job that I hadn't seen in other parts of the country. If customers knocked on the door late at night, it didn't matter that the business was closed. According to family and friends, Elsa would turn on the grill again. "No, he needs a little something to eat," she would tell her employees. "We'll make it real quick. We can do that."

Two Kopp's locations are run by Elsa's son Karl, a restaurateur who owned Bar 89 until it closed. The Brookfield Kopp's is owned and operated by Richard McGuire.

The three Kopp's locations have a slicker, more corporate feel than Leon's, as if the aim is to transport you to a place where gourmet food reigns. Walking into the Greenfield location, you could be at Danny Meyer's Shake Shack, the New York City–based high-low food chain that blends convenience food with an upscale atmosphere. At Kopp's, glistening aluminum surfaces reflect your joy back at you. Outside is a tree-lined pit with a waterfall. When I visited around lunchtime, most people were eating burgers, and many were devouring them in their cars, hearkening back to the days when many of Milwaukee's custard and burger stands were drive-ins (as opposed to the modern-day drive-through). Perhaps they wanted to revisit the childhood memories of being a kid at a custard drive-in, where eating in your car with your family was a form of temporary escape.

Karl is a bit of an eccentric by Midwest standards. He and his partner publicly advocated legalizing marijuana and turning it into a cash crop grown in Milwaukee.[39] Kopp mostly declines to talk to the press. He oversees the menu at Kopp's but has little to do with the day-to-day operations of the business.

Jeff Feist, manager of the Greenfield location, has been working for Kopp's for thirty-three years. When I saw him, he was helping out in the slammed hot food line. But he followed up with me later on, via email, about spending more than three decades of his life working for Kopp's. Like everyone else whom I'd talked to in the Midwest custard business, he couldn't resist claiming top custard honors. He attributed much of the company's success to the Galloway family, who started a custard craze when it was introduced at the Chicago World's Fair in 1933.

"The custard mix we have had produced for us by the Galloways since the beginning is to our specifications and is at 16% butterfat, which is higher than the majority of custard restaurants," said Feist. Classic Mix Partners, LLC, is a subsidiary of the Galloway Company. All the frozen custard makers I'd spoken with got their product from Classic Mix.

A representative of the company clammed up when I asked for a basic frozen custard recipe, citing concerns about salmonella and homemade ice cream. He laughed when I asked about Linscott's theory that the Wisconsin cows were the reason that Midwest frozen custard is the best in the nation. "Frozen custard people are a secretive bunch. I'm surprised they talked to you at all."

I went back for another round of Kopp's with Heidi, Luke, and Symone at the Glendale location, where the flavor of the day was Bark in the Dark—dark chocolate custard with dark chocolate sea salt almond bark. We ate outside near the *Black and White Cows* sculpture commissioned by Kopp. The cows stood like soldiers at attention watching us eat our chocolate fill. Half in a sugar coma, with melted brown custard smeared over our hands and faces, we headed home to collapse from overeating.

After four days, I had eaten my fill of Wisconsin dairy and talked to the custard kings of Milwaukee—my work in the city was done. I'd planned a final hurrah—a lunch with Heidi and our friend Ruth from graduate school at Milwaukee's public market. My rented Nissan Altima was parked in front of Heidi's house. As I got ready to go to lunch I saw a teenager approach me out of the corner of my eye. I realized half a second too late that I was about to become another one of Milwaukee's crime statistics, and I couldn't believe that my quest for frozen custard had led me to this point.

So far on this trip, I'd heard a lot of shouted offers that I could not refuse. It was as if the custard beckoned, loudly. "Eat another scoop! Try this flavor! I don't care if you're feeling sick." The teenager, quickly approaching me, shouted a very different sort of request. "Give me the keys, bitch."

"No!" I replied. "Get away from me."

"Give me the keys," he repeated, now just an arm's length away.

The sensible thing to do would have been to hand him my keys and watch him peel off with my rental car at seventy-five miles an hour. But I grew up with two older brothers, and it had left me with an instinctual response to anyone trying to grab something that belongs to me, whether it be the last pinwheel cookie in the carton or my much-beloved cardboard model of the starship *Enterprise.*

I was just about to get into the rental car when the teenager approached me and pulled at the key fob in my hand, and I pulled back, screaming and waiting for a Good Samaritan to come along and shoo this guy away. Before that could happen, the fob pulled off the key ring I was clutching. He managed to grab the purse off my shoulder as he maneuvered his way into the car. I tugged at the purple strap of the purse even as he rolled off, until it became clear there was no chance of winning this particular tug-of-war.

My desire for frozen custard had put me in peril and left me penniless, at least for the last days of my trip, and with no phone on the streets of Milwaukee. My first thought was that the attacker had taken all my identification so that I had no way of getting through TSA security and on the plane the next day.

A Good Samaritan named Joe eventually came out to help me, but only when the danger had passed; by then, the carjacker was speeding down the street.

The police came to take my statement. Heidi and Luke both came home from work early, and we picked up Symone. After hours on the phone with police, the rental car company, my husband, and the bank, we did what we had to do. We went out and had another round of frozen custard.

Something was clearly the matter with me. A police investigation was under way, and for all I knew, a dragnet was searching for the miscreant who stole my car. At that moment, the brigand might be careening through the city, committing more crimes, smacking into trees, roaring down alleyways, and knocking over trash cans, and I wanted frozen custard? Again?

At least I had a historical precedent in enjoying ice cream during or after a traumatic event. Eating ice cream during or after a near-death experience is a time-honored American tradition. During World War II, military doctors prescribed ice cream as a curative for combat fatigue. A US Navy psychiatrist said that shell-shocked soldiers needed "showers, rest, fresh air, sunshine and wholesome food, especially ice cream." US Air Force mess sergeants reported that ice cream was the only food pilots would eat after missions. During the war, Japanese bombers attacked the USS *Lexington* and the captain ordered the men to abandon ship. While they waited for rescue, some of the sailors calmly ate ice cream to cool their nerves.[40]

Earle Swensen, founder of Swensen's Ice Cream, made ice cream on US Navy ships during World War II. After, he went on to open his first ice cream parlor in San Francisco in 1948. When Grandma came to town when I was a kid, she'd take us to Swensen's, where the motto was: "Where happiness never melts."

I usually ordered the atrocious bubble gum flavor, watching the cone turn rainbow colored from the dye melting off the broken bits of gumball. But even a bad ice cream cone to a kid is better than no ice cream at all. Those fleeting moments in the ice cream parlor were, by far, the best times I ever had with my grandma, who died when I was thirty-seven and she was ninety-two. (I guess the yoga and juice fasts paid off.) Grandma and I never really got along, but we could put aside our differences for the length of time it took to finish a cone. That is the beauty of the frozen treat; you can't really get a cone and save it for later.

Now I had a new understanding of the relationship between good food and harsh circumstances. When you find yourself in painful circumstances, or live in an unforgiving place, you must take life's treats where you can. Perhaps this explains why Wisconsin ranks as the drunkest state in the United States, where more than 65 percent of the population imbibes (and doesn't stop for long). It's a state where minors can consume alcohol in bars and restaurants if accompanied by a consenting parent or guardian (at the bartender's discretion). Walk down the streets of Milwaukee and you'll even find coffee bars that serve alcohol.[41]

I now understood this need to numb, through booze or custard or fried cheese curds. This explains why I, and my badly rattled friends, decided to head to Northpoint Custard on the shore of Lake Michigan. On a summer day, this place gets busy, but it was blustery and there were only a few other customers. As soon as we walked to the window I could see one major difference between Northpoint and the Big Three custard shops I'd visited: Northpoint had a different kind of machine, a newfangled model from Stoelting.

At that point, I didn't care if the machines weren't up to Ron Schneider's exacting standards. I'd had the scare of my life and I was seeking the cold comfort of fat and sugar in any form.

And perhaps because of my traumatized state of mind, the custard tasted better than I expected. But as I kept enjoying that scoop, the post-carjacking shock wore off just enough that my custard-ian fussiness came right back in again. The consistency was less firm than Leon's, Kopp's, or Gilles. I stuck my spoon in the center of the scoop and it stuck straight up, but not with the confidence of the spoons I'd stuck in the other custards I'd tried.

Nevertheless, sitting with Heidi (who was enjoying a pecan turtle) and Symone (who was drinking a bright blue Slurpee) returned me to the basic childhood moment of ice cream as a comfort, a distraction, an innocent reminder that things will get better.

After custard, we took a tour of downtown, where we strolled along the river and had our pictures taken with the *Bronze Fonz.*

My husband, Dan, overnighted my passport, and it arrived via FedEx by ten A.M. the next day. With my ID I was able to get cash from the bank, and Heidi and Symone took me to the Milwaukee Art Museum, where they were featuring Mark Rothko and Jackson Pollock. As we were making our own art in the kids' room, Heidi got a message from Dan that my cell phone had been found in an abandoned alleyway in a shady part of the city. Heidi was nervous about going into the neighborhood, and we decided there wasn't time to pick it up on the way to the airport.

Arriving at the airport, waiting to fly home, I thought my joyous and traumatic Milwaukee adventure was over. That's when I saw the police detective at the gate, just a few minutes before my flight was scheduled to board. Before she ushered me into the hallway, she told me what had been going on while I'd been eating custard and packing. "We found the car. It was in a wreck and there are fingerprints all over it. I need to get your prints and a DNA sample."

The airport's family restroom was occupied, which is how I wound up in the stairwell being fingerprinted and swabbed. An airport employee was coming up the stairs as witness. He looked like he was about to turn around and head back the way he came. "She's the victim," the police officer explained.

"No one is going to want to sit next to me on that plane," I said.

I boarded the flight, a bumpy ride back to the West Coast. Twenty minutes before the plane landed the flight attendant poured a glass of cold water in my lap and I burst into tears.

Dan and Julianna greeted me at the airport by running to me and enveloping me in their arms. My lap was still wet and left a little imprint on my daughter's white dress.

A few weeks after the attack, I got a package wrapped in brown paper from the Milwaukee Police Department. I opened it and discovered my wallet, bright blue with an embroidered owl staring back at me. A Good Samaritan had found it and turned it in. I inspected it. The five-dollar bill I'd had was missing. Everything else had been returned to me.

A few days later, I was startled when the Milwaukee custard maven Ron Schneider called to check in on me. "I heard you got into some trouble out here. I just want to make sure you're okay."

"How did you hear about what happened?" I asked. "Did the police call?"

"No, I was at an event over the weekend and I happened to be sitting next to your friend Ruth."

It took me a minute to understand that he was talking about my friend from graduate school, whom I was supposed to have lunch with when the carjacking happened. In that moment the Midwest felt like a mysterious epicenter of friendship and hardship—where cold comforts led to pain and unexpected delights. I was still craving the butter pecan, but I resisted the urge to beg him to send me a pint. After all, what would be the point? We both knew I needed to suffer in Milwaukee to really enjoy it.

After my time in Milwaukee, I was looking forward to returning to the innocent pleasures of ice cream. I would pursue it by chasing down the all-American tradition of the ice cream truck. After all, what could bring us back to childhood like those ringing chimes that signal summer? Little did I know that the ice cream truck wars were escalating in New York City with fistfights, bloody noses, road rage, vandalized vehicles, and more police intervention.

NGB2 (NEVER GOING BACK TO) MILWAUKEE BUTTER PECAN CUSTARD

1½ cups half-and-half
1¼ cups heavy cream
½ cup skim milk powder
1 cup sugar
¼ teaspoon salt
7 large egg yolks
2 teaspoons vanilla
1½ tablespoons butter
1½ cups pecans
¼ cup coarse salt

- Heat the half-and-half and cream in a saucepan over medium heat. Whisk in the skim milk powder, sugar, and salt. Simmer until the solids are dissolved and the mixture has reached 110°F. Lightly beat the egg yolks in a separate bowl. Pour a teaspoon of the heated milk mixture into the eggs to temper them.
- Add the eggs to the cream mixture and heat and stir constantly until the temperature reaches 165°F (10 to 15 minutes). Strain through a metal strainer into a large Pyrex dish. Let cool and add the vanilla. Mixture should be refrigerated for at least 2 hours.
- While the mixture is cooling in the fridge, make the butter pecans. Preheat the oven to 350°F. Melt the butter in a skillet over medium heat. Remove from the heat, add

the pecans, stir, and sprinkle with the coarse salt. Spread the pecans on a baking sheet and place in the oven for 10 to 12 minutes, stirring so the nuts don't burn. Let cool.

- Churn the ice cream according to the manufacturer's instructions.
- Add the salted butter pecans right at the end of churning. Freeze for at least 4 hours before eating.

5.

BAD BLOOD, GOOD HUMOR!

The sun was blazing down on the streets of Bensonhurst when the ice cream truck came to an abrupt halt in front of the Twentieth Avenue subway station. Maria Campanella, aka Maria the Ice Cream Girl, likes to make a big and brassy entrance. She announces her arrival with a *whoop-whoop-whoop*ing sound like a police siren. She pulled up alongside the curb, waving. Her long bleached-blond hair and pink lipstick made her look a bit like Glinda the Good Witch from *The Wizard of Oz.*

"This is Bensonhurst and I'm the Ice Cream Girl," she said. "And this is how we roll." Maria was wearing see-through skin-tight black ruffled leggings, a black chemise, and a brown wrap pulled tightly across her ample chest.

She leaned out of the window of her vintage 1974 truck, proudly showing off every exposed curve.

But it was really Maria's truck that caught my eye. *Daddy I Love You* was painted in pink cursive letters on the rig. A photo of her dad, Angelo Campanella, dressed in Good Humor garb, is blown up and taped near the sliding window. Maria explained that her truck is a moving piece of history; she refuses to let go of this old clunker, in spite or perhaps because of its clattering limitations. Her family has traveled the same Bensonhurst streets hawking ice cream for more than seventy years. She's one of the few vendors who are still trying to make a living peddling Good Humor bars and other novelties in a changing, often violent New York ice cream landscape.

Despite my strong reservations about the cramped interior of the vehicle, my family and I piled into the ancient, clattering truck. Pink and red glitter hearts were stuck to the ceiling, with more tributes to her dad, who was known around town as Chubby, even after he slimmed down from 225 to 150 pounds.[42] Chubby started selling ice cream in Bensonhurst in the 1940s. Customers considered him their benevolent grandfather; making his rounds through Bensonhurst, he refused to sell treats to kids unless they went to school. The need to make a profit never stopped him from handing out free treats. He never let a kid go away empty-handed or embarrassed in front of his friends because he had no spare coins for an ice cream. After Chubby died at age eighty-three in 2009, Maria successfully fought city hall for five years to get a street in town named after him.

Maria may be Italian through and through, but her truck reminded me of a Día de los Muertos display—a lavish shrine of sweets to celebrate and communicate with a beloved ancestor. Julianna and I sat on a cooler filled with Orange Crush and Dr Pepper—a makeshift seat. "Be careful, it might roll," Maria warned.

Maria Campanella sells treats from her truck in Bensonhurst.
Michael Wright

Proper seats with proper seat belts in a four-decade-old ice cream truck? Fuggedaboudit! I felt like I was being transported to the 1970s, when my mom used to drive me around in her Plymouth Valiant without a car seat or even a lap belt. Maria's truck was such a throwback that the modern rules of car safety didn't seem to apply.

Maria started the engine with a loud roar. She honked the horn and ran the police siren. "We got to make some noise and wake these people up." It was five P.M. The noise struck me as a form of aggression and territorial marking, in keeping with a New York City ice cream truck tradition. The sounds of ice cream trucks are a common reason for complaint calls to New York City's 311 help line. In 2015, the year I visited, City Councilman Daniel Dromm introduced a bill to muffle the truck jingles, which he ranked among "the most annoying noises assaulting New Yorkers' ears every day." The *New York Post* ran a story about the controversy, entitled "Shut the Truck Up."[43] The city has a long-standing animus toward the twinkling ice cream melodies; in 2004, then mayor Michael Bloomberg attempted to impose a ban on the Mister Softee song.[44] In 2005, a survey showed that New Yorkers considered ice cream truck sounds even more horrifying than loud bar noises and the clamor of barking dogs, though they didn't think these melodies were quite so awful as car alarms.

Instead of the cloyingly hypnotic tunes you hear from most ice cream trucks, Maria blasts hip-hop music including Jungle Brothers' "I'll House You," which begins with a deafening blast of funk, the sounds of a DJ scratching wildly, and united voices shouting *"Can you feel it? Can you feel it?"* As we rolled past squat brick buildings and tree-lined sidewalks, Maria despaired about the quiet streets and the changing neighborhood. "These blocks are all dead," she said, with a thick Brooklyn accent I thought had gone extinct fifty years ago.

"There are no kids out like there used to be. Used to be tons of people sitting in front of their houses on beach chairs. Used to be thousands of rosebushes all over the place." I looked out at rows of minivans lining the streets and the well-manicured lawns.

"Well, there's still a lot of plants and stuff like that; people still maintain their gardens," said Maria, "but I'm saying the Italians loved the rosebushes. You see, if they have the rosebushes—" And then she paused and pointed to two large potted plants sitting on a doorstep with pink flowers. "That ain't a rosebush. If you see the rosebushes, then you know they're Italian."

Maria, who was in her early fifties when I met her, remembers the way Bensonhurst used to be and won't let us forget it. The neighborhood was traditionally Italian, filled with old-world trattorias and greengrocers, along with a legacy of wise guys and gangsters. The Gambino brothers ran a café on Eighteenth Avenue. The world-famous crime family's connections in the area date back to the beginning of the twentieth century.

Bensonhurst used to be predominantly Italian, but there's been an influx of Asian immigrants since 2000. Maria's old customers used to spend fifteen dollars a night on treats for their kids. The tradition of buying from an ice cream truck in the afternoons and evenings stopped when the Italian families migrated toward Staten Island to "live a better life."

Maria has had to try to adjust to the new reality, yet she hasn't changed routes, even though it's now barely lucrative, and her old truck regularly breaks down, eating into her bottom line.

The new immigrants in Bensonhurst and even the old-timers now have an appetite for soft-serve. "I wish I had a soft truck," Maria said. "Fuggedaboudit. I'd have an empire."

But getting a new truck that could serve soft would cost about 135,000 dollars, with a thirty-thousand-dollar down payment.

And what would she do with her old truck, her tangible connection to her dad? It seemed to me that her daily pilgrimage was less about making a real living and more a way of keeping Chubby's memory alive. Images of Chubby stared at me from every corner of the truck.

Steam seemed to be rising from the sidewalk and blowing into the truck.

What had brought me here, shvitzing and anxious, on a wild ride through a strange part of my ancestral borough? I was only miles away from where my mother and father grew up in Flatbush. I wanted to see firsthand the ice cream truck wars that rage on the streets in New York in summer. I wanted to learn how these truck drivers carve up their routes, and what happens when you cross into someone else's territory, especially when a way of life and a livelihood are at stake. But I was also chasing a childhood dream. I'd spent many hours as a kid waiting for the elusive ice cream truck to appear. Back in her Brooklyn days, my mother also whiled away the afternoons, looking out the window, waiting for the boxy truck to creep up along the side streets, luring children with its insidious melodies.

My mom remembers a Good Humor truck coming down Martense Street in Flatbush in the 1950s every night, just five miles away from where Chubby was selling his treats. Grandma would throw a quarter out the window to my mom, who was playing in the streets. Occasionally the money would fall through a drain grate, and Mom would use a stick and a piece of gum to fish it out. The drama seemed to be part of the ice cream truck fun, and also a character-building exercise. If Mom was successful in recovering the coin, she'd buy a Creamsicle. I'm sure Grandma did it on purpose, to give her slow-moving daughter a little extra exercise.

My mom was reacting to the ways that ice cream trucks induce a kind of synesthesia in young children; sound turns into hunger, and the sight of a white truck triggers memories of sweet smells. These trucks give rise to an enormous sense of want, stimulating the salivary glands with the disembodied and tinkling music that floats from the truck. I don't ever remember hearing the telltale jingle in Silicon Valley in the 1980s. And yet

I spent countless hours during the summer anticipating and looking down the street for a truck that wasn't there. My family had relocated from the East Coast when I was four, and I must have had some deep-seated memories of the ice cream truck coming around the corner at our old house in Rochester, New York. The idea that a truck might come by our new house in California had created a desperate wanting within me, to the point where I sometimes heard a phantom jingle. I didn't know that the trucks were mostly an East Coast phenomenon. When I think of waiting for the ice cream truck, I can feel the scratchiness of our yellow living room swivel chair beneath my sweaty legs, my mouth pressed against the window, breath fogging the glass, and time moving slowly as it can only when you are a kid desperately waiting for the fun to begin. Silicon Valley in the 1980s was a boring and stifling place where you were expected to find adventures, show some moxie, and discover or invent your own treats.

So, thirty-odd years later, I traveled across the country to my parents' old borough for an authentic ice cream truck experience. I wanted to show Julianna a moving piece of New York City's ice cream history. But Maria was not the East Coast ice cream ambassador I had inside my head. She had a loud pluckiness that brought to mind another figment of my childhood: Penny Marshall from one of my favorite childhood sitcoms, *Laverne & Shirley.* I could imagine Maria hanging out with Lenny and Squiggy, and blundering her way through Hasenpfeffer Incorporated. Meeting Maria reminded me that it was the ritual of consumption, the stand-in for family togetherness, and not the quality of the product, that mattered.

When her daddy, Chubby, put Maria on the truck, she was nineteen and a bit of a troubled teen, hanging out with a rough crowd. She saw the gesture as an act of faith—her dad's belief in her despite her wild ways.

"I tried to do the best that I could do for everybody. I taught myself to do that. I taught myself to become a better person. Only you can."

But as I listened to the rest of Maria's story, I discovered a hitch in her transformation narrative from troubled teen to law-abiding ice cream truck driver. Despite her best efforts to be an ice cream bodhisattva, Maria's anger, kept at bay during most of her life, is unleashed on the Mister Softee trucks that have invaded the borough. "I used to have eleven fistfights a year. I used to drag them out of their truck 'cause they come on my route. I was female, and they used to try and intimidate me."

She looked at Julianna, suddenly self-conscious that she was frightening my young daughter. "I'm not a bad person. You'll see when I make you a snow cone later." Julianna nodded and then scooted closer to me on the cooler, practically settling in my lap.

We drove down a few blocks more until Maria spotted her nemesis—a Mister Softee truck that was encroaching on her territory. Mister Softee started doling out treats in the 1950s, but it's only since the beginning of the twenty-first century that things have gotten violent. As she explained the politics of negotiating an ice cream truck route, her Brooklyn accent became stronger along with her anger.

"There's always gonna be one soft truck on each route and there's always gonna be one hard truck on each route. I let this guy stay here seventeen years. He put three trucks on my route. He's a pig. I want to beat him up."

Even though Maria's old truck can't make the modern, more lucrative switchover to soft-serve, she's not giving up her territory, her truck's real or imagined connection to the simpler times of the past, and her dad's Good Humor traditions. Back then there were no fistfights. Chubby stayed true to the company image of men doling out treats in white shirts, white pants, bow ties, and hats.

The Good Humor truck is such an important part of Americana that a 1938 Chevrolet truck, which apparently once rattled its way through the streets of Boston, is part of the Smithsonian Institution's collection.[45]

Looking at a picture of that endearingly awkward snow-white Chevy, which looks like an oversize freezer box mated with a farm tractor, it was hard for me to believe that this clunker was once considered cutting-edge. But Good Humor's ice cream parlors on wheels were once regarded as revolutionary, and they swept across the nation just as fast as their red-rimmed tires would carry them.

Half a century before the distribution giant Amazon arrived on the scene, Ohio candy man Harry Burt Sr., inventor of an unremarkable sucker on a stick called the Jolly Boy, discovered how much consumers enjoyed the conveniences of quick delivery. Burt also made ice cream on a small scale in his basement and delivered it to hungry customers around town. Burt started selling ice cream on the same wooden sticks he had set aside for the Jolly Boy sucker. This new treat was a riff on the success of a previous chocolate-covered product called the I-Scream, which got a new name—the Eskimo Pie—in 1921. Burt's brand-new ice cream product got the name Good Humor, apparently because Burt believed that "the humors of the mind were regulated by those on the palate."[46] In the 1920s, his son, Burt Jr., figured out that if he borrowed some bells from a family bobsled and attached them to his primitive truck, the tinkling could entice customers and save his vocal cords. Burt caused a sensation, and he was one of the first to witness that all-American phenomenon of little children mobbing the trucks in summer.[47]

Good Humor did its best to foster a squeaky-clean reputation, with superpolite drivers maneuvering boxy white vehicles through the streets. Perhaps they were reacting against the early seedy reputation not only of ice cream but also of ice cream salespeople. As Anne Cooper Funderburg noted in *Chocolate, Strawberry, and Vanilla: A History of American Ice Cream,* early street peddlers of goods—frozen treats included—were labeled as undesirables or socially seedy types, including a number of unattractive women and jobless midgets.[48]

The clean and safe image turned out to be an effective marketing strategy.

Good Humor trucks spread across the country. Harry Burt Sr. died in 1926. Not long after his death, the company went public, with franchise down payments going for a hundred dollars a pop.[49] By the midthirties Good Humor trucks traveled the streets throughout most of America. The white shirt and cap the drivers sported helped create a mythology around the Good Humor brand of trustworthiness and dependability. That lasted until the mid-1970s, when the Brooklyn District Attorney's

Office filed a 244-count indictment of Good Humor charging the company with falsifying records to hide excessive amounts of bacteria in its products in one ice cream making plant, located in Maspeth, Queens. Whistle-blowers who worked in the company's lab provided stomach-churning information.

The grand jury report said that the Good Humor products were "not securely protected from dirt, dust, insects and parts thereof, and from all injurious contamination."[50] The company pleaded guilty to some of the charges and was fined eighty-five thousand dollars.[51] Good Humor sold off its fleet of white trucks in 1976. The individual trucks were bought up by entrepreneurs like Chubby, who became an independent ice cream truck man. Chubby worked long hours supporting his family. He was the ice cream rock star around town and would show up at Maria's elementary school and deliver ice cream to her class. But when Chubby was in his late seventies, he developed heart problems and Maria took over.

"I had to keep my father's route. I wasn't giving it up to anyone," she said. "They would curse at me. These men were so ignorant. I fought. You have to because you're a lady."

She's a large woman—tall and muscled—and I can imagine it would be frightening for anyone to be on the receiving end of her wrath.

One particular ice cream vendor sets off her animus. "A lot of times I yell at him. I'll be on a block and he'll come from around the corner and just do the block before me. I'm aiming to get to the block. He has no respect."

She also railed against the New York City Department of Health because she claims that its regulation of Brooklyn trucks is pretty spotty. Each ice cream truck driver is responsible for getting the two-hundred-dollar Mobile Food Vendor License and renewing it. Other Brooklyn ice cream truck drivers have complained that not everyone is as diligent as they should be about the protocols. "Kool Man" Godfrey Robinson went on the local news and claimed that many of the soft-serve trucks, which have cut into his bottom line, do not have the proper permits from the New York City Department of Health.[52]

Maria has similar complaints, but a less tattletale attitude. "What are you going to do about it? I'm not a rat."

Her Bensonhurst upbringing seems to play a huge role in how she handles herself on the streets. She takes pride in the fact that she keeps quiet to the authorities, while her combativeness is almost glorified. In the years just after September 11 she was at her most aggressive. "Back then, I had beams coming out of my head. I could see ice cream trucks. I would backtrack and come up behind them. I used to take their keys and roof them. I used to punch them. I used to break their windows. That was years ago."

Maria seemed so single-minded in her one-woman ice cream turf wars that I assumed that this was the only job she'd ever wanted. Actually, she once had dreams of becoming a police officer and almost entered the academy. But she had to make an abrupt choice: go through with officer training or stay on the ice cream truck route and help her ailing father. She stayed on the route, and the violence in her territory escalated.

Six months after giving up on becoming a cop, she ran into trouble with the law.

"I was spit on and he cursed my mother just because I was

trying to protect my route," she said. She retaliated against the foul-mouthed invader by vandalizing his truck, and she wound up in jail.

Getting arrested was a life-altering event. She decided to redeem herself. And that same year, Maria was also invited to the New York mayor's mansion. She chuckles at the highs and lows.

"In 2004, I get the lifetime achievement medal at Gracie Mansion onstage in front of the biggest people in New York City. I'm talking about the whole place was packed with big-timers. I'm talking about baseball owners. Regis was there. Governor Pataki handed me the award. I deserved it. Maybe I did one thing wrong in my life. I stuck up for what was mine. If they knew what I had to go through! I got spit on. And cursed on. Believe me, I deserved that award." She got the honor for the "many different ways she finds to help her neighbors," according to a *New York Post* article.[53] Riding through the same streets every day is not unlike walking the cop beat she almost trained for, and she does find herself stepping into a Good Samaritan role. "I saved a baby's life with CPR. I also saved a man with the Heimlich maneuver."

After recounting these tales of bravery and fisticuffs, Maria dropped Julianna and Dan off at L&B Spumoni Gardens, which has been a fixture on Eighty-Sixth Street since 1939 and serves Sicilian-style square-cut pizza. I hadn't seen two people look so eager to get off a vehicle since the end of Rihanna's disastrous #777Tour, during which 150 journalists and fans were deprived of sleep, food, and bathroom privileges on the singer's private jet for a week before ultimately being given their freedom.[54]

I was left alone with Maria, and I took a moment to collect

myself. Maria wasn't exactly what I had in mind when I thought of a lady bringing cold treats to the masses. But that's not Maria's fault. As a culture we have a warped idea of ice cream truck drivers—they have their own lore. Sure, there's the dependable image of the Good Humor man. But there's also the creepy movie version of the ice cream truck driver.

Have we all been brainwashed by schlocky movies whose directors seem to have the same attitude toward ice cream trucks as they do toward clowns? There are so many horror movies featuring ice cream trucks that they form their own separate subgenre: ice cream trucksploitation. One of the earliest offenders was the director John Carpenter, whose 1976 movie *Assault on Precinct 13* shows a little girl getting shot, fatally, in the chest, when she approaches an ice cream truck and tries to tell the driver that he gave her the wrong flavor. Another gory example is *Maximum Overdrive,* a 1986 horror film about machines coming alive because of a comet and slaughtering humans. Among the murderous vehicles is an ice cream truck, its fender smeared with blood as it patrols the streets, searching for people to crunch down upon.

These images whirled through my head as Maria and I drove off and Maria honked her horn a few times to muster some excitement. She drove a few more blocks through the hot, quiet streets until we pulled up to the Marlboro Houses—a brick-and-metal group of high-rises at the end of Eighty-Sixth Street. It ranks as the forty-first most neglected development under the New York City Housing Authority's management, with residents waiting years for the most basic upkeep.[55] A few months before my tour with Maria, two police officers were attacked there while searching for a robbery suspect.[56]

The drab brick buildings seemed like a dismal spot to try to make a living. But it was the last area of territory Maria seemed to think of as hers alone. As it turns out, even this ice cream no-man's-land was not entirely free of incursions from Maria's business foes. I could see a Mister Softee truck lurking on a side street just half a block away. But Maria's reputation precedes her; when he spotted us, the driver started up his engine and drove off.

"I took back my customers," said Maria as she watched the guy drive away. "I didn't have no customers left. The other trucks, they have electric, they have air conditioning. They're flying high. They're not even hustling."

Maria played her music and in less than a minute a dozen African American boys, all around age ten, surrounded the truck. The energy was overwhelming, as kids loudly started demanding treats, hands outstretched.

"You have slushies?" one asked.

Maria shook her head. "I have snow cones for a dollar," Maria said.

The kids looked disappointed but couldn't argue with the price.

The group looked through the window as Maria took a Bible-size block of ice from the freezer and placed it between the golden jaws of the machine. With its garish red and gold paint, the snow cone machine looked like it belonged in a museum of medieval torture devices. It reminded me a bit of the head crusher, used to great effect during the Spanish Inquisition.

"A friend bought me this from Chinatown," she explained, glancing at the machine. "I'm going to pay him back when I can."

Maria set out a cone-shaped paper cup and started hand cranking the big block of ice. Without electricity in the rig, she had to make the snow cones the old-fashioned way: by spinning a wheel thirty to forty times and collecting the shavings. It took about forty-five seconds of vigorous cranking. She collected the shavings in a paper cup. A few spilled over and she sighed and cranked again, harder.

"What syrup do you want?" she asked the boy. "Strawberry, mango?" She continued before he even had a chance to answer. "Try the mango; it's really good."

Before the boy could disagree, she grabbed a plastic pouring bottle and squeezed out a little bit of the goo, which turned the ice bright orange.

She handed it over. He took a few bites.

She started taking other orders when her customer interrupted.

"Can I have more syrup?" he asked.

"The syrup's expensive," she said. "I charge two dollars for everyone else. But I give it to you for a dollar."

"It needs more syrup," he insisted. She ignored him until he finally ran off.

Maria knew she had a captive audience—and she kept her prices cheap enough to entice them. Plus, she'd scared off the competition. But it was clear, the product wasn't satisfying, even on the hot evening.

Other kids came up to the window, asking for Skittles, hands outstretched.

"These cost money," she said, pointing to the boxes of candy at the front of the truck. "Do you have money?" They clearly did not.

She opened up a small bag of Skittles anyway and poured some into the boys' hands. She reminded me of Aubrey Woods, the puckish, bow-tie-wearing actor who played the candy vendor in *Willy Wonka & the Chocolate Factory,* grabbing a scoop of goodies and sprinkling them into the hands of eager youths while warbling out the song "The Candy Man Can." Maria pointed to one boy. "Where did you go? You haven't been here for a while." Her tone was like that of a school principal—concerned and authoritative, proving that she's been paying attention to the gaggle of ice cream truck kids.

She didn't get a response and moved on to the next boy in line.

A few more boys put in orders for snow cones, and she repeated the laborious ice-grinding process about ten times. Now she was sweating. She paused to rub her upper arm muscles. I could feel the energy of the kids getting more impatient, more demanding.

A few asked for a few more squirts of syrup and she complied, but with a marketing message that the boys couldn't ignore. "You don't buy from other trucks, right? You only buy from me."

But the kids had other things on their minds besides customer loyalty.

"I want more candy!" one boy demanded.

"That's enough. That's all," Maria shouted at them.

Where the freebies end and the payment starts is unclear to me. By the sound of her customers, that line is a little blurry for them too. And sometimes Maria hands out more than just snow cones. "I was out here yesterday with a cake," Maria said. "I sliced it up and we had a party." She points to a shelf in the truck. "I bought school supplies for these kids the other day." She showed me a plastic bag filled with pencils and notebooks.

A few boys came up to the truck, asking for a freebie snow cone. She looked them over, trying to gauge whether they had a dollar to spare. She finally decided that it didn't really matter.

"Put your hands together and hold them out," she said. She dumped in a few lumps of ice and squeezed a small dollop of syrup.

"Just eat the top part," she said. "Your hands are dirty. Just eat the top."

The boys scattered back to the playground. "My dad would never let a kid who didn't have enough go away empty-handed."

She moved to the driver's seat and started up the truck again. After thirty minutes in the projects she'd collected ten dollars.

There were no other potential customers standing along the sidewalks, or waiting on a fire escape, hoping for her arrival. I wondered if she regretted that long-ago decision to say no to police work; she could have patrolled the same streets, but in a squad car, blaring a real-life police siren instead of an ersatz one. But if she had such second thoughts, she didn't cop to them. When I asked her about possible regrets, she just changed the subject. As far as she was concerned, her career choice was sound; it was the unfair and intrusive competition, the changing demographics, the harsh economic realities, the ever-changing ice cream world, that complicated a simple and noble dream.

Maria pulled up to the driveway in a row of neighborhood homes, blazing her sirens. A boy and his dad eventually emerged and the son requested an ice cream bar. "It's been discontinued," Maria said.

"It's stupid, the way the most popular items get discontinued. It's like how they took away the Mello-Roll."

Maria was referring to an ice cream novelty that continues to inspire passion and mourning, long after it vanished from grocery store freezer cases.

Google *the Mello-Roll* and you'll be taken to threads labeled "I Want a Mello-Roll" and find YouTube tributes that make its loss sound like one of the great cultural tragedies of the twentieth century. Rose Dosti, a *Los Angeles Times* staff writer, rhapsodized about the ten-cent "three-inch-long ice cream drum . . . wrapped in peel-away paper with blue print on it that sometimes blotted onto the ice cream itself." The texture, she wrote, was "sheer velveteen, a texture so silky the tongue actually slid across the ice cream with each lick."[57] The loss of the Mello-Roll represents collective baby boomer angst. Gabe Kaplan's stand-up routine "Holes and Mello-Rolls" became the basis of his smash-hit TV series, *Welcome Back, Kotter,* which helped launch the career of John Travolta. "Up your hole with a Mello Roll was a common 'rank' or put down," Kaplan explained.[58]

Maria was able to convince the boy and his dad that another bar was "just as good," although I doubted that the boy would be nostalgic for it years after it had been discontinued.

The sun was starting to set, the drab Bensonhurst skyline turning the color of the mango syrup. I was starving, and it had finally cooled off enough that I could reasonably think about eating something other than ice cream. For me, a few hours in that rig was just about as much as I could handle. But Maria seemed to take comfort in the sameness of her route—the routine a childlike comfort that I found claustrophobic.

Maria dropped me off near the subway, and I reunited with my family. She told me she'd like to head out and eat at Carmine's, a popular Italian comfort-food institution in Manhattan. Her voice softened as she talked about "the city." Manhattan is that so-close-yet-so-far-away borough where an ice cream truck driver can really make a good living. But it's a place where you need start-up capital and enough youth or hunger to fight the turf wars that make national headlines. In 2013, a Yogo driver pulled a knife on a Mister Softee driver in Midtown. Both men were arrested, and the New York *Daily News* couldn't resist the headline dig: "Mister Softee brought a sugar cone to a knife fight."[59]

The dynamics of ice cream truck territories changed after an influx of immigrants made their way into the ice cream truck world, hoping to cash in on the American Dream, Mister Softee vice president Jim Conway told me when we talked on the phone.

"We got younger guys from countries other than the US coming in. Their culture was such that if they felt someone was infringing on their territory, they would retaliate," said Conway.

Conway and his cousin, John, took over the Mister Softee company from their dads. Brothers William and James Conway worked at a Sweden Freezer, one of the largest manufacturers of ice cream machines in the United States. They rolled out the first Mister Softee truck in Philadelphia on St. Patrick's Day in

1956. Like Maria, Conway practically grew up on a truck. But the way he talked was nothing at all like the proud, brassy prattle of Maria the Ice Cream Girl. Conway has a soft, measured voice when he talks about the perils of the business. The guiding voice of Mister Softee brings to mind the patient and consoling Mr. Rogers—which was jarring, since I was expecting someone more like Tony Soprano.

"As a kid I started working here in the summer after eighth grade," Conway said.

It sounded like an ideal summer job, but Conway assured me it wasn't glamorous. He and John would clean and stock the trucks, which he started driving in the seventies. He remembers getting along with the Good Humor driver who shared his territory, despite the fact that they were competing for customers.

"When I was driving my trucks in the 1970s, the Good Humor guy and I would stop and chat," said Conway. "There was a guy who had a truck on one of my territories. Rather than bang heads, we'd go to opposite areas of the same territories."

Conway said the perfect size for a route is a territory with about fifty thousand people. The Mister Softee fleet includes six hundred trucks in fifteen states. In New York City, a group of distributors has the authority to assign territories to Mister Softee trucks. But some longtime Mister Softee franchisees have a larger piece of the pie—with an area serving 250,000 people—and aren't giving it up.

A disgruntled group of Mister Softee drivers seceded from the company and began rolling through the streets of Manhattan. Originally, they called themselves *Master* Softee, with trucks and a cartoon cone design that were dead ringers for the

Mister Softee vehicles and logo. Not surprisingly, the Mister Softee people took notice and fought back. A judge ordered Master Softee to change its name. They rebranded as New York Ice Cream. But the legal wrangling didn't end. There has even been a legal dispute about the Mister Softee jingle—which was written by Les Waas in 1960 and is copyrighted.[60] In 2005, after outcries over the earworm in New York City, the company agreed to have trucks play music only when they are in motion. But the New York Ice Cream trucks are using the same tune to lure away Mister Softee customers.[61]

Not surprisingly, there's bad blood as well as actual blood between New York Ice Cream and Mister Softee. Conway said that the rivals are run by "very street-wise guys."

The rivalry between the two companies has led to death threats and bloody noses.[62] And Conway said that Mister Softee drivers are being edged out of Midtown.[63]

"People are hesitant to go in and compete because they fear for themselves and their truck. We are actively seeking people who are willing to go in and do so and we're offering monetary incentives."

Basically, the routes are so dangerous, the company can't pay people to go on them. It was hard to keep track of who was the bully and who was the victim in these ice cream truck wars. From Maria's perspective, the bad guys were the Mister Softee drivers, who were encroaching on her territory. But she'd fought back with her own brand of violence and intimidation. And then there was this other faction of rogue soft-serve drivers, who operated with what was being described as a Mafia mentality. I couldn't help but think that Maria was wrong and that New York City had more of the old Bensonhurst spirit, with its Mafia history, than she realized.

After my ride-along with Maria, I started paying careful attention to the ice cream trucks in the East Village, where my family and I were cat sitting and gobbling up pints of ice cream from throughout the city. I noticed the same New York Ice Cream truck was parked in the same spot at Fourteenth Street and First Avenue. The owner of the truck, George, was guarded but willing to talk a little bit about his background for the price of a drippy cone. He said that he was originally from Argentina and denied that things get ugly in the ice cream truck world. He gave no indication that he may have had ties to a group that puts pressure on other ice cream truck drivers to stay out of his territory.

"This is respect. If I go to your house—what do you do?" George said.

I wasn't sure what he was getting at. Was he asking a rhetorical question or attempting to show me a general helplessness you feel trying to share a territory with someone so much larger? It reminded me of how my brothers and I all had our "spots" where we sat when watching TV. Mine was always on the pea-green shag of Steve's floor, and if I ever tried to sit on the end of the bed (Mark's spot), I was swatted at until I remembered my place.

"It's just luck. It's a big city," George continued. He said he'd never had conflict with other ice cream truck drivers. But for all I know, his denial may be the most telling sign of the power he or his friends wielded on the streets.

For those with enough guts and start-up capital, the ice cream truck is still the metallic embodiment of the American Dream. The trucks are a relatively cheap way to venture into the ice cream business in extreme-foodie, high-rent areas like Los Angeles, New York City, and San Francisco. Coolhaus started in a truck, as did the now immensely popular Big Gay Ice Cream, which has grown to include multiple brick-and-mortar shops and no longer has a truck. The company made headlines back in 2009 with its audaciously named concoctions, such as the Salty Pimp.

One of the few companies in the country that makes from-scratch ice cream and sells it from a truck is Van Leeuwen Ice Cream, named one of the top ten ice cream spots by several media outlets, including *Bon Appétit.* There's a regular line on a hot summer night a few blocks from Washington Square Park, where the truck is parked most evenings.

Brothers Ben and Pete Van Leeuwen both drove a Good Humor truck in the summers during college. Ben married Laura O'Neill (the couple later divorced but remained friends and business partners). While married, Ben and Laura developed recipes at their home in Greenpoint, Brooklyn, and the three launched the company after borrowing eighty thousand dollars from friends and family.[64]

I asked O'Neill how she handles the truck in the competitive, dangerous world of New York City. She's got a laid-back Australian demeanor, which is jarring in the context of the cutthroat ice cream truck world. And because she's a transplant from the land down under, she acts like the ice cream truck rules (and laws) don't really apply, at least as far as she is concerned. The

Van Leeuwen drivers stake out their spot earlier in the evenings, sometimes setting up shop near a fire hydrant, because the trucks are merely "standing," she explained. "They are not technically parked."

Still, location is everything.

"It's really important to get the right spot. A block in either direction can make a big difference."

Van Leeuwen now has a fleet of trucks in New York City and LA, as well as several storefronts. The company's success means that, like Big Gay, they could park the trucks in the junkyard for good. But Van Leeuwen won't retire the trucks.

"It's a huge part of our brand identity," said O'Neill. "We are keeping the trucks."

I couldn't help but wonder where that left old-timers like Maria.

Long after my ride-along through Bensonhurst, I kept tabs on Maria via Facebook, where she's extremely active and posts photos and updates multiple times a day. A few months after my time with her on the truck, she noted that she was going to a wedding of a longtime customer.

"I'll be attending the Wedding of that little blonde girl I remember so well who loved Chipwiches and chocolate bars," she said. "I was around for all her childhood through her schools & her first job and second and third and everything in between—through family's sad times."

I admired Maria for maintaining such a long-lasting connection to a customer. But I wondered how far that loyalty would get her in a cruel world where a truly "good-humored" ice cream man seems to be going the way of the Tasmanian tiger and the dodo. Would the new hipster ice cream truck drivers create the same neighborhood connections that Maria had? Were we trading an important social connection for artisanal ice cream? Wasn't Maria like a de facto youth counselor? And who would step in and take her place, the twentysomethings with their tattoos and pigtails?

We now want our ice cream trucks to bring us something we can't get at a 7-Eleven freezer. We want the trucks to finally roll down our street, bringing us something that's made to order, unexpected; something even better than what we remember from or hoped for in our childhood.

After my look inside the ice cream truck wars, I felt like I needed a shot or two of something fizzy and restorative. Eager for a cure from my travel- and conflict-induced malaise, I went to a place where weary and rattled Americans have gone for more than two centuries: I went straight to the soda bar. But I would soon discover that America's saloon keepers put some very strange things in their soda water.

A TRIBUTE TO POPS

This recipe requires an ice pop mold. I use the Silikomart Easy Cream Mini, but there are several other brands that would work just as well.

1⅔ cups whole milk
1⅔ cups cream
¾ cup sugar
½ cup skim milk powder
3 egg yolks, lightly beaten
2 teaspoons vanilla

Hard-Shell Sauce

1 cup chocolate chips
⅓ cup coconut oil

- To make the ice cream, heat the milk, cream, and sugar in a saucepan over medium heat. Whisk in the skim milk powder. Heat until dissolved. Temper the egg yolks with a teaspoon of the warm milk mixture, then carefully add the egg yolks to the milk mixture. Stir continuously until the mixture reaches 165°F. Remove from the heat. Strain into a Pyrex dish and add the vanilla. Store in a Pyrex dish in the fridge for 2 hours or longer, and churn according to your ice cream maker's instructions.
- *Or* you can cheat and soften a quart of your favorite vanilla.
- Pour the vanilla ice cream into your pop molds. Don't forget to insert a stick in each one. Cover with plastic wrap and place in the freezer for 4 hours or longer.

- To make the hard-shell sauce, heat the chocolate chips in the microwave until melted. Add the coconut oil to the warm melted chocolate and stir. The mix will have a runny consistency that will harden when layered on ice cream.
- When the pops are frozen, carefully unmold (this is the trickiest part). Dip the pops into the chocolate sauce, wait 30 seconds until they've hardened, and enjoy!

6.

SHAKE IT OFF

Russell Davis travels the world collecting stories and tidbits for his drinking encyclopedia, which is how he'd wound up in a hoarder's house on the outskirts of the San Francisco Bay Area. He was face-to-face with a man with a scar from ear to ear, who walked through the cluttered hallway of his home and disappeared. The scarred man searched through dozens of boxes littering the room until he found what he was looking for: a box marked with a skull and crossbones. Pleased with his bounty, he handed it over to Davis, the Indiana Jones of drinking.

Davis recounted the story with the enthusiasm of someone who is well versed in the suffering that follows a day or night of risk taking. He's a cerebral libation nerd. In social media photos he has two gravity-resistant peaks of brown hair that rise above his high forehead and a faint scruffy beard. He gestures with his hands a lot. Davis gives off an air of informality, bonhomie, party-hearty enthusiasm, and aw-shucks humility. He resembles the country singer Travis Tritt during his glory days in the nineties, but without the crooner's famous mullet.

Just by going to the house, he faced the risks that come along with meeting a complete stranger he'd contacted on Craigslist. The house, crammed full of oddities, was one of the strangest places he'd visited. The scarred man was eager to show off the hazardous, centuries-old loot.

"These are radiated tinctures," he said, shoving the dangerous box in Davis's direction.

Davis immediately covered his private area with his hands and searched for the nearest exit.

"I don't think I should have gone there alone," he told me in his East Texas drawl when we spoke on the phone between his international research jaunts to Costa Rica and Barbados. His job sounded made-up, a high school kid's idea of what he wanted to do when he needed to make a living. I could relate.

Davis grew up on a four-hundred-acre peach farm near a Texas town with only eighty residents. He left the Lone Star State to tend bar at Rickhouse in San Francisco. That gig launched his freelance consulting business, gave him material for his drinking encyclopedia, and led to a stint on Spike TV's *Bar Rescue,* a reality show where the drama centers around revamping failing bars around the country.

As Davis told me the story, I couldn't help but feel like it would be a lot of fun to have a drink with him, or many. He seems so happy and centered. He made me wonder if drinking would help me get to his level without all the yoga and the bother.

During our phone chat, I felt like I was talking to a friend who was entertaining me with carefully spun yarns about messy houses, drugs, booze, soda fountains, and so-called cure-alls that could kill you. "In the early twentieth century, doctors would radiate syrups and tinctures," Davis said. He told me all about a substance that sounded like something from a pulp horror novel: Radithor, a popular status drink that cost a dollar a bottle. The makers of Radithor boasted about its allegedly health-inducing radioactive ingredients: radium and thorium. Naïve consumers drank it by the bucketful, dooming themselves in the process.

Eben Byers, a Roaring Twenties playboy, steel magnate, and avid golfer, was one of the most prominent Radithor victims. After he hurt his arm in a bad fall from the top berth of his private Pullman compartment following a Harvard-Yale football game in 1927, he went to a doctor who urged him to drink Radithor to ease the ache in his joints. Following the physician's orders, he gulped the irradiated potion regularly for two years. He was so thrilled with the product that he gave bottles of Radithor to his friends and fed it to his racehorse. Unfortunately, he experienced a few side effects. For instance, all his teeth fell out. His entire upper jaw and most of his lower jaw had to be removed. "Holes were actually forming in his skull," according to a lawyer for the Federal Trade Commission who visited and interviewed Byers. He died at the age of fifty-one.[65] So much for the notion that radiation could cure what ailed you. After Byers's death, the government cracked down on the sale of Radithor and doctors finally acknowledged that radium was unfit for human consumption.

Davis read about the miseries of Radithor users during his

research. The evidence frightened him. "You can find all these pictures of people with holes burned in their throats," he said, hence his quick dash to the exit of the hoarder's home. Davis didn't even stand around long enough to find out if the collector really had genuine Radithor.

That noxious drink is just one of the many dark corners of American history that Davis has explored. He wanted to tap into that feeling of heedlessness without the actual hazards.

To create the menu for the Ice Cream Bar Soda Fountain in San Francisco, Davis immersed himself in the lore of Victorian-era soda parlors, which were filled with unsavory characters and unsavory substances. Delve through the recipe books from the turn of the twentieth century, as I did, and you'll fall into a mole hole of horrific, bizarre, and disgustingly funny pharmaceutical fixes. For instance, I discovered a highly suspicious "cure" for smallpox by reading *Lee's Priceless Recipes,* published in 1895. Apparently, a mixture of cream of tartar and water does the trick. The book also offers "Piso's Consumption Cure," consisting of morphine, spearmint, sugar, and cannabis.[66] The best of these recipes were little more than snake oil, while the worst gave patients life-threatening cases of mercury poisoning. The book also lists a broad range of treats, from Philadelphia-style ice cream to dozens of syrups to add to fizzy drinks.

While researching the nostrums and potions of the past, Davis also came to realize that the fizz of soda pop has something in common with Radithor: Americans once believed that the small, stinging bubbles could perk up their health.

Drinkers have ascribed healing and even magical properties

to bubbly water since the beginning of recorded history. Primitive societies thought fizzy waters banished disease.

If you've ever come across a natural sparkling spring, you may agree that it does seem to have magical properties, even for someone like myself who worries about the horrors of E. coli and giardia. I once found a natural soda spring at Mineral King in Sequoia National Park. Against my better judgment, I couldn't help but sample it—after putting it through a filter, of course. When I gulped down that faintly carbonated water, I was taking part in an all-American fixation with bubbly cure-alls that dates to the birth of the country. Even then we were a nation of neurotics. We had self-inflicted environmental degradation (all that tea in Boston Harbor to clean up) and the political vitriol of the original Tea Party. We had terrorist acts and the threat of a looming war. Inevitably, certain forward-thinking Americans started searching for cure-alls.

In 1773, a Philadelphia doctor named Benjamin Rush hailed the healthful, invigorating properties of dank, smelly water from a well in a backyard at Sixth and Chestnut Streets. The water source was close to an outhouse, which accounted for its pungent flavor and foul aroma. The stench of that polluted water did not keep people away; quite the opposite. "Philadelphians, convinced that water which tasted so foul must be medicinal, flocked to this well to cure their ailments," wrote Anne Cooper Funderburg in her soda fountain history, *Sundae Best.*[67] Spas at the time included Bristol Spring, Saratoga Springs, and the unfortunately named Yellow Springs and Ballstown. You would think that our founding fathers would have looked down their glasses at this sort of quackery. Sadly, that's not the case. George Washington made a trip to Saratoga Springs while waiting for the Revolutionary War peace treaty to be signed.[68]

By the nineteenth century, soda water was a reputed cure-all for everything from neurasthenia and epilepsy to asthma, obesity, and gallstones. The spas gained huge popularity for the A-listers of the time.[69] But what about the average American, who couldn't leave the family farm to travel to a remote location and spend days soaking up a cure? The chronically mopey Benjamin Silliman, a Yale chemistry professor, pondered this question. After realizing that the masses could not afford to travel to some remote spa and take the waters, he decided to bring the waters to the masses in 1806. Silliman was drawing from personal experience. He'd gone to Saratoga Springs to recover from a bout of depression and was so impressed with the water's curative powers that he bought a twenty-five-dollar machine that could "impregnate" still water with gas bubbles. Silliman and his partners opened a "fountain shop" in New Haven, Connecticut, but it took a while for the concept to catch on. In the first half year of operation, the shop made only two hundred dollars.[70] Undaunted, Silliman and his cohorts opened fountains in New York, only to watch them founder and fall into financial ruin by 1809.

An Englishman named John Matthews was far more successful, and he helped elevate the status of early American soda fountains in the process.

Matthews set up shop on Gold Street in New York in 1832, using marble dust mixed with sulfuric acid and purified to give his waters a fizzy kick. This forward-thinking businessman bought up all the marble from the construction of St. Patrick's Cathedral in New York and hoarded the ground-up church bits, which were used to make twenty-five million gallons of soda water.[71] His understanding of this weird chemistry, along with his state-of-the-art steel soda fountains, allowed him to build a soda fountain empire. But his success came at a gory and painful cost for one of his employees, "Old Ben" Austin, a former slave who was forced to place his thumb on the stopcock of a water barrel to help Matthews measure the water pressure. Matthews had no other reliable method of calculating this force. At one point, the pressure became so intense that it blew Old Ben's thumb clean off, convincing Matthews that his water was now ready for public consumption.[72]

As the years wore on, the line between "tonic" and "treat" began to blur. By the mid-nineteenth century, people started buying soda water just because it tasted good. But soda water could also be dangerous. A story in the *New-York Daily Times* in August 1854 pinpointed the reason why a cold glass of soda water could kill you bit by bit. It wasn't just the water that sickened you. The water containers and pipes could harm you too. Soda vendors came to realize that corrosive and highly acidic fizzy water would eat into the low-cost tin and alloy linings in the fountains. As a result, some nasty dissolved metals ended up in unwary customers' glasses. All too often, unscrupulous soda vendors just covered up the metallic flavor of the fizzy water by dumping intensely flavored syrups into the liquid, according to John B. Williams, a physician and drugstore owner who pumped soda water through a "long leaden pipe."[73]

But many customers and shady storekeepers were all too

willing to risk lead poisoning in the water. By the mid-1850s, most of the prosperous towns in the United States had a fountain—and soon, people all over the nation would be craving any relief they could get. In the years following the Civil War, the entire country was suffering from a form of PTSD and looking for something—anything—to ease the anxiety of four years of bloody fighting. The inventor and pharmacist John Stith Pemberton—now best known as the inventor of Coca-Cola—had a personal reason for coming up with a new elixir. For one, he was a Confederate war veteran with an addiction to morphine. A luckless soldier, he was both hit by a bullet *and* slashed by a sabre during one of the last fights of the war.[74] Pemberton decided to make his own version of Vin Mariani, a potent, exhilarating, and unwise combination of wine and cocaine. This thrilling and risky cocktail gained many admirers, including Thomas Edison and Pope Leo XIII. At one point the manufacturer suggested a daily "dosage" of three full glasses of the stuff.[75] When cocaine and alcohol mixed, they created a third unique drug called cocaethylene, which functions like cocaine but gives an even stronger feeling of soul uplift and outright bliss. Almost immediately, the *Atlanta Constitution* stepped in to spoil the fun; in 1885, the editorial staff ripped into Pemberton and called him irresponsible. Curiously, they front-loaded their criticism with praise for the curative value of cocaine. "The new drug cocaine will do almost anything," the editors wrote. "On the other hand, the injudicious use of cocaine will make a man more brutal and depraved than either liquor or cocaine. Herein lies a new danger. Before long a remedy will be demanded for the cocaine habit."[76]

In a long, rambling interview in 1885, Pemberton defended cocaine as a universal cure-all. "I wish it were in my power to substitute the Coca and compel all who are addicted to the use of opium, morphine, alcohol, tobacco or other narcotic stimulants to live on the coca plant or any of its true preparations. It is perfectly wonderful what coca does . . . We [Americans] are a great army of nervous invalids."[77]

But Pemberton quickly changed his formula because of the temperance movement, which was gaining momentum in his county in Georgia and pressured the government into making Pemberton's cocktail illegal. The inclusion of cocaine was just fine as far as the law was concerned; this substance was so popular and mainstream in those days that you could have it shipped to your house in the mail. Cocaine was considered so harmless and delightful that the Lloyd Manufacturing Co. used the image of chubby-cheeked, innocent children to hawk "cocaine toothache drops" on a widely circulated advertisement broadsheet. It was the wine, not the cocaine, that got Pemberton into trouble. In response, he kept the caffeine and the cocaine kick, swapped out the booze for sugar, and called the resulting drink Coca-Cola.[78]

Trace elements of cocaine remained in Coca-Cola until 1903, when the company entered into an arrangement with Schaefer Alkaloid Works, in Maywood, New Jersey, to "decocainize" the leaves, retaining the flavor but eliminating much of the kick.[79] Officials from the Coca-Cola Company have denied repeatedly, and even under oath, that the product ever contained cocaine. But the historian Mark Pendergrast, in his exhaustive unauthorized history of Coca-Cola, insists the beverage started off as a "nostrum, a patent medication with a distinct cocaine kick," and that the list of ingredients in the original "Pemberton Formula" speaks for itself. He also pointed out that Victorian consumers of early Coca-Cola often referred to the drink as "dope."[80]

Coca-Cola was just one manifestation of America's great fondness for cocaine. By the end of the nineteenth century, Americans had learned to love it so much that national producers could not meet the demand. Workers unloaded roughly 1.5 million pounds of coca leaves in the United States per year in the early 1900s.[81] Until 1914, you could walk into most drugstores and buy morphine, hashish, and opium in addition to cocaine. Many pharmacies included soda fountains, so these substances often ended up in drinks. Patrons would get their liquid fix multiple times a day, and you couldn't beat the price. In June 1885, the price of a cocktail in New York ranged from fifteen to fifty cents. You could buy Coca-Cola for five cents, cocaine included.[82]

Man at a soda fountain getting his fix. Date: circa 1890.
Courtesy of the Minnesota Historical Society.

The end of the nineteenth century was a high time at the American soda fountain. The bartending guru Davis told me that he turned to the old beverage formulas when looking for a blueprint for his Ice Cream Bar drink menu. He had only about two weeks to develop the concoctions before the place was set to open. He wasted no time poring through old recipe books, even risking radiation to get a feel for what the old soda fountains of the 1890s were like. "They were dangerous places, where crazy people sometimes went for their medicine," Davis said.

Contemporary press reports bear out Davis's descriptions. In 1902, the *Los Angeles Times* ran a story with the headline THEY THIRST FOR COCAINE, drawing attention to well-dressed "fiends" showing up at soda fountains throughout the day in search of their next fizzy fix.

Those desperate customers gave the fountains a sense of danger and medicinal debauchery. Davis decided to riff on that sense of risky pleasure, with help from Canadian mixologist Darcy O'Neil, who spent years researching his book, *Fix the Pumps,* a twenty-first-century homage to classic soda fountain recipes. It includes formulas for lactarts, a mostly forgotten fountain drink made from lactic acid, various tinctures, and modern substitutes for the illegal coca leaf, such as green tea. He left out many of the compounds and herbs, including hydrochloric acid, strychnine, and the toxic mushrooms that were once part of Hamburg Bitters. However, he made sure to list an unappealing recipe for Leroy's Vomito-Purgative Elixir just to give people some sense of the bad old times. "I'm not sure people want to drink the old folk remedies, but . . . they want to taste history," said O'Neil. "That's a significant motivation for me: What did drinks at an 1800s soda fountain taste like?"

Davis said O'Neil's *Fix the Pumps* was a big inspiration for his drink menu. "I didn't copy any recipes from the book," said Davis. "I was copying the ideas of recipes more than anything." The idea was to give San Franciscans a sense of the heady pleasures and dangers of the old soda fountains—drinks with a kick that evoked the turn of the twentieth century.

After talking to Davis I needed to try some of his recipes and check out these world-famous soda jerks, so I headed to the Ice Cream Bar, in San Francisco's Cole Valley neighborhood. It's a few blocks from the Haight-Ashbury section of town. It seems like the perfect geography for a nineteenth-century-style soda fountain, with its vagrants in various states of cleanliness lying on the pavement and the scent of marijuana swirling in the air. To test-drive the fountain that Davis had likened to a Ferrari, I ordered a Ginger Beer. It was the greatest embodiment of what a ginger beer tastes like—the bubbles delivered a spicy zing to my tongue—before the drink flattened out. It left me more than refreshed, without being jazzed from caffeine or sugar. The effect was similar to a post-workout high, without any of the messy sweat or exertion. I felt like a better version of myself. The pinprick bubbles are minuscule—regular bubbles seem like underinflated beach balls compared to these wonderful, tongue-stinging little beads of effervescence. It took a while for my mouth to get used to those surprising tiny blisters of air; the carbonation was almost subliminal.

The Ice Cream Bar's most famous drink is the Dublin Honey. This drink sure does have a strong effect on the human body. I watched as the soda jerk popped open a can of Guinness and poured half the contents into a fountain glass. The dark black beer had a layer of foam on top. He grabbed the glass, walked out from behind the bar, and headed to where the ice cream was kept, avoiding the crowd of rowdy San Francisco kids waiting not so patiently for their numbers to be called. The atmosphere was charged—as if a post-soccer-game sugar riot could break out at any moment.

The soda jerk's triangle hat didn't budge as he reached in and scooped out a hefty amount of homemade caramelized honey ice cream and dropped it into the fountain glass. The ice cream on its own is rich, and I couldn't wait to see how it would taste with the Guinness. He reached behind to grab the Graham's Port, pulled off the cork, and poured a generous portion into the glass.

He eyeballed the contents and topped off the Guinness. Before he served it up, he grabbed a metal set of tongs, picked up a homemade piece of dark chocolate, and set it carefully in the middle of the scoop of ice cream. Then he placed it before me with a spoon.

"Do I need a straw?" I asked.

He looked at me like I needed more than just a fountain remedy to cure what ailed me. Who, after all, would willingly drink beer through a *straw*? After an awkward moment's pause, I put the cold glass to my lips. The drink was dangerously sweet—in a way that covered up its potency. It reminded me of newspaper stories about barkeepers covering up strychnine-laced potions with sugary syrups. A few sips left me off-kilter. After I finished the drink, I left the soda fountain feeling wobbly.

I asked the mixologist O'Neil to explain the phenomenon.

"As for potency, sweet drinks tend to hide the bite of alcohol," he said. "Cream has the same effect, so if you add alcohol to something sweet and creamy, you probably won't notice how potent they can be, and often this means you drink them quicker or more of them. That's why some of the sweet sodas were used to cover up the bitter taste of medicine."

These newfangled drink makers are following a long tradition of using dairy products to smooth out a drink. At some point in soda fountain history, a scoop of ice cream got dunked into a soda fountain glass, but no one seems to know where that history-making plop and fizz first took place. The most popular account is that a scoop of ice cream and a glass of soda got together for the first time during the Franklin Institute's Philadelphia Exhibition of 1874.

Robert McCay Green, who claimed to be the inventor of this winning combination, was operating a soda fountain at the exhibition, and for one reason or another—some say he ran out of cream, while others accuse him of just trying to stand out—decided to combine the two. This was a time when competing soda vendors were trying other ways to distinguish themselves. Soda fountain makers would show off their architectural and engineering skills with elaborate fountains. Boston druggist James W. Tufts caused a sensation at the Centennial Exposition of 1876 when he unveiled his Arctic Soda Water Apparatus. Aside from just dispensing soda water and seventy-six flavored syrups, this thirty-ton, thirty-three-foot-high giant had drooping ferns, a chandelier, and a device that squirted clouds of perfume into the crowd.[83] His invention, which resembled a goliath wedding cake, included a marble fountain, with metal cooling cylinders.

Soda fountains embraced this over-the-top garishness around the same time that their "jerks" began adding ice cream to the concoctions.

It must have been fun to stand there marveling at these expensive contraptions while waiting for your daily dose of cocaine or sugar. Those early fountains encouraged loitering and soon became social centers for towns across America. In an 1891 edition of *Harper's Weekly,* the writer Mary Gay Humphrey did her best to make these places seem as exciting and glamorous as possible: "On a bright exhilarating day, to achieve a cup of ice cream soda, a place should be engaged some time in advance. Beauty and fashion surge about the counter. One of the sights of the town is the rows of bright faces, two and three deep, bent over their cups, and fishing within with long-handled spoons."[84]

These businesses got an unexpected boost from prohibitionists, who pushed drinkers out of the saloons and into the soda fountains. The trade journal *The Soda Fountain* called ice cream sodas "a greater medium for the cause of temperance than all the sermons ever preached on that subject, and in this capacity is doing better and more far-reaching work all the time."[85] But the trade journal's glowing picture misrepresented the seamy reality.

Owners of the soda fountains made themselves out to be advocates of good, healthy living and a wonderful alternative to rank saloons, even while serving some drinks that were far from healthy.

Early fountain operators weren't always being up front and honest when they bragged about their clean, booze-free soda concoctions. Many pharmacists took cynical advantage of the Volstead Act, which let them sell whiskey to cure the ailments of their loyal customers, so long as they had prescriptions for the booze. Even after the nationwide crackdown on liquor began, many bartenders turned soda jerks spiked the soda water with moonshine. Some cynical barkeeps dumped a lethal ginger-based hard liquor called "jake" into glasses of Coca-Cola. The mixture left between fifteen thousand and one hundred thousand people with a condition known as "jake leg," a jaunty euphemism for impotence or partial paralysis, according to the author Tristan Donovan in his history of soda.[86]

Despite these deleterious effects, moonshine remained a popular mix-in, and the soda fountain was a hopping industry. Some things haven't changed. Clearly we are a country of people who seek pleasures and distractions at all costs, and if someone takes one away, we will rush out and find a lethal but legal substitute, regardless of the cost to our bodies and our billfolds.

Some of the greatest beneficiaries of Prohibition were savings banks, the motion-picture industry, soft drink makers and vendors, and ice cream makers.[87] The government aimed to obliterate liquor sales, but they couldn't stop people from guzzling soft drinks that could change their body chemistry. During the 1920s, alcohol and cocaine were outlawed, but vendors peddled soft drinks that elevated moods. The original version of 7Up, named Bib-Label Lithiated Lemon-Lime Soda, contained lithium, the same substance that is used as a mood stabilizer for those with bipolar disorder. Charles Leiper Grigg invented the drink in October 1929, the same month the stock market crash set off the Great Depression.[88] Grigg's lemon-lime beverage contained the mood stabilizer until 1950, when it was forced to rejigger its ingredients after the FDA banned lithium from drinks.[89] But the company found other ways to sell the notion that its drinks could make depressives smile. It also urged soda fountain owners to offer a 7Up float, a mix of 7Up and any kind of ice cream the customer desired.[90]

Even when Prohibition ended, the soda fountains did well because soda was cheaper than liquor. But where did the booze lovers go? To the soda fountains, of course. There they found the camaraderie they craved and learned to replace their jones for drink with a knack for sweets. These days, recovering alcoholics still seek the same kind of solace. In a piece that appeared in *Salon* in 2014, the writer Jenny Chu remembered going to Alcoholics Anonymous meetings and hearing people rhapsodize about "eating pints of ice cream at night to get through those first days and months—or even years—of life without booze and drugs." Chu developed a specific addiction. "I became obsessed with a specific flavor of Häagen-Dazs ice cream called 'Bananas Foster,' and I'd walk for blocks looking for a deli that sold it."[91]

Today's old-fashioned pharmacy revivalists are well versed in the long-standing American tradition of vice swapping. In the old days, fiends and addicts swapped morphine for cocaine. Drunkards swapped a plug of whiskey for a scoop of vanilla slathered in chocolate and buried in whipped cream, a sickly sweet cherry on top.

The new breed of pharmacy-style old-fashioned ice cream

counters likes to riff on the suspect "cures" and palliatives of their predecessors while catering to sugary addictions and over-indulgences.

Seeking that curious combination of cure-alls and decadence, I visited the Brooklyn Farmacy & Soda Fountain during the hottest day of the summer and experienced a new definition of the word *gluttony.* I sat at the back table as a dozen sodas and sundaes appeared before me. First out was the Princess Float, a pink concoction with seltzer, raspberry syrup, and vanilla ice cream. Despite my best efforts to let the ice cream melt into the drink, it kept spilling over the sides. Next up was the Affugazi Affogato, which came in a ramekin with whipped cream and chocolate flakes, a vanilla scoop slathered with chocolate hard shell, and a vanilla cake that soaked up the hot coffee the soda jerk poured over it. The Sundae of Broken Dreams was next, featuring vanilla ice cream with caramel sauce, whipped cream, and salted pretzel bits. The shattered pretzels were meant to evoke the "broken dreams" of the sundae's name.

Finally, I was presented with the Elvis—two scoops of vanilla ice cream, with caramel sauce, candied bacon, a banana, peanut butter, and a sour pickle. (Poor Elvis is living on at ice cream shops all over America, where chefs can't help but poke fun at his piggish appetites.)

The display of fountain treats before me reminded me of a trip I took as a kid with my grandparents to visit my aunt Lily in New York. She was a large woman with a big heart and a genetic predisposition to show that love through food. I sat in her immaculate living room as tray after tray—cakes, cookies—was presented before me. I spent the rest of the afternoon sick. I barely made it to her newly remodeled bathroom before all the love she had showed appeared again. The story has become a family legend about the need for moderation.

I tried to remember that lesson as I sampled the floats and sundaes that were presented to me. The problem was the delay between bodily satiation and a feeling of fullness. I've read that it takes twenty minutes for the body to inform the brain that enough is enough. That's how long it takes for the stomach's "stretch receptors" to go online and for a signal of "I can't eat another bite" to work its way up to our brains.[92]

By that time, it was too late. It was a hundred degrees outside and I had more than a dozen sundaes and floats starting to sag and melt, which only increased the urgency of the eating and slurping. But with each bite of ice cream, cake, whipped cream, and chocolate, I was getting closer to the edge of what would turn from pleasure to pain.

The tender age of the soda jerks at the Farmacy (most are teenagers) means that for now the Brooklyn spot doesn't mix booze with its fizz. But their creations seemed to follow a pattern similar to that associated with overdrinking—pleasure, overindulgence, and regret.

What almost pushed me over the edge was the Green Gorilla, a pesto and mozzarella cheese sandwich I ordered just to line my stomach. It made me wonder if food items at the fountain are nothing but afterthoughts, obligatory offerings in a neighborhood that had few other food options nearby. The green sandwich tasted like it was made under duress.

"People come all this way and we feel like we have to feed them," said Gia Giasullo, who owns the Farmacy with her half brother, Peter Freeman.

Giasullo was raised as a shopkeeper's daughter in Greenwich Village, where her life unfolded within a five-block radius. Freeman grew up in Queens with his father. (Giasullo and Freeman have the same mom but different dads.) The siblings led very separate lives until the dream of owning a soda fountain came to life when Freeman found the Farmacy tucked away in Carroll Gardens.

The building dates back to at least the 1880s, when it was a boardinghouse. At some point it transformed into Longo Prescription Pharmacy and was doling out doses of morphine and opium. However, the illicit dealings at the pharmacy weren't confined to just addictive drugs. In 1968 the pharmacist's son, a clerk at the drugstore, was arrested on suspicion of "selling guns across the counter like bottles of aspirin."[93] Then the neighborhood eccentric Mark Stein moved into the building and started his pharmacy in the 1980s.

After his business shuttered, Stein became a reclusive hoarder and the building became the focus of neighborhood gossip, said Giasullo. In 2008, *The New York Times* sent a reporter to talk to the neighbors. By then, the building was becoming a mysterious holdover from the past. "It's frozen in time," said Franco Ficili, the president of La Societa di Pozzallo. "I'm here 30 years. He just closed his door. What he does in there, I have no idea."[94]

According to Giasullo, Peter Freeman arrived on the scene in 2009 and became friends with the recluse. He started renting rooms in the building and helped Stein start to clean up the filthy building. Once he'd moved in, Freeman explored the back stairway and discovered bottles, tinctures, and knickknacks from every decade since 1870. More than two thousand bottles littered the building. "It's like no one ever moved out," said Giasullo. "It was like a time capsule." Apparently, the gun traffickers hadn't had time to box up their stuff, and Stein didn't have the heart or motivation to throw anything out.

While Giasullo explained the history of the building, it occurred to me that the soda fountain revival in some ways owed itself to the human tendency to hoard. It was as if the collective need to hold on to certain parts of the past played out in certain individuals' cluttered minds and abodes.

Freeman helped Stein clean up the place and open it back to the community (albeit briefly). *The Brooklyn Paper* reported that the initial reopening lasted only one day.[95] Freeman also hosted pig roasts and lobster feasts as a way to gain community support for the business. Then he convinced Giasullo to get on a plane from Israel to take a look. "I fell in love with it," said Giasullo. "It was so beautiful even in its craziness."

The building needed eighty thousand dollars in renovations, which arrived, unexpectedly, in the form of a reality TV building makeover show called *Construction Intervention.* The producer, in desperate need of a finale for the season, just happened to be scouting locations nearby. Freeman talked her into making the Farmacy her grand finale. The crew spent five days refurbishing the place, cleaning the penny tile, getting rid of the junk, and restoring the building.

The soda fountain at the Farmacy came from a boys' detention center. "It was in good shape because it was the boys' punishment to clean it," said Giasullo. She bought the red twirling stools on eBay.

Many of the other objects at the Farmacy—from the antique prescription bottles to the mortar and pestle—have been there since the nineteenth century and are remarkably convenient. A dumbwaiter in the back room brings heavy bags up from the basement with a pull of the rope.

The Farmacy building seems dripping in luck (or savviness). The brother-and-sister duo were also given first rights on buying the building and convinced a bank to loan them enough money to do just that. They were lucky in this respect. The cost of real estate in New York (either renting or owning) is a deal breaker for so many businesses and individuals.

Indeed, when I told the folks at OddFellows Ice Cream Co. in Williamsburg that Giasullo and Freeman owned the building five miles away, chef Sam Mason stopped in the middle of cooking a batch of Thai ice cream and laughed. It sounded like a mixture of pain and disbelief. The New York rents are a constant headache for businesses, even for the most highly acclaimed restaurants. It's no wonder so many New Yorkers long for the area's low-rent past.

Giasullo thinks the modern soda revival is due to our society's need to get away from technology, if just for the time it takes to eat a sundae. "It's the reflection of the idea of us being makers again." The siblings themselves were longing for a more hands-on life. Freeman was "searching for relevance," said Giasullo.

Relevance, it seems, is a relative term. Freeman made it his mission to bring back the egg cream, known as "the original New

York drink." Even the innocent-seeming egg cream has a link to unsavory characters. A quick concoction of siphoned soda water, milk, and a pinch of chocolate syrup, the egg cream was a cheap alternative to the ice cream soda. In spite of the name, the cocktail had no actual egg or cream. No wonder it became popular among soda vendors on the Lower East Side. In 1929, an entrepreneur named Harry Solomon Dolowich organized a "soda-syrup racket." He announced his plans for a syrup "association" that would let members set prices, bully and harass competitors who resisted the racket, and divvy up their customer base. Herman Fox, the maker of Fox's U-Bet Chocolate Syrup, joined in. Dolowich's syrup racket became an unstoppable force by 1931, when he had firm oversight over half of the syrup sales in the city.[96]

But Dolowich was taken by surprise when a few mom-and-pop syrup makers, sick of the threats and coercion, got together and took their case to the state attorney general's office. The "syrup racket" soon faced fifty subpoenas as the office examined charges of extortion and other crimes. At first the plaintiffs snickered, but the charges stuck. To his great surprise, Mr. Dolowich was convicted and sentenced to up to three years at the prison on Welfare Island (now Roosevelt Island). After his release, he moved to Philadelphia, where they take their ice cream very seriously. But Dolowich, by all accounts, stayed out of the soda fountain trade.[97] In Philadelphia, the egg cream is actually made with both eggs and cream, along with syrup and vanilla extract.[98]

The Franklin Fountain in the Old City, a historic district of Philadelphia, sells both the New York– and Philadelphia-style egg cream for five dollars and six dollars, respectively. The owners are two brothers, Eric and Ryan Berley, who choose to ignore much of the unsavoriness of America's soda fountain history. Instead, they seem to have created a period in American history that exists only in our imaginations. Yelpers liken it to the movie *Pleasantville.* The fountain's mission statement is framed at the front of the store: "The Franklin Fountain aims to serve an experience steeped in ideals, drizzled with drollery, and inspired by the flavors of America's forgotten past."

"We want the store to be a reminder of the good in things," said Eric. He reminded me a bit of Bilbo Baggins—both naïve and mischievous, but determined to fulfill his quest to satisfy every conceivable sweet craving.

Eric says the fountain spans a few decades of the early twentieth century (the heyday of the fountain before World War I) but sans the dangerous tinctures. It's a revised feel-good version of the soda fountain. Judging from the popularity in the summer, with waits of forty-five minutes plus out the door, people are buying into it.

The brothers grew up in Media, Pennsylvania, a suburb of Philly. Their mom, Carole, was an avid antiquer. The family would take ten-to-fourteen-day vacations every summer around the country, stopping in at candy shops and soda fountains between touristy trips to the museum or zoo. Eric says the pair had an idyllic 1980s childhood that resembled what they imagined the 1950s to be like. It's that *Leave It to Beaver* fantasy the brothers seem to cling to—*Stepford Wives* be damned.

Pore over the menu and you'll find little hints to some of the soda fountain's earlier incarnations. The Hemingway, for instance, is absinthe flavored. But most of the drinks and concoctions are a PG version of the past.

The soda fountains weren't just history for the Berleys; they became an intrinsic part of the family.

"It's in our DNA," said Eric, who worked as a tour guide for nearby Christ Church.

The Berleys bought 116 Market Street in 2002, and after a year of renovations the family was inspired to open an old-style soda fountain of their own.

From the beginning, the Berleys started paying tribute to one of Philadelphia's most famous politicians and raconteurs. Ben Franklin began his adult life just steps away from the site of the fountain and now lies in a grave just a few blocks away. Franklin, like Jefferson, was an early ice cream fan. The fountain is literally cashing in on the Franklin legacy. It features a nickel-plated cash register with a hand-painted saying from Ben Franklin. Eric is shameless about having the long-dead American icon shill for his store. "I like to think the way Franklin would have looked at it," said Eric. "He would have appreciated branding in order to connect with customers in a meaningful way."

Eric says he and his brother went into the business backward—with more of an interest in antiques and history than in ice cream.

But he's found a way to merge the two.

The brothers own the entire building as well as the Shane Confectionery at 110 Market Street. Eric led me on a tour of the buildings, which reminded me of a constant recurring dream where I discover hidden rooms in old houses I have lived in. The back areas of the Franklin Fountain seem to lead to a kind of dream world. On one floor, chefs rolled out sheets of candy, like dough. Candy and ice cream molds filled the cupboards. The brothers attend auctions of old businesses and buy up these items of Americana for rock-bottom prices. They have drawers full of Santa shapes.

In hoarding these objects, they were deferring to another little-known corner of ice cream history in America. Ice cream molds were trendy as far back as the eighteenth century, and their cachet increased during the late nineteenth century. Dessert chefs used ice cream to make scale models of the Statue of Liberty and Eiffel Tower.[99] Top chefs, among them Charles Ranhofer of Delmonico's, made a splash with artful and elaborate presentations of wacky ice cream flavors including Pumpernickel Rye Bread. He created an asparagus ice cream that was shaped to look like asparagus spears, which he lashed together with a fancy ribbon.[100]

The Berley brothers are known for some of their elaborate molded ice cream concoctions. Eric proudly showed off the Benjamin Franklin mold, tucked in a drawer next to hundreds of other molds. "Ice cream molds are hinged because they need to be pried open. There's dry ice required to dunk them in water."

It's a laborious process. "We like to use it just for a TV show or a special event."

When Pope Francis came to Philadelphia in September 2015, the Berley brothers made ice cream bars out of a 1940 mold of St. Charles Borromeo Seminary, which the pope visited during his trip to the city. They also created an elaborate still life concoction for the Philadelphia Museum of Art that included a Licorice Ice Cream Obelisk, complete with hieroglyphics.[101]

The attic of the fountain is a collector's—or hoarder's—paradise.

It's a place where you could lose yourself for hours. There are dresses made from feathers for window displays, a 1912 milk shake machine with pulley ropes, an old-style machine for chopping up ice, and boxes of artifacts designated to go to a future museum the brothers hope to open.

On the top floor of the building is the office, with shelves of ice cream books (including the kind of old recipe books that Russell Davis pored through). On the walls are framed photos of old soda fountains, displayed with pride, the way a father might show off pictures of his kids.

Eric showed off the pièce de résistance in the former apartment—a Ben Franklin sculpture that's been soldered together with an old fountain. They got the sculpture from an auction for Franklin-related collectibles. It reminded me of the elaborate soda fountains that were created by Tufts and Matthews in the nineteenth century.

In America, if you know where to look, you can find people who are obsessively devoted to almost any pastime, trinket, or artifact that you can ever imagine. If you are passionate about something, someone out there cares about that same thing even more passionately. That's how the Berleys came to be part of a group of soda fountain fundamentalists known as the Ice Screamers who formed in 1982 and hold conventions in Lancaster, Pennsylvania. These 450 devotees collect and celebrate little-known and sometimes unappreciated remnants of the soda fountain culture, including ice cream cartons and "penny licks." The Screamers produce a sixteen-page quarterly newsletter stuffed with arcana relating to issues that most Americans have overlooked, including straws. There are 103 US patents related to straw jars, straw holders, and straw dispensers. The Ice Screamers want to share their fervor with the rest of the country and have successfully lobbied the US Postal Service to print booklets of "20 Soda Fountain Favorites" Forever Stamps, which feature photos of floats, sundaes, and cones.

All of the memorabilia is devoted to reliving the great age of the soda fountains. But it turns out you can get a taste of it in your home. In this age of home entertainment, where you don't have to leave the comforts of your home to watch a movie, you can also re-create the buzz of the soda fountain (if not the camaraderie).

While the Ice Screamers may come across as a fringe group, the nostalgia that drives its members is drifting into the mainstream. Breweries across the country are cashing in on our desire to make ice cream sodas appealing for adults. You can buy hard root beer from Small Town Brewery—which is based in Wauconda, Illinois, and makes a product called Not Your Father's Root Beer—Coney Island Brewing Company, and Mission Brewery. This popular trend is another revival. As far back as the 1700s, home brewers were experimenting with slightly alcoholic "small beers" flavored with substances ranging from ginger to sassafras. Others enjoyed beers that tasted like trees. "Once upon a time, spruce beer was so common that people regularly boiled the tips of spruce branches so they could have bottled extract on hand for quick use," remarked the writer Charles Perry in a story about the trend in the *Los Angeles Times.* Perry said the initial goal of fermentation was tiny bubbles, not intoxication: "The ginger beer recipe in 'The Virginia Housewife' (1824) promises, 'Cork it very well and it will sparkle like Champaigne [*sic*].'" He also pointed out that mid-nineteenth-century home brewers tried to goose these small beers by making them "artificially carbonated" in a crude sort of way: by stirring baking soda and ice water together with "a sassafras-molasses extract."[102]

Not surprisingly, a pharmacy man is behind the root beer craze. Charles E. Hires, a Philadelphia druggist, is credited with bringing root beer to the public at the 1876 Centennial Exposition. In the late nineteenth century, fermented and tipsiness-inducing root beers were so popular that members of the Woman's Christian Temperance Union screamed and shouted about a conspiracy being waged against the men and women of America. The perpetrator was Satan himself. Root beer was nothing less than "the devil's plan to induce people to drink alcoholic drinks without knowing it," the WCTU complained. The group even agitated the state legislature to ban root beer altogether.[103]

Several major newspapers wrote witheringly sarcastic responses to the WCTU's angry protests. *The Washington Post*, reacting to the accusation that hard root beer produces "alcoholic sensations" and "a craving for itself," remarked that other liquids are equally addictive. "Drink some tea, and after a while you will find that you want more tea," the *Post* stated. "So with water. After an interval, you will want more water."[104] *The New York Times* defended intoxicating root beers on the grounds that nonfermented root beers were simply too sweet and disgusting for public consumption. "It is, we believe, true that root beer is not palatable even to those who find it drinkable at any phase until it has been allowed to ferment," the *Times* declared.

The *Times* argued that the WCTU had not compiled sufficient evidence to prove that makers of root beer were "horrible malefactor[s]." Then, in a sarcastic and nettlesome conclusion to their argument, the *Times* mentioned that its editorial board had never come across any definitive evidence regarding "the awful ravages by root beer on the coats of the human stomach. We have never heard of a man, woman, or child who had succeeded in getting tipsy on root beer, although tramps have been driven for stimulation to eau de cologne and Worcestershire sauce."[105]

These days, one of the top-selling hard root beers comes from the Brooklyn-based Coney Island Brewing Company and is carried by Whole Foods. The root beer debuted in June 2015 and took off almost immediately; six months after its release, Chris Manca, senior specialty coordinator of Whole Foods' Northeast region, reported that month-to-month sales were growing at a rate of 400 percent.[106]

I picked up a bottle from Whole Foods on a Wednesday evening when I needed a tonic. It had been a long day—between work and the science fair and the always-headache-inducing brattiness of first-grade girls.

I decided to pair it with Polar Bear Ice Cream, a local Santa Cruz–made vanilla bean that I thought would be airy enough to soak up the bubbles and the booze. The first sip of the root beer activated the part of my brain that reminds me to proceed with caution. It was appealing—a moment of danger and delight during a humdrum weekday evening. I added a scoop of the vanilla to a pint glass and poured on a frothy layer of the root beer. I had even procured a few straws for the occasion, figuring it was okay to drink hard root beer through a straw. But as soon as the fizziness hit my tongue I regretted the effort.

The second sip reminded me why our sense of taste has evolved—to protect us from imminent death. I tasted something that reminded me of Everclear, followed by a Listerine aftertaste. The wintergreen was overpowering. It tasted medicinal.

"I feel like it's now time for me to go back to sleep and put a cold compress on my head," said Dan after swigging down a quarter of a bottle. After three sips, I couldn't continue and poured the remainder of the bottle down the drain. I was left to an even more disappointing evening, which I tried to fill with Facebook status checks, the twenty-first-century equivalent of neurasthenia. Research shows that our collective screen obsessiveness is making us unhappy; we may be more in need of the soda fountain experience than ever before. Our self-imposed isolation is making us lonelier, and social media and smartphones are making things worse. In fact, many believe that loneliness is the next health epidemic.

But the good news is, we can counteract some of that with our own human capacity to sink into the past, collecting old memorabilia and remembering the good old days. Nostalgia has been shown to counteract the negative effects of loneliness, boredom, and anxiety. Remembering past happiness can actually help you feel warmer if you're stuck in a blustery winter storm.[107]

So there may be a scientific reason for the Ice Screamers and for the hoarders who have our collective past stored in attics across America. But some brands do a better job of evoking that nostalgia than others. When I tried a different brand of hard root beer, Mission, a few months later at a party at my house, it was a delightful treat. Granted I added a scoopful of homemade vanilla and the flavor was better, with less of a wintergreen aftertaste. But the experience was uplifting because of the joy of sharing something that reminded people of their childhoods, with an unexpected adult kick. The combined scent of vanilla and root beer created such an olfactory trigger for one friend that he was brought back in time forty-five years to when he first tried to swallow a mouthful of root beer foam only to have it dissolve in his mouth.

I couldn't help but wonder if maybe the old-style soda fountains, even with their questionable tinctures and habit-forming narcotics, were doing something to keep us healthy. Perhaps we have something to learn. And maybe the soda fountain revival is an attempt to give us another place to socialize in an ever-more screen-centered world.

The soda fountain trend reminds us that sometimes the best medicine is to go out and enjoy a sugar-laden treat with a loved one or even a complete stranger—who, if nothing else, may one day become your Facebook friend.

SWEET HONEY IN THE ROCK

Caramelized Honey Ice Cream with Deschutes Brewery Obsidian Stout

¾ cup honey
Water
Lemon juice
1⅓ cups whole milk
½ cup plus 2 tablespoons sugar
½ cup skim milk powder
2 cups heavy cream
3 egg yolks

To caramelize the honey:

- Heat the honey, 1 teaspoon water, and a few drops of lemon juice in a saucepan over low heat. Stir constantly until bubbles begin to form. When the mixture begins to simmer, stop stirring and let it heat for another 1 to 2 minutes, until the honey darkens. Remove from the heat.

To make the ice cream base:

- Heat the milk, sugar, and skim milk powder over medium heat. When the sugar and skim milk powder are dissolved, add the cream and the caramelized honey. Heat the entire mixture to 110°F.

- Lightly beat the egg yolks. Temper the egg yolks by adding a few drops of the warm milk mixture, then add to the warm milk mixture. Stir constantly until the custard reaches 165°F. Remove from the heat and strain. Refrigerate for at least 4 hours. Churn the mixture in an ice cream maker according to the manufacturer's instructions. Freeze overnight.

To make the beer floats:

- Add two scoops of honey ice cream to ¾ of a glass of the Obsidian Stout. Wait 2 minutes, until the ice cream melts slightly. Enjoy.

- NOTE: The caramelized honey ice cream is extremely sweet on its own. It's best when paired with a beer.

7.

WILD COOKIE

I walked through the Culver City Arts District in Los Angeles, trying to eat a made-to-order Coolhaus ice cream sandwich that looked like the Flintstone House.

I'd insisted on two scoops of ice cream—Kahlua Donut with Salted Caramel squished between two cookies peppered with potato chips and a pretzel. The center could not hold. A mere anarchy of pretzel and potato chip bits was loosed upon the sidewalk. The ice cream was spilling out from the sides with each attempted bite. The crunchy bits in the middle were not helping my cause.

My pilgrimage for the perfect ice cream sandwich had led me to the Los Angeles epicenter of furniture and design. So what had gone wrong? Blame it all on the folly of human choice. I had created this five-dollar made-to-order monstrosity. This sammie was a reminder of my adult freedoms and that I alone was responsible for all my bad judgments.

In fairness to myself, I didn't know Coolhaus was capable of making such messy, impossible-to-eat sandwiches. In fact, one of the reasons I was in LA was to talk to Natasha Case, the architectural mastermind behind the brand. If you buy a premade Coolhaus in a store, it comes perfectly wrapped in an almost sterile-looking metallic envelope that looks a bit like a bento box or a Thermos. A prepackaged Coolhaus sandwich is a well-designed ice cream delivery system. It's a perfectly constructed snack—the ice cream carefully measured to fit between the two cookies without overflowing down the sides.

The cookies have a give, a touch of honey that keeps the baked good soft and pliable and allows you to bite without fear that the entire thing will collapse into a pile of crumbly rubble.

Unwrapping one gives me the same giddy excitement I had when eating Rolo caramels as a kid. Half the enjoyment came from unpeeling the metallic wrapper and flattening it out as my teeth sank into the chocolate and caramel.

The silver Coolhaus packaging is something you feel like saving. It serves as a CliffsNotes on the major players in architectural history. As the high fat–sugar combination hits your bloodstream, you can learn about architect Ludwig Mies van der Rohe. The packaging describes Mies van der Rohe as a historic innovator of twentieth-century modern design; Mies van der Rohe once remarked that "architecture is the will of an epoch translated into space." He described his simple, elegant works as "skin and bones" architecture. Coolhaus honors his memory—in a left-handed sort of way—with its "Mies Vanilla Rohe" cookies. The company also offers IM Pei-Nut Butter, and Mintimalism. These well-constructed delights are distributed to four thousand stores nationwide.

My made-to-order sammie, however, was an ugly experimental structure—its contents spilling out in an unseemly fashion. The messy quality of the sandwich, the shambolic heap of elements that didn't really belong together under the same roof, or between two walls, reminded me of my childhood home and the slovenliness I still try my best to hide. My dad was a messy hoarder, collecting old tools and spare radio parts that used to line our living room floor and piling car manuals and house blueprints on the dining room table.

Dad was the nucleus for my mom's entire cleanup nagging, and I took advantage of her preoccupation. Using my father as a distraction, I trashed my room from floor to ceiling. You could barely see the top of the red shag carpet in my bedroom with all the stuffed animals and dress-up paraphernalia I had scattered around.

I'd sidestep the embarrassment of hosting playdates by always going over to my neighbor's house. Looking at the ice cream sandwich brought all my childhood shame and defensiveness back to me. The ice cream and my room were both disaster areas, but at least they were mine. Both reflected the idiosyncrasies of personal choices, and those choices aren't always necessarily pretty.

CEO Natasha Case's architectural background inspired Coolhaus. Shortly after enjoying my disaster of a sammie, I sat down to talk with Case and her wife and longtime business partner, Freya Estreller, for afternoon drinks at a chic spot on Beverly Boulevard near their West Hollywood home. They comprise one of the few successful female ice cream duos in a predominantly male profession. Think of the names that come to mind when you think ice cream: Breyers, Ben and Jerry, Steve Herrell, and Baskin-Robbins. I wanted to talk to Case and Estreller about how they started and how they've handled the sexism in this sometimes cold business.

Estreller showed up twenty minutes late with two dogs in tow. Case arrived a few minutes later—wearing a black blouse, high-rise jeans, and bright red lipstick. She bears a striking resemblance to Laura Carmichael, the British actress who played the sad-eyed, ill-fated Lady Edith Crawley on *Downton Abbey.*

I settled in to listen to the triumphs and travails that come from starting your own business. In many ways the story was similar to a British PBS melodrama.

Like so many Masterpiece plotlines, the genesis of Coolhaus started with panic and despair. Case was working at Disney Imagineering in 2008, the recession had hit, and making ice cream and cookies at home was a relief from news about the layoffs.

Case started baking cookies at home and naming them after architects. New rounds of layoffs were spreading through Disney, and the couple decided to launch the ice cream sandwich business. "We didn't have money for a brick-and-mortar shop," said Estreller. "I thought, 'Has anyone reinvented the ice cream truck? We have to be the first to market the hipster ice cream truck.'"

Estreller looks like she could lead an army of hipsters, in fedoras and ankle boots. She studied sociology and business at Cornell and worked in real estate and finance.

To get Coolhaus going, Case and Estreller bought an old postal truck on Craigslist for twenty-nine hundred dollars. This sounded like the adorable beginnings of an indie ice cream success story when in fact it was the first slap of unforgiving reality. The truck looked great, but there was just one drawback. "It didn't work," said Estreller. "We had to get it towed to us."

In an only-in-LA turn of events, they had a friend who had a friend at the Coachella Valley Music and Arts Festival—arguably the most powerful, trendsetting multiday arts-and-rock-bands conclave in the United States, with musical acts like Arcade Fire, the Cure, and Daft Punk taking the stage while entrepreneurs hawk everything from gourmet walnuts to pedicab rides. This friend of a friend booked the pair into the campground for the April 2009 festival. Both were working full-time and realized they didn't have one spare moment to make the cookies and ice cream themselves. "We decided to look for someone to make the ice cream and cookies for us," said Estreller.

As soon as I heard the words, I could feel my face freeze as solid as an almost impenetrable chocolate-covered It's-It. The revelation that no one at Coolhaus makes the cookies or the ice cream for the sandwiches was like bad special effects debunked—reminding me of the moment I learned that the Incredible Hulk was in fact not a monster, but Lou Ferrigno in green makeup, and despite my hours of wishing it, he was unlikely to show up at my front door and offer to beat my brother Steve to a pulp.

But my need to know had led me to this moment of confusing awkwardness, when the idea of "gourmet" took on a new meaning. After all, wasn't the point of artisanal food a sense of going back to the basics of simpler times—when you knew what was in each treat? I wanted Mom's homemade chocolate chip cookies—well, not *my* mom's creation, but someone who knew how to bake and put love and care into each cookie and reminded me of what I always longed for when I came back from school. It was an alternate reality to my latchkey childhood, which usually involved store-bought boxes of Nabisco Pinwheels cookies that I devoured while watching episodes of *Scooby-Doo.*

Of course it was clear that neither one of these hip ladies was a Mrs. Fields. As twenty-first-century entrepreneurs, they had decided to outsource the domestic part of the business. I was having a hard time coming to grips with the idea that nobody within the company they'd created actually made the cookies or the ice cream. And I must admit I was confused by what I'd heard after seeing the many photos of Case standing in her truck or behind the scoop counter at her shop, holding ice cream sandwiches that looked like she'd just put them together.

Natasha Case holds a made-to-order ice cream sandwich at the Coolhaus Shop. *Viet Nguyen*

In the food world, companies hire contract packers (aka co-packers) to manufacture food. It's a common enough practice in the ice cream sandwich world. It sounds so absurdly simple. Get out a couple of cookies. Daub some ice cream onto one of the cookies. Squish the sandwich together, and you're done. Actually, an ice cream sandwich is a difficult creation. I'd recently attempted to make a dozen classic sandwiches, the chocolate rectangles with the hole-punched tops. I'd even whipped up a batch of fresh vanilla ice cream. It was like trying to build the Taj Mahal out of plasterboard. Cookies crumbled almost explosively, as if to teach me a new meaning to the old cliché. As for the ice cream, a perfect consistency in the maker became liquefied when I scooped it between the chocolate cookies. Ice cream spilled over the sides and dribbled through the holes. Trying to put the sandwiches together reminded me of my fourth-grade mission project—where I'd attempted to create Mission San Juan Capistrano out of flour and water. The result was a gloopy quarter-inch wall structure in the shape of a rectangle, which earned snickers from my fellow Gifted & Talented classmates, who were smart enough to get their parents to do their projects for them.

Still, I found myself reeling from the idea that no one within Coolhaus was baking or making ice cream. Couldn't we all just buy premade cylindrical, shrink-wrapped packages of Toll House dough and pints of Dreyer's and do it ourselves? As a society have we really become so lazy? Apparently, we have.

Most important, how did we get to the point where we will pay five dollars for an ice cream sandwich? The novelty was invented as a cheap way of selling ice cream to the masses.

The first ice cream sandwich was created at the turn of the twentieth century as a convenient ice cream delivery method a few years before the ice cream cone was invented.

The cone seems like such a simple feat of engineering—something that should have been around since the Egyptian pyramids. But in fact, the first successful airplane flight took place before the ice cream cone was invented in America.

The Wright brothers were flying in the air above Kitty Hawk before we as a nation had evolved enough to find a way to plop a scoop onto a handheld edible conical structure and have it hold together for long enough for us to enjoy the treat.

Different types of ice cream cones were popular in Europe, but there's a good deal of debate about who invented the ice cream cone in the United States. Most accounts point to the 1904 World's Fair in St. Louis, where at least six different vendors tried to take credit for the invention. Ernest A. Hamwi, a Syrian immigrant, is the top contender for cone honors. Hamwi operated a waffle stand next to an ice cream vendor at the fair. His customers would buy a waffle, then go next door to get a scoop. As the story goes, Hamwi and his employees experimented with different ways to combine the two foods. According to Hamwi's own published records, he was the one who suggested rolling the waffle into a funnel shape before scooping in the ice cream.[108]

But ice cream historians still waffle on the issue, pointing to an Italian immigrant, Italo Marchiony, who claimed to have invented the cone in 1896. Marchiony applied for a patent in 1903 for "ice cream cups and the like." However, the baffling patent for this invention suggests an object that was more of an edible coffee mug than a conical structure. Imagine eating Chunky Monkey out of an edible coffee mug.[109]

The Lyon family eating ice cream cones at the 1904 World's Fair.
Date: 1904. Photographer: Unknown.
Courtesy of the Missouri History Museum.

Before ice cream entrepreneurs made the huge evolutionary leap from cup to cone, pushcart peddlers had to use their ingenuity to bring ice cream to the masses in a cheap, convenient way that left few dirty dishes. Hence the ice cream sandwich.

A pushcart peddler in the Bowery in 1899 invented the ice cream sandwich, according to the ice cream history *Of Sugar and Snow.*

The peddler, as the story goes, originally sold the sandwich for two cents, but boys in the neighborhood demanded that it be available for just a penny. The ice cream sandwich brought the ruffians and knickerbockers of the Bowery in contact with the white-collar workers on Wall Street. According to an article in the August 19, 1900, edition of *The New York Sun,* "[Wall Street] brokers themselves got to buying ice cream sandwiches and eating them in a democratic fashion side by side on the sidewalk with the messengers and the office boys. Blue and white collars alike huddled around pushcarts on hot summer days."

The ice cream sandwich brought ice cream to the masses—before the cone. By its very existence, the ice cream sandwich was a populist sensation. It was good enough to please Manhattan elites but cheap enough for wage slaves to afford it.

During a brutal heat wave in 1900, the *New-York Tribune* described the popularity of the treat, with its questionable ice cream.

> The ice cream sandwich man, who sells quarter-inch layers of alleged ice cream between tiny slabs of water wafers, did a big business during the hot spell. The field of operation was within the district inhabited by the Russians, and his push-cart was elaborately decorated with signs in Hebrew characters. He made the sandwiches quickly in a tin mold, and was kept so busy that he could not make change, and insisted on receiving the actual price of each ice cream sandwich—1 cent.[110]

So how did we get from paying one penny per sammie to forking over five dollars?

Even factoring in for inflation, were we now overpaying in an amount that the street boys of New York City would be ashamed of?

Or should I think of Case and Estreller truly as architects of my ice cream cookie consumption, who are getting premium pricing for creating the experience that my little-girl self craves? Sure, they are not the construction crew—they aren't making the materials or building with them—but they are, in their own way, the Howard Roarks of the frozen treat world, dedicated to creating their vision of what the experience should be. They have put a lot of time and effort into manufacturing a perfect ice cream sammie moment—from the shiny packaging to the clever names. In that sense they really are the ice cream sandwich's answer to Frank Gehry, who most certainly doesn't bend and shape his curlicued museums and office buildings all by himself, or artists like Jeff Koons, who have teams of artisans doing the grunt work for them.

Besides, research shows that packaging plays an important part in how we experience food. For instance, "a cookie seems harder and crunchier when served from a surface that has been sandpapered to a rough finish," according to food scientist Charles Spence, quoted in a *New Yorker* article.[111]

And here I was, eating an ice cream sandwich that was very good when it was the product of outsourced labor, attempting, like a Communist worker, to seize the means of production, only to make a foul mess of it.

I had learned with my Flintstone House of Shame how difficult it could be to try to do it yourself, even if you're given the basic materials.

I had more questions about how Coolhaus—which made a name for itself as a gourmet ice cream sandwich company—was able to pull off this amazing feat of outsourcing and still build a successful company based on on-the-ground customer satisfaction.

"We found a co-packer who made ice cream for Trader Joe's and a baker who was making cookies for Angel Stadium and McDonald's," said Estreller. She added that the company now has different co-packers but declined to give details. "Co-packing" is food business–speak for a company that manufactures and packages food for other brands. It is the ice cream industry's worst-kept secret—so many big brands do it, and no one is really willing to admit it—as if the illusion of how the ice cream sandwich is made (by some mom-type figure) is as important as the taste.

So now the two young entrepreneurs had a plan to conquer Coachella—but there was no way of getting there in the derelict ice cream truck. They didn't make the cookies or ice cream, and they had even outsourced the ice cream truck's very mobility.

Estreller convinced AAA to tow them to Coachella, where it became the most popular vehicle in the campground—selling about five thousand dollars' worth of sammies.

Listening to the Coachella story reminded me of when Ross becomes the cookie dude on the sitcom *Friends.* Ross breaks a girl's leg and winds up selling Girl Scout Cookies for her to stoners in the NYU dorms.

Wasn't Coachella a great outdoor version of the same phenomenon, aka the munchies? Even at five dollars a sammie, what hot stoner could resist such a cool treat offered under those circumstances? They sold out. Estreller and Case filled in a niche, discovering a truth that would help catapult their business: Stoners love ice cream. In fact, many of their flavors, such as the Doritos-containing "Netflix" and Froot Loops Cereal Milk, cater to that niche.

"It's the zeitgeist of lowbrow and highbrow," said Estreller. "These things are junk food but they taste good for a reason. They've been developed to be addictive."

But potheads weren't the only ones who had a sammie addiction.

Four months after Coachella, Coolhaus had forty-three hundred Twitter followers, who would stalk the truck. That number has steadily grown to more than seventy-nine thousand. The company was getting notice from major media outlets including *Time* magazine. In 2014, Case made the Forbes 30 Under 30 list.

Estreller and Case finally had enough money to begin the business in earnest.

But even after the success at the music fest, there were some major setbacks. Case, who had been quiet during the early part of the conversation, became more animated when discussing her business humiliations.

The Craigslist truck was both nonfunctioning and illegal. It was permitted for premade food, not the made-to-order food Coolhaus was offering. The health department cited the truck and Natasha went to court. Her defense? She feigned ignorance, or at least managerial incompetence. She said she didn't know what the people she hired were doing, so how could she be blamed?

"I basically threw my employees under the bus," said Case. "I said I didn't know they were making made-to-order sandwiches."

Would Lady Edith ever have conducted herself so? Perhaps, if she'd been targeted by the LA health department. But then the health department caught her a second time, when she was the one scooping on the truck. It was First Friday, there was a long line, and then, while she watched in horror, a health department worker showed up with a bottle of bleach, took the cap off, and dumped it into her batch of ice cream.

She still sounded bitter about it—like the bleach had left a permanent bad stench that lingered. But it wasn't enough to make her quit the business.

In fact, as she told the story I saw a determination that seems to have kept her going. Her business mottoes define her desire to rebel against the female business stereotype. She says she refuses to act like a victim or give up easily.

The run-in with the law motivated the pair to buy a legitimate second truck. The couple took out a thirty-thousand-dollar friends-and-family loan to buy another truck, which was fully functional and properly permitted.

They had no intention of just standing there in the sun all day scooping out the treats themselves.

"We knew we didn't want to scoop ice cream out of a truck for the rest of our lives," said Estreller.

For the third truck, the duo got a "hard money lender" who was known for financially backing taco trucks. He charged a whopping 18 percent interest.

"It was fast and a catalyst for growth," Case added.

Finally, the two found an "angel investor," Robert "Bobby" Margolis of the Cherokee clothing line, who put one million dollars in the company. When the couple met with him for the first time, he asked what goals the duo had for Coolhaus. They laid out their big plans.

"We want to be the next Ben & Jerry's," Estreller said. "In 2000 Ben & Jerry's sold to Unilever. We want to do the same thing."

I couldn't suppress a surprised gasp. The Ben & Jerry's sale to Unilever is still the subject of debate among businesspeople and legal scholars.[112] Ben & Jerry's, which started in a renovated gas station in Burlington, Vermont, in 1978, made a name for itself with its wacky flavors and commitment to social responsibility. In 1981 *Time* magazine hailed it as "the best ice cream in the world."[113] In 1985, the company tendered a national stock offer and set up a foundation with 7.5 percent of its pretax profits.

But by 1998 company stock was lagging. Dreyer's tried to buy Ben & Jerry's, but the bids were rejected.[114] Takeover rumors boosted stock value. In 2000, Ben put together an offer to buy back the majority stock and take the company private again. The plan fell through. Unilever offered forty-three dollars and sixty cents a share, or 326 million dollars in cash. Neither Ben nor Jerry wanted to sell. But the Ben & Jerry's board approved it. Both Ben and Jerry did well in the sale, making about 40 million and 10 million dollars, respectively.[115] But was it worth it? When I'd spoken with Jerry Greenfield, he'd sounded wistful about having an "undefined" role at the company that holds his name.

"We have limited influence," Greenfield said. "It's as much influence as the company decides we have."

Unilever started as a seller of soaps and margarine, but these days it owns about one-fifth of the world ice cream market and has been trying to beat out top brand Nestlé in the United States. Unilever has gobbled up Breyers, Klondike, Good Humor, Talenti, and Ben & Jerry's.

If Unilever bought Coolhaus, couldn't it result in the indie brand's ice cream sandwich annihilation?

Unilever has its own line of ice cream sandwiches, including ones made with Mrs. Fields. Who can forget the ill-fated Chipwich? The story should serve as a cautionary tale—but I was getting the impression Case and Estreller were using it as inspiration.

Chipwich is a classic tale of raising a business from nothing, fighting back against vicious competition, then stepping away from it as a huge corporation takes it off your hands for loads of money.

On May Day 1982 Richard LaMotta sent sixty khaki-wearing street-cart vendors into Manhattan, with matching pith helmets on their heads. These workers looked like the French Foreign Legion but they were there to sell ice cream, not fight on the western front.

The sandwiches were four and a half ounces—including three and a half ounces of ice cream—and sold for a dollar apiece. Customers swarmed the vendors and bought up that first run of twenty-five thousand Chipwiches in just a few hours. Copycats lost no time getting into the sandwich business, coming up with unimaginative names such as Chilly Chips and Chips 'n' Chips. A Chipwich competitor explained the ploy to *The New York Times*. "One guy comes up with a good idea, and everyone rips him off. It's the American way." But these fakes weren't enough to push Chipwich out of business. By 2002 the Chipwich was being sold in almost four thousand markets across the country. The company was eventually guzzled down by Nestlé, which discontinued the sandwich to avoid competing with its own novelty.

I couldn't help but wonder if that was the fate Estreller and Case wanted for their business—to lose control of their brand for the sake of a bigger business win. They are two powerful women who own their own company—although Estreller admitted she's stepped aside from the day-to-day operations at Coolhaus "for the sake of our marriage." She still owns stock in the company, and if the business sells, Estreller will reap the rewards.

It's easy to see why Case and Estreller would seek out the similarities between their company and Ben & Jerry's—even though Ben & Jerry's doesn't make ice cream sandwiches. It's obvious that they studied the Ben & Jerry's success recipe—quirky flavors cleverly marketed with a hip, fun joie de vivre and a left-leaning pro-weed mentality. Ben & Jerry's came up with the idea of putting weird things in ice cream. (Pretzels! Cookie dough! Brownies!)

It seemed to me that Case and Estreller had carefully studied the Ben & Jerry's story—and were picking up some key lessons along the way in ice cream entrepreneurship, including the importance of wholesale distribution.

After the success at Coachella and aided by their Twitter fandom, Coolhaus broke in early to Whole Foods—where Ruby Jewel, a Portland-based ice cream company, was selling an ice cream sandwich for three dollars and forty-nine cents. "The Whole Foods contact recently told us he didn't think we'd succeed," said Case.

Now Coolhaus is distributed all over the country, including Hawaii. When I sat down with them, Estreller and Case were plotting ways of breaking into new markets.

Case seems a twenty-first-century feminist—the kind of woman entrepreneur who has a power she's created for herself through the long hours she's put in creating and maintaining her brand.

There's a long history of women getting left out in the cold in the ice cream world, starting with Nancy Johnson, inventor of the artificial freezer, who got a patent in 1843. She sold her rights to the invention to Williams and Co. for a mere two hundred dollars.[116] When the patent office dealt with her, it sent her an impatient, snippy letter addressing Johnson as a "*he*."

Case and Estreller are part of a group of modern women trying to make real money in the ice cream world, after centuries of the gender losing out on that slice of the ice cream sandwich. A 2014 Bank of America survey showed that things are looking particularly hopeful for women in the ice cream business.[117] Take, for example, the success of Robyn Sue Fisher, CEO of Smitten Ice Cream, who started selling her product out of a Radio Flyer. Smitten produces ice cream to order using a patented Brrr machine. You order a scoop and they take a base, put it in a below-zero machine, and blast it with nitrogen, and the scoop is ready within minutes. A Smitten scoop is dense and sweet and is popular in the Bay Area, where instant gratification feels like it takes too long.

Smitten expanded into Los Angeles and has more than a handful of locations in the Bay Area, with plans to open more shops. Fisher earned an MBA from the Stanford Graduate School of Business but said that pulling her wagon around the streets of San Francisco taught her more about running a company than her time at the prestigious school.[118]

Case and Estreller admit they knew almost nothing when they started Coolhaus. The pair are now teaching other young women how to run a business in a world where both men and women still prefer a male boss.[119] During our meeting, they mentioned they were preparing a TEDx Talk on the subject of female and millennial entrepreneurship.

The two have a confident and almost mischievous energy when they are on the stage talking about business. The topic of the TEDx Talk was how to change the ratio of women to men as business leaders. They discussed society's different reactions and expectations of male and female bosses.

"We are never assumed to be the owner of our business," said Estreller.

Case explained how they were able to grow Coolhaus by raising money from investors, launching in strategic cities, and diversifying their revenue stream from trucks to a scoop shop. "We put organization systems in place. We grew our team," said Case.

Unfortunately, Case noted that Americans still prefer male to female bosses. Men who are in positions of authority are seen as decisive. Too often women in authority are seen as bitchy.

I couldn't help but wonder: Was I expecting Case and Estreller to be more mom-like (actually the ones baking the cookies and mixing the ice cream) because they are women? Was that ingrained sexism part of the initial disappointment I'd felt on learning that they relied on co-packers?

Coolhaus's business strategy has always been dependent on co-packaging, and I wondered if other ice cream sandwich brands used a similar business tactic. After I said good-bye to Estreller and Case and walked back down Beverly Boulevard, I wondered about the issue of outsourcing. Certainly there were companies in the country that were making the sandwiches from scratch, weren't there?

I felt like I needed to access the inner workings of the

mysterious ice cream sandwich world, and what better way than touring the It's-It factory in Burlingame, California? But the It's-It factory was cloaked in as much secrecy as Willy Wonka's chocolate plant.

It's-It dates back to 1928, when George Whitney created the novelty at his amusement park, Playland-at-the-Beach in San Francisco.

He took two oatmeal cookies, placed a scoop of vanilla ice cream between them, and dipped the entire concoction in dark chocolate. Legend has it that the treat was declared, "It!" and that's how It's-It got its name.

Playland was demolished in 1972, and two years later, Charles Shamieh and his three brothers purchased the It's-It name. The cookie operation moved to South of Market and then to its Burlingame location, off Highway 101.[120]

It's-Its are brick-hard cookies with a chocolate shellac covering. They look and feel like hockey pucks. Growing up in the Bay Area in the 1980s, I damaged a few teeth enjoying the treats. People outside the Bay Area have a hard time understanding how anyone could enjoy these sometimes painful creations. But there's something nostalgic about the slight discomforts of childhood. Don't we all get a twinge at memories of riding backward in an old station wagon or emptying a bag of Pop Rocks on our innocent tongues?

I requested a factory tour (or an interview with the It's-It creators) and was rebuffed. I Facebook stalked the Shamiehs for a few weeks and discovered through Internet sleuthing that the cookies are baked by Stella Shamieh at Stella's Gourmet in

Suisun City, California. She emailed me immediately when I asked about the company, and she confirmed that she provides all the cookies for the It's-It. I could tell Stella is the pleaser in the family. Like her cookies, she seems to be trying to hold everything together.

She tried to be the bridge between me and the elusive ice cream cookie overseers of the family, talking to her cousin Alex McDow.

But McDow was less than enthusiastic about giving me a tour. Why the secrecy? Why wouldn't they let me in?

I wanted to know how It's-Its were made. The cruel denial to my pleas felt like the worst childhood punishment.

The company website has a video of the factory that was broadcast by *Eye on the Bay.* I watched it several dozen times. The announcer proclaimed: "It's a winter wonderland where tasty treats are made by the thousands."

It shows oatmeal cookies stacked in a conveyer, ice cream made in giant pasteurizers, machines cutting ice cream and plopping it on the cookies, sandwiches naked of their chocolate being spun around in a dizzying rack. The cookies pass through an enrober where the "chocolate waterfalls coat fresh cookies." Maybe it was a good thing I couldn't get in. How could I resist dipping my fingers into a never-ending lake of chocolate? Wouldn't I be at risk of contaminating the stream of chocolate with my human writer hands and wind up being sucked into the factory's pipes like poor Augustus Gloop?

In the video, according to Charles Shamieh, the president, one hundred thousand It's-Its are made every day. They spend one to two weeks in the freezer (to make sure that each sammie has the consistency of granite when you bite into it) before being shipped out to stores.

It's-It is like a Soviet bloc country from the 1960s, with its squat, boxy-looking building and its fear of transparency. What are they so scared of? Defection? Or spies from other ice cream sammie companies who will steal the company secrets?

I would have to look elsewhere on my ice cream sandwich journey. Fortunately, the Berkeley area seems to have a shop on almost every corner—it's as if the entire region is preparing for an ice cream sandwich Y2K.

Jimmy and Gus Shamieh (distant cousins of the It's-It Shamiehs) started CREAM in Berkeley in 2008. CREAM is an acronym for Cookies Rule Everything Around Me (a riff on the Wu-Tang Clan song "Cash Rules Everything Around Me").

Step into a CREAM store and you're greeted by the smell of fresh-baked cookies. The scent is so appealing that Realtors advise sellers to bake cookies in a home they are trying to sell. It's almost impossible to smell it and not want to spend money.

Buoyed by its Berkeley success, CREAM expanded into Palo Alto and Cupertino, where it caters for Apple, Google, and Facebook.

Gus, who studied law at Northwestern University and looks like he's spent more time at the gym than in an ice cream sandwich shop, said customers are drawn to the superpremium ice cream and highest-quality ingredients. The company uses a "proprietary recipe for both the cookies and the ice cream." When I pressed him, he admitted that both were made at non-CREAM facilities (i.e., by co-packers).

I was soon to learn that co-packers are just as bound to secrecy as the people who partner with them. Co-packing is like an underground brotherhood, where oaths are sworn and sealed in chocolate fudge.

I tried to infiltrate this co-packing world by talking to Ted Castle, the president of Rhino Foods in Burlington, Vermont. Rhino Foods co-packs ice cream sandwiches for brands across the country, but Castle would not give me the names of the companies for fear of spoiling the magic.

"It's supposed to be their brand," he said. Castle did proudly proclaim that his company creates the cookie dough inclusions for Ben & Jerry's. Castle started his company more than three decades ago with his wife, Anne. He was an assistant hockey coach at the University of Vermont when the couple decided to open a small ice cream shop. He started buying up cookies from the shop next door, making ice cream sandwiches with them, and selling them under the brand Chessters.

Chessters ice cream sandwiches are sold for two dollars in Vermont (but I'd heard about them from a mom in California, who smuggled an ice chest full of them for a friend's wedding). I'd never heard of an ice cream mule before, and it left me jonesing to try one of these sammies. What makes Chessters something people talk about across the country, even though they can buy it in only one state?

Castle said it's the homemade feel and taste of the cookie and the quality of the ice cream.

Instead of the entire process being done by machine (like the It's-It video shows), someone places the cookie top on by hand. This gives the entire sandwich a more handmade feeling, according to Castle. The skeptic in me laughed. How could a cookie assembled by robots taste robotic? But the rest of me believed that a cookie placed by hand on the rest of the sandwich would, in fact, taste more homemade.

Unfortunately, it's impossible to get these treats outside of Vermont. Distribution has become more competitive in the past three decades, said Castle. The big brands (Unilever and Nestlé) own most of the freezers that you see in convenience stores and gas stations across the country, and they control what goes in them. That's why you see the same brands in Bismarck, North Dakota, that you do in Reno, Nevada.

And it's why Castle got into the co-packing game of creating ice cream sandwiches for other companies.

"So basically you are competing with yourself?" I asked.

Castle hesitated for a moment before replying. "Yes."

And he's doing so with the utmost efficiency. His machines can churn out 150 ice cream sandwiches a minute. Rhino Foods has more than one hundred employees.

The company has a certain mystique, which comes across in the Rhino Foods *Wikipedia* page. The people who wrote this entry seem to be baffled and intrigued about the company and its business practices.

"The company produces cookie dough and baked pieces for most major brands in the ice cream industry [which?]. The company also co-packs ice cream cookie sandwiches for national and international companies [which?]."

So, when I open a grocery-store-brand ice cream sandwich, I could be eating something that was made at Rhino Foods and never know it.

The prevalence and secrecy of co-packing seemed completely at odds with the twenty-first-century foodie movement. In an age where we want to know the name of the chicken that lays our eggs, we don't even know the name of the companies that are producing our ice cream novelties.

My attempts to create my own made-to-order sandwich showed the messiness of human creativity and freedom. But what's the price of perfection? Outsourcing our food prep to soulless machines felt like an even bigger disaster. Where was the art that comes with the potential for real failure? If given the choice, I would pick the chaos of human foibles every time.

I wanted to meet others who felt the same way, which is why I found an ice cream maker in Northern California who was doing it all from scratch. He was caring for dairy animals, milking, churning ice cream, and distributing almost entirely by himself. And to make things even more challenging, the animals he was raising weren't even cows. They were hulking, snorting, temperamental long-horned creatures that had already led many American dairymen to financial ruin.

8.

BEASTS OF BURDEN

The baby buffalo sucked my finger and swirled her large gray tongue along my hand. She nuzzled, then licked again, searching for a bottle.

I was hanging out with this slobbering animal because she's part of a growing water buffalo herd at Andrew Zlot's Double 8 Dairy in West Petaluma, California, about an hour north of San Francisco. It's an area of hilly land that's become a world-class foodie mecca. It's situated a few minutes from the Bodega Bay Oyster Company and within striking distance of the California Cheese Trail—a sort of Camino de Santiago for dairy lovers. Or the Ninth Circle of Hell for the lactose intolerant.

I was on a very specific pilgrimage—to see the first US dairy that's turning buffalo milk into gelato. And to answer the question: Can you really find a decent scoop of gelato in the United States?

I ate gelato twice a day both times I was in Italy. I sampled as much as I could on my trip to Florence and then Lake Como.

Giving in to temptation and eating the treat as many times as I could was part of the allure of being in Italy.

But American gelato has always been a disappointment to me. It's too grainy. You can feel the individual pieces of sugar crunching between your teeth. So often, it lacks the smoothness you find in Italy. So I was curious if the buffalo milk would create a more satisfying alternative to commercial gelato, which is so varied in quality. And I wanted to unlock the mystery of what is in gelato. The name has an infuriating nonspecific meaning—which translates as simply "frozen."

I longed for the specificity of the German language, which has its own terms for the complex relationships people have with eating. For example, *Kummerspeck* is the perfect word to describe what so many ice cream lovers experience—it means excess weight gained from emotional overeating. But Italy, my adopted food culture, has a lackadaisical approach for the words for its frozen delicacies.

Gelato usually has between 3 and 8 percent butterfat and an overrun—the air pumped into the product—of 20 to 40 percent. But when I think of gelato, I always think of the texture—smooth and dense. Certain optimists claim gelato is a less fattening version of ice cream, with a lower calorie count. But that's not necessarily true, because some gelato makers use a butterfat content similar to that of ice cream. There are even vegan desserts, made out of cashews, that are marketed as gelato, but no amount of soggy, pulverized nuts can make up for the shameful lack of dairy.

Consumers play a greater role in defining *gelato* than the manufacturers. In fact, there is no standard of identity for gelato in America. Why? There's no accounting for this wishy-washiness. How can we live in a country where the percentage of egg yolks in custard is maniacally monitored, the minimum amount of butterfat in ice cream is carefully controlled, but you can take out all dairy from a product and still call it gelato? It's the sad stepchild of frozen desserts, along with sorbet, which also lacks any federal production standard.

The government may choose to treat gelato with disdain, unworthy of standardization, but those of us who've been to Italy have our own rules. When we look for gelato we seek certain traits—just like we'd look for on a blind date. Can it take us away from the mundane misery of our daily lives, if only for the few minutes it takes to consume it? It's something more exotic than ice cream—it can do things to you that normal ice cream can't do. The flavors are bolder because the gelato is usually served at room temperature so the taste buds aren't numbed. Gelato is like a studly hazelnut gigolo. Ice cream is like the vanilla husband who makes you long for adultery.

So perhaps it was fitting that I'd left my husband behind and taken off with my daughter on this adventure in search of the water buffalo.

The Double 8 Dairy had no signs—and there was no cell reception on the road. After a few missed turns, I parked in the dairy's unpaved lot. I had brought Julianna with me because it was a rare opportunity to see the large dairy animals up close.

Andrew Zlot came out to greet us. He had a five-o'clock shadow that looked like it had started at five A.M. the day before. A group of pastry chefs from the upscale restaurants Delfina and Locanda in San Francisco were sitting around on white plastic chairs eating chocolate soft-serve cones. Delfina, a top-rated spot in the Mission District, serves Double 8 Dairy's gelato, as does Locanda, its sister restaurant. You can order Zlot's *fior di latte* (another vague Italian term that translates to "milk flower") in an affogato. The menu doesn't mention that the gelato comes from water buffalo. The dairy also supplies the soft-serve base to San Francisco's beloved Bi-Rite creamery.

If you've ever come late to a birthday party, where the cake's already been served and the kids have smug, self-satisfied grins, you can imagine what walking in on that scene felt like.

I saw the remnants of a picnic—watermelon rinds and artisanal cheese crumbs. It was like entering a scene at the end of a women's travel fantasy movie—such as *Under the Tuscan Sun*—where all the fun is over and all that's left is the cleanup. A few of the women were still finishing their ice cream cones. I had never in my life wanted to grab food out of someone's hands more than I did at that moment. I was unlikely to see these people ever again, and my ice cream id (stoked by the heat and the childhood feeling of being left out) was overpowering my rational self. After watching me drool and stare, Zlot took pity on us. We followed him out back to where his partner, Curtis Fjelstul, was making the gelato using fresh milk from the hulking animals that were standing just a few hundred yards away.

Fjelstul, the former production manager for Three Twins Ice Cream, reminded me of my father-in-law, with his tall and lanky body. Zlot seemed restrained, even taciturn, but Fjelstul was smiling and energetic as he handed us the cones. I couldn't help but think that Zlot seemed a bit buffalo battle worn.

The gelato had a half-melted consistency, reminding me of

slow summer days, like someone had left out the ice cream just long enough that it hadn't become soupy. It felt like chocolate cotton candy in my mouth. It was an instant mood enhancer, recalibrating my brain and making me forget the runaround it had taken me to get here.

A preternatural calm settled on Julianna. It was the kind of quiet in a child that usually rouses suspicion. If we'd been at home, I would have wondered if she was coloring her bedroom walls with a green crayon. I hadn't heard a sound in her room until a great fit of giggles, signaling that her mural was done. But this was a quiet of complete concentration, as if she didn't dare miss a single bite.

The cone was delicious but completely different from the smooth, stretchy gelato I'd discovered in Italy. This was a soft-serve, some of the best I've had in my life. As I enjoyed the soft creaminess, I couldn't care less if it fit a definition of gelato—whatever that might be. As I lost myself in the cone, Zlot explained how water buffalo are different from the American bison. "You can't milk a bison," he said. He prefaced his explanation by complaining that everyone in the United States seems to confuse bison with buffalo. To complicate matters, bison, which were hunted almost to extinction, are commonly called American buffalo.

But Americans have an appalling lack of knowledge about these creatures, or about where they live, which can perhaps be chalked up to our general ignorance about geography, world affairs, and animal husbandry. Water buffalo, aka *Bubalus bubalis,* are the largest member of the Bovini family. Five millennia ago, Asian farmers domesticated buffalo. By comparison, cows were domesticated more than ten thousand years ago. Farmers introduced the creatures known as *bufali* in Italy between the sixth and eighth centuries. They've since been grazing and producing milk for a much-sought-after cheese. The brilliant and persecuted Galileo Galilei had buffalo mozzarella on his mind while he was under "house arrest" in Siena in 1633. He wrote his daughter a letter letting her know that he hoped to send her a gift of seven gooey cheese rounds known as *uova di bufala,* which literally means "buffalo eggs." Unfortunately, Galileo's daughter was not as bright as her dad. She was living in a convent and was confused about the nature of his gift. "I believed them truly to be eggs, and planned to fry a huge omelet."[121]

Buffalo have been a snorting, moist-eyed facet of Italian food culture for so long that some gourmands understandably mistake them for native creatures. In spite of their high standing in Asian and Italian food culture, they are still a marginal presence in the United States, with a population of between five and six thousand. Dr. Hugh Popenoe first saw the enormous animals in Thailand in 1951. More than twenty years later, he established the first commercial herd of buffalo in the United States.

Before the Civil War, the owners of a South Carolina rice plantation imported water buffalo from Constantinople. During General Sherman's march, his troops came through destroying buildings and eating some of the animals. Those that survived the onslaught of hungry Union troops wound up in Central Park, some seven hundred miles to the north.[122] After a brief stint in the urban jungle, they wound up in several North American zoos.[123]

In spite of these heroic efforts, the boring old Holstein and Jersey cows still dwarf the buffalo in popularity in the United States. But it's a different story up in Canada; Zlot told me that farmers are milking lots of water buffalo up there "and making a lot of cheese."

Water buffalo are extremely common in Asia, where Zlot worked in finance for fifteen years and, feeling burned out, wanted to move back to his hometown of Marin. "I worked for people my whole life. I thought: I don't want to die like this." He confronted the stark truth about life in the foodie area. There are only two real options if you want to make a living in this West Coast food mecca: "Out here you either make food or serve it."

Zlot started the dairy in 2013 with about a dozen water buffalo he bought in Texas. His original plan was to make buffalo mozzarella, regarded as the Great White Whale of American cheese making, "a dream so exotic and powerful that it drives otherwise sensible people into ruinous monomaniacal quests," *New York Times* reporter Sam Anderson once wrote.[124]

Zlot soon found out just how hard it would be to start a viable cheese-making operation with his small herd. The dozen animals he'd bought didn't yield nearly enough milk; water buffalo, for all of their bulk, produce less milk than cows. The average happy Holstein can pump out nine gallons per day. In comparison, a water buffalo makes a measly one to five gallons per day. Zlot simply didn't have enough animals to turn a profit.

But Fjelstul's experience at Three Twins had taught him that air is the free secret ingredient in ice cream. Pump some into your product, and you will double the volume of your milk and cream. Desperation drove the pair to devise a new plan: Why not take the small amount of buffalo milk and whip it into gelato? Zlot had an expired California Department of Food and Agriculture permit, which was easy enough to renew, making it possible for Zlot and Fjelstul to milk the buffalo, make ice cream base, pasteurize, and sell it all at the same facility.

Buffalo milk has a higher fat content than cow's milk—it's more like half-and-half. The butterfat ratio of the buffalo milk is a whopping 8 to 10 percent. If the butterfat were to fall below the 10 percent benchmark, it wouldn't be considered ice cream. But labeling the product "gelato" gives them some leeway; the product can have as much or as little fat as they wish. Nobody in charge of overseeing these things checks or cares.

Zlot walked us over the hot, dusty ground to the milking parlor and showed us the eponymous setup. The dairy is named Double 8 because eight buffalo get milked on the right side and eight get milked on the left. The milking machines are for cows, but that doesn't matter. As Zlot pointed out to me, "the anatomy of the buffalo and the cow are very similar."

I explained that I wanted to see the process of milking the large beast. Zlot was not enthusiastic about my idea. He said it doesn't really work to have strangers in the barn during milking. As friendly as they may be to people they know well, these animals are notoriously skittish around strangers. "Buffalo are more intelligent, curious, and affectionate than cows," Zlot told me. "Those are traits that have been bred out of Holsteins." On the other hand, they have a certain cussed determination and willfulness you don't see in standard-issue bovines. "It's hard to make a buffalo do something it doesn't want to do. They're strong-minded."

As he showed us around the barn, I picked up on the animals' personalities. Once I looked past their massive gray shapes, their enormous curved horns and beady eyes, I detected their various quirks. Some curious water buffalo wandered over to Julianna and me and didn't care when I gave them affectionate pats. Others stared us down as if we were fierce and getting ready to pounce.

I have a strange fear of even mild-tempered Holsteins and tend to run for cover when I'm hiking in Santa Cruz and come across a herd of free-ranging cattle, which have the run of some open pastureland just off Highway 1. They hang out on one of my favorite trails and moo ominously at me when I try to pass. It has occurred to me, on more than one occasion, that I might suffer from bovinophobia, an irrational fear of cows or cattle. You can find tips on how to conquer this fear, including articles with pictures that recommend studying "bovine body language." I doubt such behavioral conditioning would work for me; their size makes them seem like bullies to me even when they stand immobile in the middle of my path.

These buffalo, with their great weight and height, looked even more dangerous, with their curly shofar-like horns. But only a few of them seemed to be aware of their own physical menace. Indeed, as Julianna and I approached one of the large animals it snorted disdainfully in our direction.

Zlot could sense my fear—as could the animals, I was sure.

"Let's go see the calves," he suggested.

The babies were lazing in their own separate barn—the equivalent of daycare that allows their moms to do their job producing milk twice a day, without the little ones underfoot. My attitude to these creatures softened when I saw the baby buffalo, which were the size of Great Danes and had the temperament of well-fed kittens. One licked my hand with its smooth tongue, searching for more food (the animals are bottle-fed because the moms are milked for the gelato). It was hard to resist their dark brown eyes. "I would like to take one home with me if it would behave," Julianna said. I wasn't quite so sure that they would make good pets. Sure, they could eat up the enormous weed patch known as my backyard and produce some fantastic milk. They can also stroll through a fence, knocking it down, along with anyone else who might be standing nearby. The adult buffalo were probably the least cuddly creatures I'd ever seen. How would I take care of him? It would be like trying to spoon-feed an elephant.

Essentially, it was as if Zlot were responsible for a preschool filled with giants that could turn on you at any moment. But Zlot sees them as fantastic milk producers that may still help him realize his dream of mozzarella. He's adding buffalo to the herd every year—he had seventy-five when I visited, but only forty-five animals were of milking age. He had all the gelato customers he could handle and seemed to have a 24-7 operation.

He was churning out about four hundred pints a week—and the nature of his work style (doing everything himself) means there's a limit to how much he can reasonably produce. One of the biggest time constraints is putting the gelato into pints to sell. He handles distribution himself. He bought an old Dreyer's truck and distributes the product to half a dozen high-end grocery stores around the Bay Area. But he's not taking on new customers. His gelato production is at capacity.

Zlot's schedule is grueling, but he seems resigned to it because of the freedom it allows. He's his own boss, in his own mind at least. From my perspective, it seemed like the buffalo were running the show.

Zlot took us to the back of a kitchen and went into a huge walk-in freezer, looking for a pint to send home with us. He frowns on the inclusions that are so popular in Ben & Jerry's and other superpremium brands.

"We don't have bits of cookie dough or brownie or that extra junk that other places put in their ice cream," he said. "Our signature in terms of taste profile is clean, straightforward flavors that feature the milk. I prefer to have subtle flavors. The beauty of this product is the taste and texture."

Julianna and I left the dairy with a pint of candy cap mushroom gelato and some tasting spoons. Despite our earlier soft-serve indulgence, we immediately sunk the spoons straight into the carton. The texture was smooth, the taste both musky and sweet. Zlot was definitely pushing original flavors. As Julianna remarked, "Ice cream is not usually made out of mushrooms."

It was a satisfying, light-feeling treat, but it had little in common with my ideals about Italian gelato. Instead it had the unmistakable airy feel of high-end American-style ice cream. It was a fantastic delicacy, and yet it left me wondering how many faux gelato experiences I'd had in my life. Wasn't there anyone out there who wanted to create an "authentic" gelato in the United States, whatever that might be? Wasn't there anyone in my country who was bold and brave enough to impose a more exacting standard for gelato? And if I was tired by the lack of consistency in the product, weren't the chefs who created the delicacy annoyed at this lack of commonly accepted definitions?

As it turns out, I wasn't the only one who had some serious concerns about the gelato standards anarchy. A little research led me to Chris Tan and Trevor Morris of Gelateria Naia, a company based in Hercules, California. Tan started the business in 2002 and soon brought Morris on board to help him create a more artisanal brand, with fresh dairy and locally sourced ingredients.

Tan and Morris looked around to see if there were other gelato makers trying to make a truly handmade product and were sadly disappointed. Morris said the lack of a standard of identity meant that what's sold under the name *gelato* accounts for a wide variety of products.

In 2008, Tan and Morris got so fed up about wishy-washy gelato standards that they wrote up the three key standards of gelato.

1. Gelato must have between 4 percent and 7 percent milk fat.
2. Gelato must have an overrun of not less than 6.4 pounds per gallon.
3. Gelato can include no artificial ingredients.

"It may seem strange that we are trying to further regulate our industry, but the goal is simply to make it clear for both the consumer and the producer what gelato is and what it is not," Morris wrote at the time.

Morris admitted to me that he and Tan perhaps overreached, especially by pushing for absolutely no artificial ingredients. The attempt to impose these standards in California resulted in an onslaught of fierce backlash and a certain amount of public humiliation. More than forty other gelato makers in the state lobbied against it. "People said, 'Who the hell are you to be defining gelato?'" said Morris. "'You're not even Italian.'"

That snipe about his ethnic identity was a cheap shot; it turns out that even the Italians don't have an authentic style of gelato making anymore, Morris said. The Italians mostly rely on premade, prefabricated ingredients—many of which come in bags and tubs.

Bags! Tubs! I hated to hear such things. The more I delve into the secrets of ice cream making, the more it makes me wonder what else the food industry is hiding from me. It feels like a fake world—a vertiginous trip down the ice cream rabbit hole. Who else is hiding information? Are the "chocolate dream cookies" from my favorite small-town bakery made from a Betty Crocker mix? Are the bakery's four-dollar puffy croissants made out of Pillsbury dough? Are the male baristas at my favorite hipster coffee shop secretly sneaking Folgers into my latte, counting on the fact that the milk will obscure the flavor anyway, and are they chuckling behind their handlebar mustaches as they do it? Who can forget the Mast Brothers scandal, involving two neck-bearded siblings who claimed to make bean-to-bar chocolate. In the early days of their operation, they melted commercial Valrhona chocolate, reshaped it, and sold it under their label. The brothers were compared to Ponzi schemers for their chutzpah in selling this reconstituted chocolate for ten dollars a bar.[125]

We're at an age when foodies are willing to pay for made-from-scratch food—but we don't want to be misled or lied to about where that food comes from or how it's prepared. As

Morris talked I could feel my food paranoia reach new heights. He confirmed some of my worst fears. "When you go to Italy, you have these romantic ideas about old grandfathers making all these old recipes that have been in the family for years," Morris said. "The authentic way to make gelato in Italy right now is out of bags and cans."

But I have no right to rant at Italy for destroying my gelato dreams. It turns out the same is true right here in the United States. Companies like PreGel and Fabbri produce bags of powder and paste. There is even a convenient powder that can be added to water to form the "base of gelato." You can buy dozens of flavorings from coconut to fruity banana and create a product without ever shredding or peeling a single piece of fruit. Gelaterias that claim that their products come from Rome are in fact importing these bags, rehydrating the ingredients, pouring them into a machine, and creating a lovely display. And the sad thing is, those gelatos are often delicious nevertheless. Morris acknowledged that those prefabricated ingredients make a tasty scoop.

"But it's not a great product," he said.

The problem with the bags and cans is that you have no idea what's in the product you're serving.

"If you're making gelato that way, you don't know what the butterfat content of your product is," said Morris. Morris said Gelateria Naia keeps its butterfat content around 6.5 percent. A lower butterfat content means that you are better able to taste the flavorings and ingredients, he said. And for an ice cream lover, and a foodie, is there anything less appetizing than thinking of gelato coming out of a squeeze bag? It's like getting a precooked turkey for Thanksgiving and not telling your guests you picked it up from the Whole Foods meat counter. The turkey may taste great, but the lack of effort and the deception are part of a lie that clouds the entire meal. It's doubly complicated when you're a customer. The "chef" knows something the guests do not, souring the flavor of the relationship between cook and diner and compromising the entire delicate relationship between those who "make" food and those who are paying for the privilege of consuming it.

Morris and Tan have opted out of "prefabricated ingredients," even though those bags of powder make a product that has a perfect consistency every time, yielding what many of us think of as the "authentic" Italian-style gelato we remember from our travels. They even contracted with a dairy to create their own base recipes. (They have six different bases depending on what flavors they are going to add to them.) Then they began sourcing local ingredients. Tan and Morris buy California pistachios, TCHO chocolate, and hazelnuts from Oregon.

After talking with Morris, I just had to rush out and try the stuff myself. But the gelato from Gelateria Naia has a consistency I associate more with ice cream. I got a cup of it at a Whole Foods in Cupertino about a mile from where I grew up, close to the headquarters of tech giant Apple. It was served colder than gelato is usually served. In fact, it numbed my mouth. The ice cream was a bit crumbly, with the consistency of halvah. At least the flavors were bright and fresh, and it made me wonder if we need to get over this obsession with consistent gooey stretchiness in gelato and embrace a more artisanal, less elastic riff on traditional ice cream.

Meanwhile, Morris and Tan have backed away from standardizing the treat.

"We were vilified for doing it," said Morris. "We never revisited it."

The contrast between what I'd seen at Zlot's dairy (with its ultralocal ingredients produced just seconds from where the gelato is made) and what I was hearing from Morris created a brain freeze. We are in an age when even my first-grade child knows the difference between organic and nonorganic. Yet I'd lived for decades not knowing that the creamy, dense gelato of my dreams was made mostly from reconstituted goo. The idealistic properties of gelato (the stretchiness, the denseness, the consistency) were some of the few romantic vices my forty-year-old self had left to cling to. And now I was learning that gelato relied all too heavily on both artifice and shortcuts.

Erin Evans, R & D food technologist, helps develop the popular goo flavors for PreGel. I met her during a talk she gave at the illustrious Ice Cream 101 course at Pennsylvania State University. Evans is a fast-talking millennial with short blond hair that conveys a certain perkiness. Before landing at PreGel she was a lab technician at Bush Brothers & Company, makers of Bush's baked beans. Evans referred to PreGel as "an ingredient solution company" and encouraged wannabe gelato makers to use it as a supplement to other products. Still, I found it unfortunate that the company sounded like more of a hair care product ("PreGel, a little dab'll do ya!") than a food.

PreGel America is based in Concord, North Carolina, on the aptly named Fortune Avenue. The company sells a lot of compounds, pastes, and powders. "Use our products as a supplement," said Evans. "You can use fresh ingredients a lot of the times, but that will increase your costs." According to Evans, it's these products more than any kind of ice cream making skill that will evoke that feeling of being in Italy. "Ingredients like this will create a uniform product year-round. It doesn't matter who makes it."

The fail-safe nature of these prepackaged ingredients must be a relief for store owners who employ apathetic teens to make and scoop their products.

Another selling point of PreGel? You can store these ingredients in a cupboard, which is much less costly than having them hog up precious refrigeration space. The powders last two to three years and are not dependent at all on pH, light, or cold. "These products have great shelf stability. That's scary in an industry that's going toward natural, but it's hugely beneficial on a business end," said Evans. "One container can last for a long time. You don't have to worry about refrigerated storage, even after it's been open."

All this talk of shelf stability reminded me of the Cold War bunker mentality, when people were building fallout shelters and hoarding MREs. Maybe we haven't come as far as I thought. Are we trapped in the 1950s with our cans of Spam and jars of Tang?

Evans makes a good argument that you can still be creative and zany with these prefabricated products. She gave some examples of successful ways to experiment with PreGel's products.

"We've done sushi gelato—but there was no fish involved," she said. "We've also done French toast gelato. French toast is not a traditional ice cream flavor. But you have a pan and you drizzle maple syrup on it. You decorate with slices of real French toast. You infuse your base with actual French toast. You create this experience that maybe doesn't taste exactly like your breakfast French toast. The customer is so engaged with it, they are with you in that experience."

Some of these products also remind me of the ill-conceived foods of the 1950s. I couldn't help but think of Heinz Carnival Cream (aka Ketchup Ice Cream), which called for a cup of cream, vanilla, a blob of ketchup, and three eggs, whipped together, frozen, and topped with maraschino cherries and almonds.[126]

The fact that this entire process could be created through bags and jars still seemed so wrong to me.

But if you've ever enjoyed the simple pleasures of a s'more (or any other almost completely synthetic food), you will sympathize with the guilty delight I experienced while sampling these reconstituted products.

In the basement of the Penn State Food Science Building, a representative from Carpigiani (the world's leading gelato maker) stood in front of PreGel bags and jars, laid out enticingly on a long folding table. The bags were white and gleaming, with pictures of bright green trees with ripe fruit falling from them.

First the man dumped in a basic dairy mix, and then he opened a jar labeled PISTACHIO PASTE (which looked surprisingly similar to a spirulina shake) and added that to the machine. Through a grated window in the front of the machine, I could see the green mixture freezing and aerating. The group of onlookers chatted amiably. After about ten minutes, the man stopped the machine and pulled the lever, and a stream of bright green gelato fell easily into a scooping bucket. It was served immediately.

I wanted to hate it on principle. But my stomach wasn't interested in the morality of locally sourced ingredients. It wanted the dense, nutty richness, the perfect consistency. This was just like the gelato I remembered, and the guilty realization that it truly was something out of a bag was enough to create a double *Kummerspeck,* if such a thing existed. I overheard a Penn State staffer complain she was going to wind up sick from overindulgence, even as she dipped her spoon in for more of the treat.

At that moment it didn't matter to anyone in the room that the ingredients were all from bags and jars. It satisfied our need for a rich, creamy, cold treat. But was it a good product? Would I have forked over money and, most important, done it more than once? I don't think there was anything special about the prepackaged gelato, and isn't "special" just as important as consistency these days?

I posed the question to Jon Snyder, who is arguably making some of the best gelato in the United States. He agreed that it's rare to find a good artisanal gelato in America. "I definitely see more poor-quality than higher-quality gelato," said Snyder, who owns Il Laboratorio del Gelato on the Lower East Side of Manhattan. And, to add insult to injury, we're paying more for the fancy name. "Put the gelato name on it and they can sell it at a higher price."

Snyder sees no real difference between ice cream and gelato.

"No one would ask us the difference between cheese and formaggio," said Snyder. "*Gelato* is just the Italian word for 'ice cream.'"

But what about all the hubbub about butterfat and overrun? Snyder, who founded Ciao Bella at the ripe age of nineteen, thinks we make too much of it. "There's all different kinds of ice cream, and that's true in Italy—where there's variations to the south and to the north. You can find some really terrible commercial gelato. Or you can find artisanal gelato. You have to look for it. You have to search; that's my take on it."

Snyder makes a pretty convincing argument. His gelato or ice cream or whatever he wants to call it is so good that it's difficult to debate semantics. And I was coming to realize through my visits to the buffalo and Il Laboratorio that maybe butterfat percentage didn't mean a thing. Perhaps the freshness of the ingredients, the work that went into it, and the feeling it evokes are really the best definitions for gelato after all.

Snyder makes all his flavors in-house, with the exception of hazelnut paste (which he buys in a can). "You can't beat the Italian hazelnuts," he explained. Everything else is cut, peeled, diced, pureed, squeezed, and maturated in his Lower East Side plant. Even the vanilla is made in-house. The base for his gelato is a proprietary recipe that's made in upstate New York and delivered twice a week to his shop.

His Lower East Side Il Laboratorio del Gelato is a sleek, modernist establishment that seems to take the romance out of gelato. The place had a certain chilly, pragmatic ambience, which was almost antiseptic. There was nothing to distract from the transporting flavors. The store, across the street from Katz's Delicatessen, is close to where my relatives lived after immigrating from Poland and Lithuania. My mom remembers that her aunt and uncle owned a grocery store in the neighborhood. Gypsy families lived in tenements across the street. There's little of the old world left now. Today the block is the brick and glass of modern Manhattan, although you can still pick up a potato knish at nearby Yonah Schimmel before getting a scoop at Il Laboratorio, which I did, of course.

Snyder's original 550-square-foot shop had only window service at one time, and the newer incarnation has a few seating areas, mostly as a thank-you to his longtime customers.

I tried his Cajeta gelato, a Mexican confection of thickened syrup usually made of sweetened caramelized goat's milk. After devouring a scoop, I bought a pint to share with friends. When that was gone, I wished I'd bought two. It created an unspeakable want inside me. And even though my friend Rose had let my family sleep in her apartment and had fed us, I can't say for certain that the entirety of that pint made it to her freezer.

Even though he comes across as an artisanal purist, Snyder is against any federal standardization of gelato. "I think there's some silliness to that." Snyder's product, with its 10 percent butterfat ratio, can technically be considered ice cream. Yet, it's the truest to Italian-style gelato that I've found in the United States.

Snyder, who has been described as "a babe" by *The New York Times* with his salt-and-pepper hair, athletic build, and air of confidence, comes from three generations of ice cream makers. His family ran a Carvel franchise for more than fifty years in the Hudson Valley. He started Ciao Bella after traveling to Italy and dropping out of school.

He didn't have much money and first concentrated on wholesale.

"I was trying to do things the commercial Italian way," said Snyder.

One of his very first ice cream customers was the River Café. "I brought chef Charlie Palmer samples [he'd just fired the previous ice cream vendor] and he asked me to make a blueberry sorbet." Snyder made the sorbet with a prepackaged can and brought it to him. "He literally spit it out. He told me you make blueberry sorbet by getting fresh blueberries. So, that's what I did."

He sold Ciao Bella when he was twenty-five, reportedly for 120,000 dollars.[127] The new owners expanded Ciao Bella into a pretty "commercial national brand" and moved operations from Manhattan to Irvington, New York. Snyder went to Columbia Business School and worked unhappily on Wall Street. After September 2001, Snyder decided to get back into the family business and opened Il Laboratorio, with much debate among family and friends about the name.[128]

He now makes more than 250 flavors for five hundred restaurants in New York City. More than 80 percent of the business is wholesale, and it feels more like a true chef's lab than a sweet shop.

"I focus on chefs and restaurants in the community," said Snyder. "This is a place where chefs can come and develop recipes."

His flavors include standards like vanilla, hazelnut, and pistachio. But he's known for his unusual flavors, including Cheddar Cheese and Thai Chili Chocolate.

Snyder admits that some people find the sterile atmosphere uninviting, but for him it's the perfect atmosphere to experiment with flavors on three Carpigiani machines. "I like the minimalism and the stark whiteness of it all."

For Snyder it's all about sticking to his vision of creating artisanal, great one-note flavors. "I've said no to people who said they want cookie dough. You can go to Ben & Jerry's for that."

He's also not looking to grow into what Ciao Bella became.

"If you get to a certain size, the product is going to suffer," said Snyder. "I'm not willing to do that."

When I first started out investigating this frozen treat, I didn't expect that there would be so much drama, nor did I expect to get my heart stomped on when I found out how people were cheating my mind, and my taste buds, by resorting to prepackaged powders and goops.

But in the end, gelato gives you cause for hope. Perhaps the people who are doing it the hard way—folks like Snyder and Zlot—will one day free gelato from the tubes and the glop and the goo. My investigations had led me to a few other gelato makers in the country who are committed to making gelato without using preprepared pastes and off-the-shelf mixes. Bryce Licht, who owns Fior di Latte in Boulder with his wife, Giulia, said his shop makes everything from scratch, including the gelato base, which is churned out one batch at a time.

Gelato may be going through troubled times, but I have some faith that artisanal manufacturers of gelato will ride Asian bovines into the sunset and lead the public to the taste of *real gelato.* Whatever that may be.

Despite its reliance on artificial goop, gelato still delivers the pleasures of dairy fat in a smooth and satisfying way. What's left when you take away that fat and add in a sprinkling of "healthy" probiotics? The sometimes fruity, sugary modern invention we've dubbed froyo.

9.

THE CULTURE CLUB

The scene I witnessed at Yogurtland looked like a Muppets horror show. A boy was stirring blue gummy worms into a mess of chocolate frozen yogurt. It looked like the aftermath of a battle to the death between Elmo and Mr. Snuffleupagus.

As I sat staring at the blond boy with the missing front teeth proudly devouring this glurpy creation, I realized I was the only one at Yogurtland without a bowl of frozen yogurt. Yes, it seemed like a supremely antisocial maneuver. Even a recovering alcoholic will order a near beer or a Coke when out at a bar. But I would rather wait and have ice cream later, even if it meant I had to eat my dessert while sitting near the front window all by myself, like some sad loner in an Edward Hopper painting.

I have despised frozen yogurt since its first wave of popularity in the 1980s, when it tried so unsuccessfully to mimic the whipped fatty creaminess of my childhood obsession. My own mother, who has never, to my knowledge, turned down a dessert item, can't stand it either. The few times I've eaten it, I've come away feeling deprived. I experience a desolate, empty feeling that is so much worse than mere hunger. The yogurt cruelly mocks the unofficial motto of all ice cream lovers: "Fat! Makes the world taste good," a rallying cry at my ice cream course at Penn State.

So how did I wind up at Yogurtland, a place I'd always considered the archnemesis of my beloved ice cream parlors?

My weekly trips started out as a form of well-intentioned parental bribery. Julianna has always longed for froyo. We would drive past it, and she would beg me to take her, claiming she'd rather go get a bowl there than eat at the French Laundry. Could this really be my offspring? Was it just the verboten nature of the treat (Mom can't stand it!) that made it so appealing? When I was pregnant, I ate a few bowls of it because the shop was closer to my workplace than any ice cream store, and maybe that had a detrimental impact on her developing taste buds. Or maybe she knew it was the one dessert she never had to share with me.

I promised my soft-spoken child that if she could read to her teacher in her big-girl voice, she'd get a visit to her beloved Yogurtland. That's when my little redheaded curly-haired angel turned into a con artist. Every day at pickup time she announced she'd read a little bit to her teacher. One week I took her there every day after school before it dawned on me to ask her to see one of the books she'd read aloud. It consisted of about eight words.

Somehow, because of her deception and my questionable parenting strategies, our Yogurtland trips had become a ritual. And despite my distaste for the stuff, I was building lifelong memories with my daughter over food *I could not stand.* Besides, I couldn't help but wonder if the garishly flavored and colored froyo was really so much less wholesome or authentic than the cloying bubble gum ice cream I'd ordered at Swensen's as a child.

And yet I sensed that things were getting out of hand with the froyo.

If froyo is so healthy, how come you are supposed to buy it by the pound after heaping it with crumbled cookies, M&M'S, translucent gummies, and those weird little beads of flavored corn syrup that dissolve and explode on your tongue? The message on my Yogurtland rewards card all but spells out the chicanery: "Sometimes I use my yogurt as an excuse to eat a cup full of candy."

The heaps of candy made me wonder if my child was coming back for the "healthy" yogurt or the sugary toppings. Suddenly, we were heading for froyo every other day and even planning Yogurtland playdates, which was how I'd come to witness the phenomenon of the blue gummy worms. Yogurtland and many other chain frozen yogurt shops charge by the pound, and bulky toppings make for a great profit. Some of the other junk foods that you have to get a child past in order to pay include: Twix, chocolate-covered macaroons, gummy bears, and Reese's Peanut Butter Cups.

Oh, and there are cut-up bits of fruit, too, but good luck pushing them on a playdate with ornery schoolchildren.

When Julianna was a baby, I had lovingly prepared her organic pureed peaches and pears, shopping at the overpriced organic produce place down the street. What had happened? At one point did I just give up as a parent and realize that it was not worth the trouble? Had my fifteen months of sleep deprivation left me with mild but permanent brain damage, diminishing my capacity as a parent? My food standards had become alarmingly low.

Every time we visit Yogurtland I see another mom I know

who has been hoodwinked into participating in this sour cultural ritual. Frozen yogurt has become one of the main parental currencies. It helps, perhaps, that it's being sold as a healthy alternative to ice cream. It caters to the health-conscious worriers who want a treat without impacting the sleekness of their thighs or increasing the cling of their Lululemon pants, and to parents who want to reward their kids for the latest soccer game win or good report card. Perhaps if we all had better parenting skills most of the froyo shops in America would be boarded up and nailed shut with pink plastic spoons.

There's always an after-school crowd at Julianna's favorite Yogurtland, conveniently situated at the area's only mall, so it was a little hard for me to believe the chilly rumors about the frozen yogurt industry's downturn. Some claim that froyo has hit its peak, although representatives from Yogurtland tell me the company is still growing at "a good clip," continuing the expansion Phillip Chang started when he founded the self-serve company in 2006. In seven years, almost three hundred new Yogurtlands opened up around the world. Things were going so well that in January 2014 Chang stepped down as CEO to focus on Christian charity work. But six months later, he returned to his leadership role at Yogurtland, laying off fifteen top executives.[129] Some of the froyo chain's locations have shuttered, including one at Harvard Square, where some Ivy League customers were "heartbroken" over the loss.[130]

The stakes are high for entrepreneurs who have bought into the Yogurtland franchise. One business owner I spoke with told me she paid five hundred thousand dollars up front and took out a ten-year loan to open her Silicon Valley location.

Frozen yogurt has gone through incredible waves in popularity—first in the 1980s and into the 1990s, before rebounding yet again in the mid-2000s with brands like Yogurtland, Red Mango, and the iconic Pinkberry. What's the reason for the latest possible meltdown? According to Jonathan Maze of *Nation's Restaurant News,* part of the current bust in the froyo industry is due to the owners' initial overenthusiasm. "In this case, it means that entirely too many entrepreneurs decided to create their own chains, leading to a rapid oversupply in many markets—particularly in colder Midwestern states where yogurt is less popular."[131]

Another reason may be that dairy fat is "in." For years, nutritionists have pushed lower-fat options to curb the rise in obesity and diabetes. But recent scientific evidence seems to discount that theory. When it comes to avoiding weight gain, full-fat dairy may actually be better at keeping the pounds off. Fred Hutchinson Cancer Research Center in Seattle found in eighteen separate studies that there were lower body weights, less weight gain, or a lower risk for obesity among full-fat dairy eaters.[132] Some researchers believe that drinking skim milk doesn't make you feel as full, or stay as full, as you would if you reached for whole milk. The documentary movie *Fed Up* looked at how America's obesity rate worsened since the 1970s, when low-fat, high-sugar foods hit the market.

This renewed zest for animal fats reminded me of the 1950s, when a leading dairy researcher at Cornell was pushing ice cream as a diet regimen—not just once but twice a day. "Two dishes of plain ice cream make a satisfying reducing for a physically active man," according to figures worked out by Dr. A.C.

Ice Cream is a Food

Famous specialists have recommended the use of ice cream for years back. One quart contains the same amount of protein as a half dozen eggs or two pounds of beefsteak. During the hot summer months it serves as an incomparable substitute for food which must be cooked and prepared--it is a zestful, appetizing confection.

THE HISTORY OF ICE CREAM

105 years ago this month Sambo Jackson, a negro pastry chef in a New York Tavern, gave to the world its first dish of ice cream.

For years Sambo had a monopoly on the sale of ice cream, because he kept his process a closely guarded secret. All that is definitely known about his discovery is that it was an accident.

Today ice cream is the national dish. Its wonderful flavor, its mildly stimulating effect, its unquestionable pureness, make it a popular favorite. Not only is it a confection but it contains protein—it is a food that builds up the body.

Big days or little days ice cream is always appropriate. Take home a quart every evening.

Either plain or as part of a sundae, parfait or soda ice cream is always a welcome morsel.

Eat a Dish of Ice Cream Every Day

"Ice Cream Is a Food" advertisement from *The Evening Missourian* (Columbia, MO), July 27, 1921.

Dahlberg at the New York State (Cornell) Agricultural Experiment Station in Ithaca, New York.[133]

The modern ice cream diet is based on a book by Holly McCord, an editor at *Prevention* magazine. It allows for daily ice cream consumption, as long as you have only low-calorie meals. There's also an ice cream "cleanse" where you can eat five pints a day of Halo Top "plant-based raw coconut cream" and *nothing else* to lose weight. Cartons boast "240 calories per pint." Writer Shane Snow tried it for ten days and wrote about it for *GQ*. He lost weight but developed an understandable aversion to ice cream.[134]

Pinkberry is one of the most well-recognized brands in the frozen yogurt world, and even it has had a shake-up.[135] In December 2015, it was purchased by Kahala Brands, which also owns Cold Stone Creamery.

In the face of ruthless froyo competition and dairy fat–positive headlines, every frozen yogurt maker is looking for a secret weapon that will help the company stay edgy and relevant. In the case of Pinkberry, that secret weapon is a wunderkind named Maya Warren. She was only thirty-one in early 2016 when the company hired her to create interesting flavors that would engage the taste buds of children and adults. Warren is one of the very few African American women who have a leadership role in the frozen-dessert industry. She is savvy, smart on her feet, and supercompetitive, thanks in part to her stint on a hit reality show, *The Amazing Race,* where she competed as part of a team called the Food Scientists. This is an inside joke; she and her team partner, Amy, had both studied food science at the University of Wisconsin–Madison. Though she was more of a scientist than a survivalist, she somehow beat out trash-talking wrestlers and a one-armed surfer to win the million-dollar prize.

Keeping a company relevant is a daunting task. Then again, Maya has faced greater risks, including the time she jumped out of a third-story window made of rock candy as part of an action stunt. After landing she analyzed the window's chemical composition before moving on to the next challenge. "It was basically made of sugar, so your sucrose, corn syrup, and water." She regretted being so rushed and not putting a shard or two in her mouth. "I should have tasted it!"

Winning *The Amazing Race* helped Maya land the gig at Pinkberry. I was by no means a frozen yogurt connoisseur, but even I could tell that each brand had its own flavor notes—some places like Yogurtland leaned toward sweet, whereas Pinkberry has a telltale tartness. Maya said it was about the amount of sugar added to each product, while Scott Shoemaker, a vice president of innovation/research and development at Scott Brothers Dairy, claimed it was the strain of bacteria each brand added. Maya is a chemist by trade, but Pinkberry allows her to use her scientific background in a practical, on-the-ground way. In seeking new flavors, she was inspired by the show *Unwrapped,* a behind-the-scenes look at how America's favorite foods are created. "I believe as a scientist you have to look beyond the goggles and beyond the beaker," Maya said. "Look at what you can do and what you can be." Searching to push boundaries, she travels all across the country, sampling flavors, striving to be open-minded, even while tasting some out-there flavors, including durian, an exotic fruit whose overwhelming odor has been compared to stinky socks and rotting meat. "We are looking for what's new and innovative," she explained.

But don't expect to see any smelly durian yogurt or ice cream wafting out of your neighborhood Pinkberry or Cold Stone anytime soon. Though Maya herself is adventurous, she must contend with cautious customers. With fifteen hundred Cold Stone stores and hundreds of Pinkberry locations, there isn't a lot of room for experimentation. "You have to be more careful. You have to be able to sell the product," said Maya. As a tastemaster, she has to be safe but different enough to draw in customers with curious palates.

The ability to reformulate has kept Pinkberry fresh in its tumultuous short life span. Pinkberry was founded in 2005, and its co-founder Young Lee left the company in 2010. A year later he was charged with beating a homeless man with a tire iron after he asked for money and flashed a "dirty tattoo" at a car full of Lee's friends, including his fiancée.[136] Lee fled to South Korea. But he was picked up at LAX by a fugitive task force in 2012 and was sentenced to seven years in prison in 2014.

Pinkberry distanced itself from Lee and created such a strong following in Hollywood that Larry David riffed on it during an episode of *Curb Your Enthusiasm* when Larry and Jeff are sent out to get a cupful of coconut frozen yogurt for Susie's dying dog, Oscar. "Get me the F-ing Pinkberry, Larry!" she screams. It's supposed to be the dog's last meal, but Larry is starving and pleads, "Come on, I've got low blood sugar!"

Jeff agrees, "One bite, but make it small, small, small." Larry takes a bite, kvelling. "Is there another spoon in the bag?" Jeff asks. Larry hands it to him, and then all of a sudden the two are snarfing down the entire cup and fighting over who gets the biggest spoonful. Unfortunately, they are spotted and eventually turned in by Vance, who breaks a vow of silence to rat them out.

But was what they were eating really yogurt? Does it matter? Some customers thought so, and they sued Pinkberry in 2007, claiming the frozen dessert didn't live up to its health claims.[137]

In most of the country there are no standards for frozen yogurt. But in California a product cannot be marketed as frozen yogurt unless it is made from milk that is fermented with bacteria, mixed off-site rather than in stores, and sold with its ingredients "prominently displayed."[138]

The Pinkberry scandal reminded me of the famous *Seinfeld* episode "The Non-Fat Yogurt." Jerry, Elaine, and George are eating froyo at a place that claims to sell nonfat yogurt. "How could this not have any fat? It's too good," George says at the beginning of the episode. A few minutes into the episode, Elaine and Jerry appear with their shirts untucked and Kramer proceeds to call them both fat. They climb on the scale and realize they've both gained weight. They then proceed to uncover whether the froyo has any fat—sending it to a lab where the blood of Rudy Giuliani is also being tested for cholesterol. Giuliani actually appears in the episode, denouncing the faux yogurt. At the end, the company changes its formula but no one can stomach it.

Pinkberry settled the lawsuit about its ingredients and agreed to pay 750,000 dollars to two Southern California charities, the Los Angeles Regional Food Bank and Para los Niños, a childcare group.[139]

You can now find Pinkberry's ingredients on its website. Its froyo competitors also list the nutritional information. Go to the sites and download the thirty-page PDFs and you'll see ingredients with names like *propylene glycol monoesters* for TCBY. I did a little Internet research to confirm that despite what it sounds like, it's a common emulsifier, not the anesthetic propofol, which killed Michael Jackson.

While finding out that certain frozen yogurt contains stabilizers like carrageenan didn't bother me very much, I was surprised to find out that lots of frozen yogurt—like countless gallons of American ice cream—comes from a premade base. Frozen yogurt shops can buy base in mass supply from companies like YoCream, a Portland-based business owned by the French company Dannon. YoCream ships out a combination of Grade A milk, sugar, and cultures in a frozen form to both franchise and mom-and-pop yogurt shops. Store owners just defrost, shake, and pour the base into a frozen yogurt machine. In other words, the "fresh" froyo we consume in many stores today is mostly prefab, like a large portion of American ice cream and gelato.

Similarly, Pinkberry gets its proprietary base shipped frozen from a dairy it contracts with, said Maya. Flavor, such as pomegranate concentrate, is added to the mix as it spins through a Carpigiani machine, or what I like to think of as the "delicious machine," which is often used to give gelato its smooth consistency.

I can't help but wonder if such premade bases—combined with consumers' limited tolerance for wildly "experimental" flavors—place some constraints on the work of people like

Maya. But it seems to me that her role at Pinkberry goes beyond mere flavor enhancement. Even before she became a public face for Pinkberry and Cold Stone Creamery, she was an advocate for women in the sciences; as a brave and resourceful competitor on the reality show, she shattered stereotypes of the nerdy female scientist. "When Amy and I were on the race, we got emails, texts, and Facebook messages from people thanking us for showing how badass a woman scientist can be."

She is also a strong advocate for diversity in the sciences. Maya was the only African American graduate student in the food science program at UW–Madison. "I wished there were more people that looked like me," she said.

I was startled to hear about the overwhelming whiteness of the frozen-dessert industry. Even the food science labs at the University of Wisconsin–Madison were vanilla white. As an ice cream history geek, I find this ethnicity gap jarring, considering the long-standing and valuable contributions of African Americans to the world of ice cream, going back for nearly two centuries. Augustus Jackson served as chef in the White House during the 1820s, decades before slavery was abolished. Jackson reportedly developed ice cream making techniques, which he took with him to open a successful business in Philadelphia.[140]

George DeBaptiste, an African American businessman, was a well-known owner of ice cream parlors. At various times, he also owned a bakery, worked as a barber, and served as a steward for President William Henry Harrison, but he is best known for the help he gave to the Underground Railroad, secreting slaves away on a steamship. Bounty hunters tried to catch him in the act and at one point tried to have him arrested, but the fearless DeBaptiste outwitted them every time.[141]

There may be a rich history of African American ice cream makers in this country, but few are studying it at the academic level. "I've met people who tell me I'm the only African American food scientist studying ice cream that they've ever met," Maya said. "I hope I'm not the last."

Maya seems to have a never-ending supply of energy and a boundless enthusiasm that has helped her rise to the top in her professional and personal life. (Along with winning *The Amazing Race,* she's also a marathoner and triathlete.) But she insists she's not a competitive person.

My conversation with Maya reminded me of an interview I'd read that featured President Barack Obama and Misty Copeland, the first female African American principal ballet dancer for the American Ballet Theatre. Copeland talked about pushing herself to be the best and to work harder. She described having a "fire inside" of herself because of her race.[142]

"I'm competitive with myself," said Maya. "I strive to do my best, not better than. If I can do my best, then rewards will come."

She's now tasked with coming up with flavors for Pinkberry that "pop." And it's that kind of experimentation that really keeps things interesting for her. "There was a time when froyo didn't exist," she said. "Someone had to think, 'How can we do this?' That's what we're still dealing with today."

I was encouraged to find out that Maya was working to make

the Pinkberry flavors more interesting, but I was still an ice cream loyalist, inimical to the dubious pleasures of frozen yogurt. As a mom, I did want to find out if it was a healthier bribe—that is, treat—for my daughter.

With this question in mind, I called up registered dietician Melinda Pine, from the University of Kansas Hospital, to help me understand what these ingredients are and to settle the question of whether frozen yogurt was really better for my kid than ice cream.

I asked Pine right off if frozen yogurt was a healthy alternative to ice cream.

"It's a great source of calcium and protein, and it can be wonderfully lower in fat content," Pine said. Frozen yogurt also has probiotics that Pine said can aid in digestion.

However, that claim is still being disputed. A team of researchers in Denmark recently published a report that probiotics are a waste of money for healthy people but can aid those who are suffering from "gut-bacteria-based maladies."[143]

But the verdict is still out on probiotics, and they certainly can't hurt, said Pine. "You have to look for the 'seal' that shows that probiotics have been added back in, since the freezing process can kill them."

The beginning of my chat with Pine was going great. Pine temporarily allayed my fears that I was failing as a parent, at least in regard to frozen yogurt.

Then things shifted when we got to the issue of serving size. Pine agreed that frozen yogurt was a good dessert choice, but with a huge qualifier. "In proper serving size and with the right toppings." When she repeated this idea a second time, I realized we might have different concepts of what a "proper serving size" looked like.

Pine explained that most froyo stores offer customers a sixteen-ounce cup in which to pour their yogurt. "We see that as four times the normal serving size, which should be about four ounces." This is when a nagging horror began to travel up my spine, to the part of my brain that handles the unpleasant realities of parenting. I had an image of Julianna and her cohorts filling their sixteen-ounce yogurt cups happily to the brim (and sometimes beyond). So the yogurt Julianna was pouring herself on an almost daily basis was about four times the recommended amount? I asked.

When Pine confirmed this sugary reality and added that at sixteen ounces—if you fill up the cup—you're looking at thirty-five calories per ounce, with seventy-six grams of sugar. That's before the toppings, which often include chocolate and other leftovers from the Halloween basket.

"Fruit and nuts are the best topping choices, but in moderation. You can easily turn a bowl of frozen yogurt into a five-hundred-calorie dessert with the toppings, if you're not careful," Pine said.

Pine has a reassuring attitude, and a way of conveying bad news in an upbeat way. Talking with her was a bit like downing an icy treat too fast—you don't know what you're in for until the pain has you clutching your head and screaming.

I have never in my life skipped lunch in favor of froyo, but apparently this is something people eagerly do, and Pine warns against it, not because of the questionable taste but because of the lack of nutrition. "Frozen yogurt is an accompaniment to a meal," she said. "Let's have some other good stuff too."

You may think you're making the "healthy" choice by

skipping the higher-sugar yogurt options in favor of no-sugar added (NSA) flavors, but Pine said those NSA options might not be the best choice.

Most NSA flavors, such as Yogurtland's French Vanilla, contain aspartame, which brings up other long-term concerns, said Pine.

Some studies have shown that artificial sweeteners can actually lead to weight gain because they mess with our metabolisms.[144]

This unintended effect can be particularly bad for kids, worsening the obesity epidemic.[145]

"The concern is that these artificial sweeteners can increase the perception of sweetness," said Pine. Pine compared the effect to people drinking a Diet Coke and thinking it tastes sweeter than a regular Coke. Pine said sticking to natural sugars is probably a better choice.

"I think we're at a point where we have a lot of chemicals in our world," Pine said. "It may be prudent to try to reduce chemicals and get back to basics."

I wasn't sure what to think of Pine's advice, as I headed out to visit the Pinkberry store at Santana Row, a kind of grafted-on quasi-downtown where hideous Starburst Fruit Chew–colored sports cars compete for spaces in a gigantic parking structure that towers over a crowded retail avenue. A burly middle-aged woman was belting out "Fire and Rain," James Taylor's heroin-and-insanity song, accompanied by a tambourine player and a guitarist. People mostly ignored the band, or swayed vacantly while pile driving free samples of pastel-colored yogurt into their throats. A dad was sampling the pear flavor and was trying to get his toddler to take a taste, when the boy burst into tears and started screaming.

The band began playing "A Horse with No Name," a ditty by

a rock band called America. I started thinking that yogurt is the easy-listening option in the frozen-dessert world. The crowd looked frantic, impatient.

Wanting to see what the fuss was about, I tried a fruit-flavored sample. My husband, Dan, informed me that it was supposed to be blood orange, but it left my tongue feeling engorged. I felt like I was having an allergic reaction. Unbelievably, it made me long for the milder flavors of Yogurtland.

How could people wait in line to pay for this? I wondered. Even with headlines about a frozen yogurt meltdown, it's a popular treat, although it's still not the craze it was when it first hit the market when I was in elementary school.

These days, frozen yogurt is not quite the force it was in the 1980s, when this treat was such an in-demand commodity that froyo purveyors had to be sharp elbowed just to grab up their market share. Americans had been familiar with this substance since at least the seventies, when an East Coast company marketed it, unappetizingly, as Frogurt, which sounds like an intestinal tract disorder specific to amphibians. Within a decade, Americans had become so obsessed with this substance that it permeated every aspect of our culture; nothing could escape froyo, not even our horror movies. In the 1980s, an auteur by the name of Larry Cohen made a widely publicized film called *The Stuff*, about a strangely addictive brand of froyo that becomes wildly popular. It turns out—spoiler alert—that the frozen dairy goo is actually a kind of calculating and intelligent parasite that turns consumers into vapid zombies.

The Stuff was not a major commercial success, perhaps because this schlocky sci-fi scenario was just a bit too close to real life. In the early 1980s, even some of the lesser-known froyo chains were adding new stores constantly, hiring armies of sales staff, and posting tens of millions of dollars in annual profits. Meanwhile, the biggest froyo businesses watched their sales skyrocket. In one hectic two-week period in 1986, TCBY's shares rose 70 percent on heavy volume; a business journalist reported the company's market value as "above $650 million." Wacky flavors and ooey-gooey sugar toppings proliferated as froyo outlets struggled to get a toehold amid the overwhelming competition. And the relationships between competitors were not exactly cuddly.

In fact, a Dallas-based company called This Can't Be Yogurt Inc. ended up getting sued by a company called I Can't Believe It's Yogurt, claiming their trademark was getting stomped on. *The Wall Street Journal,* in a brief and cheeky news item, pointed out that the suit was filed just one day before This Can't Be Yogurt Inc. had scheduled a public offering. The reporter pointed out that the defendants "can't believe" that the timing was not intentional.[146]

This was all part of the early 1980s frozen yogurt boom that changed America; yogurt emporiums were as ubiquitous then as Starbucks are now. "From San Diego to San Antonio to Raleigh, N.C., hundreds of entrepreneurs have started frozen yogurt stores, only to watch competitors open shops across the street and around the corner," noted *Wall Street Journal* reporter Karen Blumenthal in May 1984.[147] "It gets real intense," noted Nancy Milburn, owner of a Texas-based froyo chain with the startlingly original name of I'd Rather Have Yogurt. "The more you know about the yogurt business, the more it looks like a soap opera."[148] In the same, hair-raising article, Blumenthal talked about charges of sneaky behavior. "Bill Brice Jr. and his sister Julie Brice, owners of I Can't Believe It's Yogurt, say they fired a manager in their Austin, Texas, store last year because they believed he was a spy."

Michael Serruya, the CEO of Kahala Brands, which now owns Pinkberry, has been in the frozen yogurt business for more than thirty years and has ridden the chilly coaster of the product's success and doom.

In fact, he's built and lost and rebuilt a food empire on it.

Several online photos of Serruya show a confident man with fashionable facial stubble and gleaming white teeth. His coiffed brown hair is flecked with gray. He looks like there's no place he'd rather be than in front of a camera.

Serruya was twenty-one when he and his brother, Aaron, nineteen, started Yogen Früz in Toronto. The siblings had seen the success of froyo in the United States and wanted to bring the trend to Canada.

The young Serruyas called TCBY and asked if they could buy the franchise rights for Canada.

The brothers were invited down to Arkansas to meet with the heads of the company.

"I think they were taken aback when they saw our age," said Serruya.

"They said, 'We're not ready to come into Canada—if we're ready, we'll be sure to give you a call.'"

The Serruyas weren't stopped by the chilly response. "We said, 'Maybe this is an opportunity for ourselves,'" said Serruya. "'Nobody has introduced froyo in Canada.' We spent the next year meeting with architects and designers. Aaron worked for nine months to develop a recipe."

The Serruyas opened their first Yogen Früz location at a mall in Toronto, and the business grew to fourteen hundred stores worldwide. My Canadian pals tell me the brand is a household name, like Ben & Jerry's. The name Serruya, however, is not, perhaps because, unlike the Vermont buddies, the Serruyas didn't put their names or faces on the product.

When I spoke to Serruya on the phone, he was polite enough to ignore my fumbling over the Yogen Früz name—my brain kept wanting to say Frusen Glädjé, the long-defunct ice cream company. It was the first time I understood the case for umlaut infringement. The brothers made up the Yogen Früz name, which, like Häagen-Dazs, doesn't mean anything.

Even though the Serruyas are in Canada, their success reads like the quintessential American Dream. The family immigrated to Canada from Morocco in 1966, during a wave of anti-Semitism. Michael's father, Sam, learned English, held two jobs, and went to university. Then he started a successful computing business.

Michael and Aaron did so well with the yogurt business that they at one point held a frozen-dessert empire. The Serruyas built off their Yogen Früz success and turned CoolBrands International Inc. into one of North America's largest ice cream producers.[149] At one point, it held the rights to Eskimo Pie. Its stock was soaring in the early 2000s, but the brand collapsed as it tried to compete with ice cream giants Unilever and Nestlé.

CoolBrands shareholders lost much of their investment.[150]

News accounts painted Serruya as a belligerent autocrat who was misunderstood when he served as co-chairman of CoolBrands.

"This is a great Canadian success story," Mr. Serruya reportedly bellowed back in 2005, when he was questioned about the company's "profligate use of stock options."[151]

Serruya stepped down from Yogen Früz. His brother, Aaron, who developed the original recipes all those years ago, is still chairman.

Now as CEO for Kahala Brands, Serruya is responsible for eighteen brands, including Tasti D-Lite, Pinkberry, Cold Stone Creamery, and Blimpie.

I asked if he felt like he was competing against himself and the other yogurt brands he owns.

"People have a tendency to like one brand over the other. They stick and stay loyal to the brand." For example, Yogen Früz is a very different product from Pinkberry, Serruya said. Pinkberry goes through a soft-serve machine. Yogen Früz is made by putting a frozen yogurt bar into a proprietary machine known as the YFM, which blends the yogurt with the added fruit. "We put in a puck of yogurt and throw in fruits. "It's a very different product than the soft-serve." I was hard-pressed to think of anything less appealing than hearing about a *puck* of frozen yogurt. But I kept my distaste to myself.

As someone who has been in the business for three decades, Serruya understands the highs and lows of the froyo industry and didn't seem too put off by it. Kahala owns Cold Stone Creamery, so when froyo is lagging, Cold Stone does well. "When froyo is on upswing, ice cream is on downswing."

Serruya says that Pinkberry and other frozen yogurt brands have saturated the market. "There are too many locations in too dense an area." That's why Pinkberry is looking to expand its market overseas.

"Internationally we're seeing a twenty-five percent growth on Pinkberry," said Serruya. One of the fastest-growing markets for froyo is the Middle East. If you happen to be visiting Dubai, you can pick up a cup of Pinkberry at the Mall of the Emirates.

It wasn't lost on me that a company owned by Jewish immigrants who'd fled North Africa because of persecution was now doing business in a state that refused to acknowledge Israel.

But maybe yogurt could bring us all together? Maybe it was the equivalent of when my grandma and dad called a truce long enough to enjoy a cone with us kids. All the years of resentments and misery were still there, but ignored for just long enough that everyone was satisfied.

Serruya says bringing families together is the best part of the froyo business.

"One thing I've always loved—despite the challenges—is that it's a product that makes people feel great," said Serruya. "It's such a family thing. It's where memories are made."

One thing I know for sure about frozen yogurt: It will be back. And maybe if these yogurt makers continue to innovate, they'll find a way to make it more like ice cream. Of course, Julianna is just at the right age that when the third or fourth coming of froyo begins, she'll bemoan the changes and long for the perfect blend of twanginess and sugar she remembers from her childhood. And who knows, I may even pine for those chaotic afternoons of blue gummy worms mixed with sugar and milk and topped with just the right dose of parental regret.

Anyway, I was soon to learn that there were worse things than fake worms in frozen dessert. Some people were putting in real insects and expecting us to like them.

10.

ICE CREAM CRAZY

I was sitting at an outdoor table at Humphry Slocombe in San Francisco, poised to take my first bite of foie gras ice cream, when I began to wonder if my life might be in danger.

The risks, as I saw them, were twofold. First, and most urgently, there was the fear of food-related aggression. Jake Godby, chef and co-owner of the ice cream shop, receives repeated death threats every time the fatty duck-liver ice cream is on the menu. When the shop first opened in 2008, animal rights activists set up a website called Humphry Slocombe Must Die, which featured a photo of Godby with a red slash across his face. Some even threatened to force-feed him until he died.

What if an animal rights activist saw me with the item, which was exposed inside a crinkly cellophane package, stamped with a bright blue sticker, and labeled *Foie Gras Sammie*?

No food item is quite as contentious as foie gras, which has been the center of a food fight in the United States and has led to bans, repeals, protests, menacing phone calls, Facebook rants, hurt feelings, lost friendships, and even violence.[152]

The concerns about foie gras center around the ethics of gavage, or the process of force-feeding, and have led to countless articles with existential titles like, "Does a Duck Have a Soul? How Foie Gras Became the New Fur."[153]

I was sitting about twenty feet from where that menu proudly proclaimed Humphry Slocombe's fatty duck-liver ice cream. There is no actual Humphry or Slocombe. The shop is named after Mr. Humphries and Mrs. Slocombe, the main characters in a satirical 1970s British sitcom, *Are You Being Served?* Godby runs the shop with his business partner, Sean Vahey. I'd met Godby six months earlier at his shop on Twenty-Fourth Street. He seemed to embrace his inner schlumpiness, proudly displaying his "I don't care" attitude in a fraying gray sweater he'd paired with shorts.

Despite the violent threats against him (or maybe because of them), Godby still makes the foie gras. Yes, he has to worry about protesters. On the flip side he's never had to pay a dime for advertising.

In addition to the sometimes violent emails, the shop receives a tremendous amount of interest—with twenty-plus phone calls a day from people wondering how they can get the foie gras (and who are disappointed when it sells out).

Godby warned me that he rarely makes the delicacy because it's expensive and labor-intensive. He advised me to check the shop's Twitter feed, which I did daily for six months before finally seeing, "DUCK, yes! Foie Gras ice cream on Ginger (oh) Snap Sammies have returned." The tweet referenced the often confusing legal wrangling in California about the food item.

California became the first state to ban the production and sale of foie gras in 2012, only to have the ban overturned by a federal judge in 2015. Chefs around the state celebrated by bringing the liver back on the menus. This led to a rash of protesting. Ken Frank, who owns the restaurant La Toque in Napa Valley, told *The Huffington Post,* "A good share of them talk about shoving a pipe up my ass or down my throat."[154]

These graphic images were swirling in my mind as I sat and prepared to take my first bite of foie gras ice cream. But the Mission neighborhood seemed sleepy, unaware of or unconcerned about the provocative food item in my hands. Several dog owners even walked into the shop and asked for a spoonful of ice cream for their dogs; I watched a poufy-haired labradoodle lap up a scoop of vanilla.

If my life was temporarily spared of human aggression, I still had to contend with another potential danger: What if the ice cream sammie hooked me on the stuff, like a foie gras gateway drug? Getting addicted could very well happen because of the fat-sugar brain reward complex, abetted by a chewy cookie. A recent bit of research indicated that eating large amounts of foie gras could actually cause death. In 2007 researchers published the results of a study showing that mice developed abnormal protein clumps, known as amyloidosis, after ingesting large amounts of the fatty duck liver. In humans, amyloidosis is a rare disease that occurs when a substance called amyloid builds up in your organs.[155] There is no cure.[156]

If true, it seemed like the ultimate karmic payback.

If I avoided both of these potential outcomes, there was always the serious concern that my vegetarian friends might stop talking to me and would keep their like-minded vegetarian children from playing with my child. Julianna had refused to try the foie gras ice cream, as any smart child would. Still, she could be seen as an accomplice.

Humphry Slocombe is as kid-unfriendly as an ice cream store can be. Godby admitted as much. He unapologetically develops his flavors for adults.

"I don't really like children," he'd told me. His most famous flavor is the Secret Breakfast, which includes cornflakes and bourbon.

Still, you can't keep kids away from ice cream, even if you douse it in mystery meat or booze. Every ice cream shop, no matter how adventurous, keeps vanilla on the menu. Vanilla sells better than any other flavor throughout the world. Julianna sat with us, happily eating a vanilla cone, while I considered my first bite.

I had to admit I was apprehensive.

Societal shunning had never before been a factor when I considered my food choices. I eat what I want, when I want. Usually I'm a cautious eater, avoiding foods that could cause illness, discomfort, or offense. It was one reason ice cream has always been my favorite food: When I eat it, nothing is expected of me.

Along with the moral quandary, I wondered how it would actually taste, this mixture of duck liver and ice cream. Dan gazed at me as if I were Diana, the leader of the lizard-alien visitors on the 1980s miniseries *V.* People change during twelve years of marriage. Your spouse can turn into a stranger, and her taste buds can lead to the ultimate betrayal. Still, I could understand his abject expression and confusion. Dan had married a woman who cooked Tofurky for Thanksgiving and experimented with different recipes featuring Veat, a discontinued mystery meat substitute. Now he was sitting across from me as I sat poised to eat meat-infused ice cream.

The foie gras ice cream was presented between two gingersnap cookies and came in a clear plastic wrapper with a bright blue label. I felt giddy as I unwrapped it, the fear adding to the excitement.

As I put it to my mouth, I could smell the ginger from the cookie. I took the first bite. The foie gras had an incomparable mouthfeel. The duck fat coated the edges of my tongue. It tasted a bit like salted caramel. I held it in my mouth and let it warm up, the slightly gamey flavors now easier to taste.

Dan took a bite. He had a look of complete incomprehension as his brain tried to work out the sensations on his tongue.

"It's a taste best described as caramel pâté," Dan said.

Humphry Slocombe has a cookbook that teaches you how to make what you're eating while you're eating it. That's how I know that a home chef would start out by caramelizing half a cup of sugar and adding four ounces of raw foie gras, cooking it in a nonreactive skillet for three minutes. Then add cream, milk, more sugar, and salt, cool the mixture, and puree it in a processor. The mixture is strained, left to cool overnight, and then put into an ice cream maker. At Humphry Slocombe they use a Straus base, add the foie gras to it, sandwich the ice cream between two cookies, and wait for the death threats.

As I took another bite, I couldn't help but feel a thrill. There was something decadent in eating a treat that so many people would be upset about. The wrath I could incur by simply opening my mouth, chewing, and swallowing made me feel powerful. And maybe that perceived transgression is itself a flavor enhancer, much like artificial coloring can ramp up our experience of "lime" or "banana" in some mass-produced, neon-colored taffy or gum.

Is that why Godby put it on the menu—so he could wield that kind of power? Why continue making food that would anger people? Was it to get attention?

Godby insisted that wasn't the case, that he was just trying to make flavors that would appeal to his own sensibilities and to those of his friends who are chefs. "We don't do anything for the sake of being weird," Godby said.

Although Humphry Slocombe put out a cookbook with exacting recipes for consumers, and in spite of its reputation for defying convention and following its own rules, Godby does not make his own base. He told me he gets it by the truckload from Straus.

Having made my own flavors, I could relate to the desire to experiment and try something no one has done before. Following a recipe, especially one from a premade mix, seems both boring and repetitive.

Despite what he says, Godby comes across as a bit of a button pusher who does what he does regardless of others' reactions. He reminded me of my dad, so uncaring about his lack of fashion sense that he was content to walk around with a slide ruler in his breast pocket. Perhaps you need to have that kind of ego to be a tinkerer and sometimes inventor, either in the kitchen or in the world of engineering. And if people don't like what he's made? So what? Godby doesn't spend a lot of time worrying about it.

"It's not my job to educate," he said.

What's the limit to what's acceptable with ice cream? I asked.

"There's a place in London that does breast milk ice cream," said Godby, the revulsion clear on his face.

He was referring to the Icecreamists, which sold pints of breast milk ice cream labeled *Baby Gaga* in 2011.[157] Just a few days after going on sale, the ice cream was seized by regulators for safety testing. The Licktators, a UK company that also sells female-Viagra-infused ice cream, brought breast milk ice cream back in celebration of the birth of Princess Charlotte and called it Royal Baby Gaga. Lady Gaga threatened to sue because of the name, expressing concern about the implied association between the Lady Gaga brand and a product that struck her as "nausea-inducing."[158] Its revival was short-lived, and it's no longer on the menu.

Breast milk ice cream is one of the few dairy products that does not draw the wrath of animal rights activists. PETA has touted breast milk as a more humane alternative to cow's milk in ice cream. "If Ben and Jerry's replaced the cow's milk in its ice cream with breast milk, your customers—and cows—would reap the benefits," wrote Tracy Reiman, executive vice president of PETA.

The trend with extreme ice cream shows that one person's gross-out experience seems to be another person's gleeful experimentation. It left me wondering about why we are eating more extreme foods. Foods that were considered ridiculous twenty years ago are now mainstream. Hence the migration of bacon off the breakfast menu and into every possible food item, including ice cream.

Dan said eating the foie gras ice cream reminded him of the novel *My Year of Meats* by Ruth Ozeki. There's a scene in the book that describes making ground meat fudge.

"I remember thinking the idea of having meat as part of the sweet is the most revolting thing I've ever heard in my life," said Dan. "It became passé to have bacon in people's ice cream."

Dan and I passed the silver-dollar-size sandwich between us, taking tiny bites. Does the ginger cookie make the foie gras taste more savory? That was one theory of the kids who scoop ice cream at the shop.

"If I'd advertised to someone on PETA that I was eating a foie gras ice cream sandwich, they would want to set my hair on fire," Dan said. "They would be very angry with me." I looked blankly at Dan's bald head and wondered if lunacy was a symptom of amyloidosis.

Food that causes such delight and rage is extreme, and it begs the question of why anyone would want to make it or eat it.

Freya Estreller and Natasha Case of Coolhaus make the argument that our palates are changing as we explore the umami taste. What's brought about this taste revolution? They say it's the melting-pot quality of America—with fusion foods bringing rise to things like a Korean barbecue taco or a sushi burrito. Now more than ever, our minds and taste buds are primed for unusual pairings.

But a little historical digging proved that theory incorrect. We have a history of unusual ice cream in America that dates back to the founding fathers.

We may have fallen collectively into a vanilla-and-chocolate rut, but we were more adventurous in our flavors during our early years of ice cream eating. First Lady Dolley Madison insisted on ice cream at her husband's inaugural ball. Her favorite flavor? Oyster. She made the fish into a kind of chowder, with onion and ham, added egg yolks and cream, and froze the entire concoction. The recipe appeared in *The Virginia Housewife,* by Mary Randolph, in 1824.

A few chefs have tried making their modern rendition of this founding father's favorite. It's been on the menu at America Eats Tavern in Washington, DC, and it's got a cult following in Japan, a country that seems to fully embrace the wacky options of modern-day ice cream, with bizarre menu items like raw horseflesh.

Award-winning chef Kyle Schutte makes his own version of oyster ice cream, which he whipped up for me at his home in Jefferson Park, a neighborhood in Los Angeles—a place he matter-of-factly referred to as the hood. His street had well-kept houses pressed so closely together that the gaps between them reminded me of crawl spaces. This informal and friendly enclave in South Los Angeles is known as "the Bungalows" because it has rows of fanciful and alarmingly similar houses that look like they came out of a kit (which is actually the case for many of them). But it's also a high-crime area where many residents can tell you first-hand stories of break-ins and "grand theft auto."

Schutte has worked at some of LA's top restaurants, but he's restaurant poor. All his resources have gone into renovating the Flats, which still wasn't open when I met him. So he invited Dan and me to the hood where he lives to taste his ice cream. He greeted us behind a locked driveway gate, wearing a T-shirt, jeans, and beanie hat.

Schutte admits he's a chef with an opinion, and that makes it complicated to appease the business partners.

"I've been told so many times that I'm too innovative." He described the humiliation of being asked to put a turkey club on the menu at one restaurant, which was also serving lamb lollipops and panna cotta with liquid nitrogen Coca-Cola. He gives the unmistakable impression that his lot in life is to be misunderstood.

It's little wonder that Schutte's taken his interest in innovative food and melded it with ice cream. He said he's an "ice cream freak" who first decided to become a chef after eating an ice cream sandwich. He was a twenty-year-old who didn't even know where to find thyme at the grocery store. But he experimented with adding zip to his food, getting creative, and eventually went on to culinary school at the Art Institute of Atlanta and then had stints at 54Twenty and Roadhouse LA.

Schutte started experimenting with liquid nitrogen during his time at One Midtown Kitchen, where he worked with Chef Richard Blais (of *Iron Chef America* and *Top Chef* fame). Liquid nitrogen has become a trendy way to make rich, dense, made-to-order ice cream at places like Smitten in San Francisco and –321° Ice Cream in Brooklyn. It is so dense that it feels a bit like frozen pudding. Schutte described scenes of chefs throwing liquid nitrogen at each other and even dunking their chef's hats in the flammable substance at One Midtown Kitchen. That's the kind of rough playfulness Schutte brings to his cooking.

"I want people to understand that I take what I do seriously, but I don't take the food too seriously," Schutte said.

You can watch Schutte make his modern version of oyster ice cream on YouTube.[159]

He shucks the oysters by hand. Then he adds milk, cream, sugar, egg yolks, and salt to a blender and mixes the base together. Schutte puts the oysters, with their juices, into a vacuum-sealed bag, adds the base, and cooks it all sous vide, at 182 degrees Fahrenheit. Then he cools it down, strains it, and freezes this saltine creation in liquid nitrogen.

After describing his food philosophy—food should be fun yet sophisticated, innovative and familiar and humane and accessible—he presented the oyster ice cream on a plate on top of bonito flakes and lemon foam.

It took several seconds for my brain to process what was in my mouth. I'm used to ice cream as a dessert, not as a kind of frozen amuse-bouche. "The first bite and the last bite are never the same," said Schutte.

Schutte messed with the rules of food—the idea that ice cream is always sweet—forcing me to juxtapose the mouthfeel of ice cream with the inescapable savor of slimy mollusks. When I eat ice cream, I'm used to my brain just shutting off and the pleasure principle taking over. But Schutte's creations forced my brain into action. When was the last time I'd had a new food or a food presented in a new way? It reduced me to an almost toddler-like state, unable to understand or contain my reactions.

"This is delicious!" I exclaimed, but only out of shock, not knowing what else to say. Schutte may have a tortured chef's air to him—a mixture of being both ornery and clever—but he looked like a little boy when he was watching our faces while we sampled his inventions.

Schutte said the waitstaff at his restaurants loved serving his newfangled ice cream creations. "They knew people would be scared and skeptical at first," said Schutte. "As you eat through it, you begin to understand it."

Schutte was right that the experience changed over the course of finishing the scoop, but for me it went from shock to distaste in a matter of minutes, skipping the honeymoon phase of sensations and flavors.

The next course was Caesar salad dressing ice cream—served on a bed of greens. Schutte said it contained milk, cream, eggs, sugar, olive oil, anchovies, and Worcestershire sauce. Dan admitted to having a harder time with it than with the oyster. But there was something refreshing about the coldness against the fresh lettuce that lessened the fishiness of the anchovies. This tangy-fishy thing behaved like an ice cream in every way except the flavor. It melted on my tongue and dribbled down the spoon. The more I ate the ice cream, the more confused I became. And the more confused I became, the more I wanted to try the ice cream again, just to see if I was wrong.

The next course was a mustard ice cream that Schutte served on a pig-shaped wooden charcuterie plate. The ice cream was accompanied by toasted bread, buffalo mozzarella, pickles, and prosciutto. He's served it in the past with crab cakes, but we'd already had our fill of fish for the afternoon. Against my better judgment, I spread the mustard ice cream on the toast with a butter knife. It seemed like a plate designed for pregnant women or a Jewish grandmother transplanted from Brooklyn who longs so desperately for a good deli sandwich that she doesn't care about the form it takes. Schutte pushed the idea that it's not enough for food to be satisfying. It should also be interesting.

The final ice cream was a mint, Schutte's favorite. He described serving it to an eighty-year-old who wept as she ate it. The taste brought back a childhood memory of gathering fresh mint in her grandmother's garden. I was having another reaction—one of joy and relief that the food I was eating was actually something my taste buds recognized.

As we were finishing our dessert, Schutte talked about the various ways in which his ice cream achieved a kind of complete meal. "It's unconventional," Schutte said. "But we did give you a protein *and* a condiment *and* a dessert."

While Humphry Slocombe plays with the idea of ice cream breakfast with its cornflakes-and-booze signature flavor, Schutte is playing with the idea of ice cream as a complete meal. At the time of my visit, he was developing a menu for a Los Angeles pop-up that would allow diners to eat a dinner consisting entirely of ice cream, for sixty-four dollars per person, with such offerings as *uni,* oyster, roasted peach, pork belly, coconut, brown butter, espresso, and mint ice creams. When I later described Schutte's creations, detailing the oyster ice cream, every single one of my friends made a scrunched-up face of horror and disdain. "I'm going to have nightmares about that oyster ice cream," one friend fretted.

How had we all gotten so closed-minded about food? When did our collective expectations begin to limit our options?

In the late nineteenth century, our adventurous palate wasn't limited to fish in ice cream. We were also sticking vegetables in cream and sugar to see how that would taste. Thumb through old recipe books from the late nineteenth and early twentieth centuries and you'll find instructions for tea or sherry ice cream. *The Encyclopaedia of Practical Cookery,* published in the 1890s, also offers a recipe for asparagus ice cream.

While this may sound like a horrible trick to get recalcitrant children to eat their veggies, the outcome can be surprisingly good. One of my first experiences eating vegetable ice cream was at OddFellows in Williamsburg, where Sam Mason makes a celery sorbet he calls Ants on a Log. It's based on the laziest of kids' snacks—peanut butter on celery with raisins on it. I was so lazy as a kid that I skipped the raisins, preferring to dip my limp celery directly into the jar of Skippy while watching the summer-long unbandaging of Meg Ryan's face on *As the World Turns.*

Mason, who made a name for himself at wd~50, the legendary avant-garde restaurant on the Lower East Side of Manhattan, makes his sorbet using celery juice; it is remarkably green. Luckily green is a color we are accustomed to seeing in ice cream (pistachio, mint, green tea). The taste was so shockingly like my childhood snack—but so much better—the flavor of the peanut butter seemed to explode in my mouth and transported me back to the hot summer boredom of my Silicon Valley living room. As my brain struggled to process the snack in its frozen form, my legs itched from the memory of my bare legs against the scratchy old family room couch.

Mason's recipes for celery sorbet and other vegetable-laden desserts can be found in *Lucky Peach* magazine,[160] for those who can't make it to Williamsburg and might want a nibble of beet ice cream or caramelized onion ice cream.

But there is a limit to what kinds of vegetables you can add to ice cream.

One rule of thumb: Vegetables that cannot be eaten alone also cannot be eaten in ice cream, especially in their powdered form.

Case in point: my taste test of the garlic ice cream that's served up at restaurants like the Stinking Rose in San Francisco and

Beverly Hills (as well as at the annual Gilroy Garlic Festival). It turns out the flavor was created at Marianne's Ice Cream in my hometown. Owner Charlie Wilcox informed me that the garlic ice cream is not available at the business's two scoop shops. As if to make up for its general unavailability, Wilcox offered me not one but two scoops of the smelly concoction, one of them using a straight-up sweet cream base, the other with a chocolate base.

I took the lid of the ice cream container and held it up to my nose. It broke one of the most important tenets of ice cream: Ice cream is not supposed to smell. The garlicky odor alone was repellant.

I picked up the spoon and dipped it into the cream base first; the taste of the garlic was overpowering. To me the idea of garlic and chocolate was unspeakable; imagine combining melted Hershey bars with shrimp scampi sauce. But Wilcox said he preferred the chocolate because it masked some of the potency of the garlic. Others like the sweet-cream version. I thought both were equally revolting.

Wilcox theorizes that in twenty years scientists will discover a gene that makes certain people love garlic.

There is a scientific context to this odd appreciation for pugnacious foods that pummel our taste buds, confounding and confusing our relationship to "yum!" and "ick!" Researchers are already discovering that the way we taste certain foods is encoded in our DNA.[161]

Scientists have discovered we have genetic variations that account for what foods we enjoy. What's disgusting or even painful to some people is addictive to others.

Take, for instance, another vegetable: the hot chili pepper. After puzzling over the reasons why certain people have a passion for fiery and agonizing foods, researchers have determined that peppers can activate the part of the brain that responds to both pleasure and pain.[162]

In the 1970s, Paul Rozin at the University of Pennsylvania studied the eating habits of Mexican children and coined the term "benign masochism" to explain why a person would develop an affinity for the "biologically aversive stimulus" of a mouth that feels like it's on fire. To him it seemed akin to the thrill of gambling or riding a roller coaster, slaking a desire for new and slightly dangerous sensations.

In studying two groups of kids, Rozin found that the difference between "just right" and "ouch" was small. "The hotness level they liked the most was just below the level of unbearable pain," Dr. Rozin said. "So that led me to think that the pain itself was involved: They were pushing the limits, and that was part of the phenomenon."

Following a similar philosophy, Scott Wilson of Sunni Sky's Homemade Ice Cream in Angier, North Carolina, developed his Cold Sweat flavor to appease his hot sauce friends. Scott described himself as the "biggest wimp" when it comes to hot flavors. But a friend of his ordered a vanilla cone and swirled some hot sauce on top. That encouraged Scott to make a jalapeño ice cream, but it was too mild. "The hot sauce people thought it was a joke," he said. "That's when I realized how crazy those people are." As appeasement or retribution, he developed the Cold Sweat—which includes pequin peppers, Thai chilis, habaneros, Dave's Gourmet Insanity Sauce, and Blair's Mega Death, a hot sauce made from habanero, cayenne, and chipotle. You need to sign the following waiver just to sample it:

SUNNI SKY'S HOMEMADE ICE CREAM 100% LIABILITY WAIVER FOR DANGEROUSLY HOT COLD SWEAT ICE CREAM

This ice cream was created with some of the hottest known peppers and extracts made. No one with any existing health problems such as:

- Expectant mothers
- Lactating mothers
- Heart ailments
- Vascular problems
- Respiratory problems
- Back problems
- Vision problems
- Sinus conditions
- Digestive problems
- Neurological problems
- Circulation problems
- Bleeding problems
- Immune problems
- Any and all known or suspected health problems

No one with these problems should attempt to sample this ice cream. Expectant mothers or any female who could possibly be pregnant should not attempt to have a sample of this ice cream.

By signing this Liability Waiver I understand and take 100% full responsibility for all risk and consequences as the result from the consumption of this product containing such peppers, extracts and hot sauces. If legal action is pursued with disregard to this liability Waiver, all legal fees and cost will be the responsibility of any such person involved with the consumption of this product.

NO ONE under the age of 18 is allowed to taste this product without legal guardian consent of both parties signing this Liability Waiver.

No one above the age of 30 should attempt to even sample this product.

It should be noted that what is painful going in, may be painful upon exit.

Scott has never done more than touch a dab of it to his tongue. "I don't think I'd live through the Cold Sweat." He said 99 percent of people are smart enough to take just a few bites.

There's a vast difference in people's tolerance to capsaicin. "I had a sixty-five-year-old lady who took it down like it was butter pecan." On the other extreme was a customer who reportedly wound up in the hospital from trying Wilson's flavor.

My neighbor Mike is part of a fringe group known as pepper heads who seek out the spiciest experiences on the planet. His reasoning sounded like an extreme version of Rozin's thrill-seeking theory.

"I want to have a heart attack but survive it," said Mike.

It didn't sound very pleasurable, and Dan suggested as much when the two of them were talking about searingly hot peppers. Mike looked taken aback, almost offended. "No, it *is* pleasurable," he insisted. "It's like doing drugs! It is the best high you can get!"

For weeks I debated using my ice cream making skills to create my own version of the Cold Sweat and inviting the pepper heads in my life over to try it. Then I started wondering about the morality of inflicting it on people, even if they wanted to try it. Daredevil pepper eaters, hoping to win bets and competitions, wind up in hospitals all over the world. Maybe I have the bias of not being a chili head, but it seemed like the ultimate stunt ice cream.

I didn't want to kill anyone, and so I decided it would be too risky to create a hot flavor. But that didn't stop me from seeking out other "dangerous flavors."

There's no doubt that we have an increased appetite for unusual flavors, and the places that are bold enough to create them are rewarded with buzz and seeing their names on national top-ten lists. But I had to wonder: Where were the limits to the boundary pushing? What was the line between delicious and delirium inducing?

Tyler Malek of Salt & Straw is determined to find out. He's gained a following from Oprah Winfrey and *GQ*'s Alan Richman for his ultrarich butterfat-laden recipes and such publicity-generating flavors as bone marrow (imagine a swarthy caveman sucking on bones). He's also created Peking duck and Thanksgiving turkey ice creams and a dill pickle sorbet. Malek's thoughtful blend of innovation, edginess, and deliciousness impresses and antagonizes Schutte, who says Salt & Straw's virtuosity almost wrecked his ice cream making mojo.

Malek has a boyish enthusiasm and admits he can't help "geeking out" when talking about ice cream. When I met up with him at an event in San Francisco at trendy Sightglass Coffee, he was calmly talking with me while scooping fresh ice cream for a techie who complained that he was being served in a paper rather than a glass bowl.

But Malek seems impervious to praise or insult.

Lines for his creations at his Portland shop are so long that people often wind up buying a scoop for the person behind them. That's what happens when a bunch of people end up waiting in the same space together for an hour or more. A few customers have met their future spouses while waiting for one of his scoops.

"I loved the idea of a neighborhood place that we could turn into a community gathering spot," Malek said.

In 2015, he created the Halloween favorite Creepy Crawly

Critters, a green matcha-infused ice cream that has real grasshoppers, ants, and other insects encased in a hard candy "amber." "It's fun to see what our limits are," said Malek.

Malek isn't the first to think of bug-infused ice cream. During the emergence of cicada Brood XIX in 2011, an ice cream shop in Missouri created a cicada-flavored ice cream. The first batch was sold out before it even made the display case, but the health department shut down the bug eating almost immediately.[163]

Cicada eaters at the University of Maryland put out a cookbook to give people an idea of what they can do with the pests, which apparently have a nutty and somewhat shrimpy flavor. I contacted Professor Michael J. Raupp to see if he had any ideas on how I could get some cicada ice cream. Periodical cicadas develop underground, sucking nutrients from plant roots, for thirteen or seventeen years, depending on the species.[164]

He broke the news that Brood XIX was underground for five more years.

"Sorry, Amy, I am out of the cicada-eating business until 2021." I felt elated—like I'd escaped the worst possible culinary fate. Yet bug eating is common practice in many countries, including Thailand and Mexico. At any given moment, somebody somewhere is sinking his teeth into a stinkbug taco, a raw termite, or a fried giant spider and calling it delicious. About two billion people already eat insects. The *European Journal of Clinical Nutrition* published a study in 2015 that suggested that bugs were a more nutritious food than pork, beef, or even chicken.[165] The pro-bug contingent insists that raising insects is cheap, costing little or nothing, and is more sustainable than raising livestock, which accounts for one-fifth of greenhouse gases.

With this kind of mathematical armor, many in the Western world are pushing bug eating as a way to help boost the world's food supply.[166]

I appreciated that the practice might help save the earth, but there was nothing I found more revolting than putting bugs in my mouth. True, I eat shrimp and lobster, which are arthropod cousins to grasshoppers and crickets. But it was impossible to whet my appetite for lizard food.

As I studied my own reaction, it left me wondering why Americans have such a revulsion about insect eating, when certain pests are a delicacy in some parts of the world. In 2013, when a plague of locusts hit Israel, they were turned into kosher snacks that were boiled, fried, and covered in garlic, chili powder, and even chocolate.[167]

A few US restaurants are catching on to the practice of turning cheap, readily available pests into food. The Black Ant in New York City is Michelin rated and serves delicacies like enchapulinados—grasshopper-crusted shrimp, aioli, and cabbage slaw. Many of the dishes are sprinkled with ant salt: salt with ground-up chicatanas—large, winged leaf-cutter ants.[168]

Meanwhile, for those of us who don't have that much zeal for bug eating, entomophagists have launched a public campaign to help us all feel less squeamish about eating pests. These campaigns range from the informative to the truly graphic.[169]

In 2015, *The Economist* magazine handed out insect ice cream in London as a way of shedding (or perhaps molting) light on the issue. The four flavors were Scurry Berry, an elderberry raspberry swirl with mixed insect parts; Choc Hopper, with chocolate-covered grasshoppers; Strawberries and Swirls, with mealworms; and Nutritious Neapolitan, for those seeking a mix of critters.[170]

The team behind the documentary *Bugs* handed out samples of escamole ice cream in April 2016 on the High Line in New York City. The delicacy was made from ant larvae, blanched in milk, added to sugar and eggs, blended, and churned.[171]

Monica Martinez, founder of Don Bugito: Prehispanic Snackeria in San Francisco, offered to pick me up some frozen escamoles on a trip to Mexico. But ant larvae are a rare and expensive delicacy. Did I want her to bring me back some? I politely declined.

Merely thinking of the squish and crunch of insects in my food made me cringe. But I had to admit to a certain curiosity. Besides, I'd read that mealworms were actually pretty delicious. And so at the beginning of summer, I ordered two packs of Martinez's toffee mealworms, which she assured me were best served over vanilla ice cream.

I felt the beginnings of excitement as soon as I placed my order, imagining the mealworms making their slow journey to my mailbox. One scorching-hot day, the insects arrived in the mail in two metallic vacuum-sealed envelopes hidden inside the small, nondescript box I found on my doorstep. Julianna couldn't wait to break into them.

With some hesitation I tore the seal and peeked in. "Oh no, oh no," I said. Julianna couldn't wait to stick her eager curly-haired head into the bag. I poured them out onto a plate. Their segmented bodies clumped together inside a translucent glop of hard and crispy toffee; the amber-colored glaze brought the natural pigmentation of each dead mealworm into stark relief.

Their bodies were taut and curly with rigor mortis. They smelled like crayfish and sawdust.

The contents of a bag of toffee-covered mealworms.

The sight of the mealworms unleashed an unprecedented hysteria in Julianna, who ran through my kitchen screaming, "We're gonna have the worms on the vanilla," over and over.

How could my overly feminine daughter, who loved to dress up and play dolls, be excited about this queasy dessert? Perhaps our insect revulsion is a learned response. Maybe Julianna was too young to let our Western cultural fussiness about foodstuffs stop her from eating bugs. But her youthful enthusiasm, and the strong encouragement of my husband, could not change my feelings of dread and disgust.

"I don't think I can do this, guys," I said, scooping myself a bowl of vanilla ice cream and wishing I could eat it straight up, with no creatures on top.

"I don't think you can back out of it at this point," said Dan.

I moved slowly, walking over to the table where the mealworms sat in the bag, waiting for me. I dipped my hand in and sprinkled a couple on my bowl.

"I can't do it. I can't do it," I said.

Dan advised me not to think about it too much; get the spoon in the ice cream, shovel down some mealworms, and be done with it. "Just get it in you," he said.

I dipped my spoon into the wormy mix, placed the spoon in my mouth, and experienced my first taste of vanilla, mixed with toffee and a shattering crispiness. It took several moments before my brain could figure out what I was tasting, followed by a moment of shock, and then a twinge of unexpected delight.

"Oh, it's really good with the vanilla," I said. "You guys need to try it."

I eagerly grabbed a handful more of the bugs and scattered them on the ice cream and handed it to Dan.

"The thing about it is the look," he said. "If I didn't have to look at that, man." He powered through and put a spoonful in his mouth. I could hear the chitinous crunch—not the sound of potato chips, not that of pretzels, but the sound of teeth on dry skin. Dan complained about the shape of the creatures in his mouth and the mealwormy residue of fish scales and coconut flakes in his throat. Even after he washed down most of the mealworms with a heaping scoop of vanilla, a few of the critters remained. He picked part of a mealworm out of his teeth.

After the initial excitement passed, there was a lingering deep regret, even an animosity among members of my family. Remembering what we had done just made it worse. This was not like cricket powder, when the insect is all ground up and added to an energy bar. In this case, we were forced to feel every contour and cranny on our tongues.

"The segmentation of their bodies is just horrific," I complained.

Julianna, who had eaten the majority of the insects in the vacuum-sealed bag, had an earthy smell that lingered on her breath. She brushed her teeth several times and then complained that her stomach hurt.

"Where does it hurt?" I asked, alarmed.

She couldn't point out any place in her stomach that felt bad. "It's just they are so gross," she said.

"So you are just thinking about it and that's upsetting you?" When Julianna nodded yes, I urged her to think of other things.

"But I can still taste them," she said, making a face.

Dan was having a similar psychosomatic reaction. "I hope you didn't give me pinworms," he said accusingly.

"Mealworms are not parasites," I informed him. I was fairly certain the creatures wouldn't colonize our guts. But just the memory of the crunch brought forth a mild but undeniable nausea. I couldn't help it; the experience of eating the mealworms—which were actually the larvae of darkling beetles and not immediate relatives of the night crawler worm—was disappointing. I had been led to believe through my pro-bug-eating readings that the mealworms might taste good. It's true that the initial flavor was not awful, but the texture was hard to forgive and the aftertaste lingered as a deterrent against future experimentation. I couldn't help but feel that I'd been naïve in thinking bugs might ever be delectable. Did I regret ingesting the mealworms? Of course, but I also had the satisfaction of having tried them.

Like any other stunt food, candied mealworms exist mostly for bragging rights, and the joy of watching other people's faces when I share the experience. Though I asked my family to keep a low profile about the insect ice cream, they could not stop boasting about it, even at a bat mitzvah reception, where two guests they told were eating pasta. At first they could not hide their looks of dismay, or their apparent regret for having chosen to sit next to us. But their curiosity prevailed. They wanted to hear about the tribulations of eating beetle babies, even while eating loops of spaghetti that looked a bit like earthworms.

Inquisitiveness had led me on this ice cream adventure to begin with, so it made sense that the odyssey would end in oysters, foie gras, and scuttling insects. To me, my gradual move toward bugs paralleled the movement of a countercultural food revolution that has been taking place in America for years. The idea of artisan foods hearkens back to our collective interest in urban homesteading that started with the countercuisine movements of the 1960s. Steve Herrell and the schlubby hippies, Ben and Jerry, were part of this group, testing and pushing at what's acceptable to put in our ice cream. Of course, their mix-ins were candy, not mealworms, but the add-ins, or "smoosh-ins," were a break with long-standing tradition. The only difference is now we have hipsters, not hippies, to push the boundaries of popular taste. We are going back to the days of gardening, pickling, canning, fermenting, and curing. We are building lists of ingredients from our gardens. Instead of just using vegetables, we're picking the bugs off plants and cooking them too. Eating bugs may seem like the extreme boundary of the homegrown trend. But maybe we need to know where the edge is so we can explore around it.

One of my favorite pleasures as a kid, besides ice cream, was watching *Star Trek*. My often picked-on, misunderstood self got lost in the idea of exploring new civilizations, never knowing what you would find when you beamed down to a planet. You never knew if you would encounter an infuriatingly docile Organian or a hostile reptilian Gorn. Perhaps it was better than what you knew; perhaps you'd meet a Horta, a monster made of molten rock, living in tunnels, fighting to protect her children, or find yourself in a parallel universe where your best friend, Mr. Spock, was now your sworn enemy. Even in this science fiction world, people of all backgrounds expressed their culinary preferences. Spock was a vegetarian, Kirk had a penchant for Saurian brandy, and Klingons enjoyed Gagh, a delicacy of live serpent worms.

I wanted to be an astronaut for a short time, but I've never been much of a thrill seeker, until I'd set out to explore the world of ice cream. I'd eaten bugs, I'd tried foie gras, and those were just some of the flavors pushing the boundaries. Who knew how many more I'd find?

I'd learned that the culinary frontier is ever expanding, just waiting to be explored.

ROCA OF AFFLICTION

The word *affliction* takes on new meaning if you use toffee-covered mealworms in this recipe for the Roca. *Note:* That version would not be kosher. I recommend using matzos.

For the Roca:

¾ cup unsalted butter
1 cup organic cane sugar
1 teaspoon vanilla extract
6 matzo crackers
10 ounces milk chocolate, chopped
⅓ cup chopped roasted almonds

For the ice cream:

1⅔ cups cream
1⅔ cups milk
¾ cup sugar
½ cup skim milk powder
3 egg yolks, lightly beaten
1 tablespoon vanilla

- Preheat the oven to 350°F.
- Melt the butter and cane sugar together in a saucepan until the sugar dissolves. Remove from the heat and add the vanilla. Line a baking sheet with parchment paper and place the matzos on the sheet. You may have to break the crackers into halves. Pour the melted butter mixture over the matzos, using a spatula to help spread it. Bake for 11 to 15 minutes, checking often and removing from

the oven as soon as the sugar begins to brown. Melt the chocolate in the microwave for about 30 seconds.

- Spread the melted chocolate on top of the matzos with a butter knife.
- Sprinkle with the roasted almonds and place in the refrigerator to cool.
- To make the ice cream base, heat the cream and milk and whisk in the sugar and skim milk powder. Temper the egg yolks with a teaspoon of the milk mixture and then add the eggs to the milk. Stir until the custard reaches 165°F. Remove from the heat and pour through a strainer into a Pyrex dish. Let cool on the counter and add the vanilla before transferring to the fridge for at least 4 hours, but preferably overnight.
- Churn the vanilla base for 35 to 40 minutes, according to the ice cream maker's instructions. While the base is churning, break up the Roca into bite-size pieces. Turn off the machine and fold the Roca into the base. Pour into a freezer-safe container and harden for at least 8 hours.

Epilogue

JERSEY GIRL

After zigzagging across the country searching for America's best ice cream, I found myself in the Capitol Hill neighborhood of Seattle on National Ice Cream Day. It was a rare sunny day, and the whole city seemed to be at Molly Moon's, where the line wrapped around the block. President Ronald Reagan created National Ice Cream Day. In 1984, the same year he joked he was "outlawing Russia forever," he proclaimed that "ice cream is a nutritious and wholesome food, enjoyed by over ninety percent of the people in the United States."

I was torn between a need to see what all the fuss was about at Molly Moon's and my refusal to stand in a crowd with the hot sun baking us. "Let's go to the park across the street instead," I said. "We'll try it again tomorrow." Julianna looked horrified, as if an apathetic replica had replaced her ice cream–obsessed mother.

Normally a fairly compliant child, Julianna pitched a fit. We attracted the stares of the millennials around us. I didn't care. I was too busy remembering the best ice cream I'd had in the past year: the Cajeta from Il Laboratorio del Gelato, the Sea Salt with Caramel Ribbons from Salt & Straw, the butter pecan from Bassetts, where a customer ran through Reading Terminal Market with a dripping cone, screaming and swearing about how great it was. Could this place be on par? Would anyone risk public humiliation for a scoop of Molly Moon's? I was skeptical.

I weighed my time in the sunny line against the potential for great disappointment. On my quest to find the best ice cream, I've endured a carjacking, traveled on a rickety ice cream truck through the streets of Bensonhurst on a sweltering August afternoon, eaten mealworms glazed with toffee, and lunched on ground-mustard ice cream served on a charcuterie platter with aromatic pickles. Hadn't I already sacrificed enough of my time, and even my dignity, to American ice cream? I pitched my own fit. I didn't want to stand in that hot line. It might be the first time in my life when I've put so much emotion behind *not* wanting ice cream. Julianna must have sensed a disturbance in the Force, because she finally relented.

The next day when we went back to Molly Moon's, there was no one ahead of us and we sampled almost everything. I found the Salted Caramel to be a touch overflavored, as if the owner were trying to defiantly prove something with all that sugar. Research suggests that ice cream is like crack[172] in the way it acts on our brains, and in my case it may be true. The more I have, the more I want, and the more difficult it is to find satisfaction. If possible, I have become a greater ice cream snob. I passed on buying a scoop.

So Dan, Julianna, and I wandered the streets of Capitol Hill aimlessly, until we saw Kurt Farm Shop, almost hidden from sight on Chophouse Row. We walked through the door and were immediately greeted by large photos of a Jersey cow—two portraits hanging close together, one showing off the cow's front, the other showing off its business end. I was intrigued. I'd learned that most milk in the country comes from Holsteins—strapping black-and-white cows that are famous for their placid demeanors and their profligate milk productivity. It was rare to find ice cream made from the milk of a Jersey, which has more butterfat and higher protein than Holstein milk. Some say the Jersey milk is easier to digest.[173]

I spotted a middle-aged man behind the counter—an odd demographic for a scooper at an ice cream shop. I was startled by the creaminess of the ice cream samples he gave me. I always have an odd reaction when I sample something I'm not expecting—a delay in my brain functioning that almost short-circuits my response. Sometimes it takes me days to figure out whether I love something or hate it. Finally, my senses began to defrost, and I was able to form a question. "Do you know where the ice cream base comes from?" I asked the man behind the counter.

"It's from the milk from my farm," he said.

It was then that I realized the man behind the counter was none other than Kurt Timmermeister, an award-winning cheese maker and former restaurateur, hailed by *The New York Times* as a "table-to-farm pioneer . . . a sometimes tetchy but always passionate, detail-driven" food craftsman.[174]

"You actually milk the cows, make the ice cream, and scoop it?"

He nodded, but then added a slight correction: He didn't

actually do the milking himself. His farm was on woodsy, sparsely populated Vashon Island near Seattle, accessible only by ferry; it has no bridge link to the mainland. He has about fifteen Jersey cows. His base is pasteurized and made at the farm before he delivers it via ferry to the shop, where he churns it himself. He grows most of the fruits that flavor his ice cream, including blackberries.

"I want things very simple and very high quality," Kurt said. "It's a pain. It's a challenge to do it every day."

The ice cream was incomparable. It's one lesson I've learned on my ice cream journey: Somehow hearing about the travails of America's high-end food suppliers makes the food taste better.

Kurt said he was the only person he knew of in the country with such a farm-to-scoop operation. He reminded me of Andrew Zlot, the water buffalo farmer, who was working round-the-clock in Petaluma, California, to create made-from-scratch gelato.

I could sense my cynicism-and-disappointment-hardened brain softening, but only a little bit. While researching the histories of the big ice cream companies in this country, from Breyers to Häagen-Dazs, I'd learned that mass-produced ice cream can turn into a competition for freezer shelf space, market share, and volume sales, while exploiting our needs for an instant "feel-good." Ice cream can make people desperate and greedy. In the stifling-hot summer months in New York City, demand for ice cream is so high that certain people are willing to pay for half-melted pints that thieves have filched from grocery and convenience stores. Between November 2015 and September 2016, shoplifters grabbed 256 pints, most of them high-end brands like Häagen-Dazs and Talenti, according to police. The thieves would shove them in freezer bags or duffel bags, then race into the sweltering streets to try to sell off their sweaty pints. They will accost any passerby and hard-sell their ice cream, hoping to liquidate their assets before they melt. It's gotten so bad that CVS drugstores have installed alarms in their coolers, letting the staff know when anyone opens the doors.[175] But the scoop I was eating reminded me that for some farmers and chefs, ice cream means more than just the bottom line. It's a way of life, a family business, an ethos. These people are working long hours to milk, churn, and hand pack pints for us all to enjoy.

I bought a scoop of Jersey Cream from Kurt. It was just churned ice cream base, with nothing, not even a droplet of vanilla, to goose the flavor. I stood outside eating it with a miniature flat wooden spoon. It was dense, but it didn't have that annoying chewiness that can ruin superthick ice creams. Kurt doesn't use nonfat milk powder. He believes in using only "extraordinary" liquid milk. Buying bagged, dehydrated milk goes against his food belief system. Instead, he uses dry tapioca to keep his product from becoming icy.

It surprised me to learn that Kurt doesn't want to bring his superior ice cream to the greater masses. "It's important to me that it's not available in grocery stores," he said. "I don't want to be a part of that. If you want it, you have to come here." His arguments against distribution sounded remarkably similar to those of Ron Schneider, the controversial curmudgeon at Leon's Frozen Custard.

A few hours later, after meeting up with friends from Seattle,

I couldn't help but rave about Kurt Farm Shop. Holly, the wife of Dan's friend Bill, couldn't wait to go. They were going to take their sons. Did we want to go with them? It was late, I explained. We'd just had some a few hours ago. I needed to get Julianna back to the hotel.

Even an ice cream adventurer has some regrets. This was one of them. As soon as we woke the next morning and were headed out of town, I regretted not going back for a second round. I'd ignored the motto I thought I lived by: Always say yes to good ice cream.

But this was the high cost of my journey. My ice cream odyssey had left me with a craving for all the good places I'd tried and I can't get back to soon enough.

Ice cream might have been my escape in childhood, a cold cocoon of safety, but it's a different kind of escape as an adult. I want it to be the best version of itself, the ultimate incarnation, an unexpected thrill, a chance to have a "first time" with something once again. It is also an opportunity to see people in a new and unexpected way. As Tyler Malek of Salt & Straw said: "Food is one of the most important things in our culture. It's one of the few ways we now have where we *have* to interact with one another."

As a child I ate ice cream seeking a balm for my wounds. As an adult I have an even greater need, a larger appetite for distraction and comfort, that's harder to satisfy. Jerry Greenfield of Ben & Jerry's asked me if all my ice cream eating had turned into a job. I'd told him no. It was still true. Despite the gallons and gallons of ice cream I'd ingested, I still had the same childish delight when ordering a scoop.

As my dad had taught me, it's the search that makes it fun; it's the shared longings, hardships, and surprises that make our memories. Dad was willing to take risks for the sake of his often misunderstood ideas. Even though Dad had what would now be considered an "unsophisticated" palate because he favored coffee shop fare over haute cuisine, he would have appreciated these self-directed ice cream mavens who answer to no one and nothing except for their obsessive need for perfection. My father loved a good scoop, but sprinkle that with a little quirky self-reliance, and it was his version of the quintessential American Dream.

And I was coming to realize that it was my father, more than anyone, who had taught me to hit the open roads searching for something that would answer my longing and justify my journeys.

On hot summer afternoons, my brothers and I would pile into our Ford station wagon and Dad would drive the dusty roads to Gilroy, stopping for cherries along the way. The juice rolled down our chins and we spit the pits out the open windows. We sang "99 Bottles of Beer" at the top of our lungs until Dad tried to drown us out with Kenny Rogers songs. When the car hit sixty miles an hour, we sometimes stopped dead in the road. Dad sometimes referred to the Ford as "Fixed or Repaired Daily" or "Found on the Road Dead."

Despite these little hiccups, Dad could not take himself off the road. He loved the adventure, the surprise, and never knowing what was waiting for him in the next town. In this way, I guess, his DNA has been passed to me.

I've taken Dad's stubbornness, his orneriness, his joy-loving sensibility, and transmitted it to the search for ice cream. It's too late to do anything about my obsession or to even apologize for it. I'm just left with an anxious delight of not knowing where I might find the next great scoop. Each time I hold a cone in my hand, I wonder: Will this live up to my ridiculously high standards? Will it set off the pleasure sensors in my brain that are now ever more exacting? Will it send me careening back in time to when each flavor was still a new experience?

I never know when I try a new place if the ice cream will be weak or creamy, whether I'll feel disappointment or rapture. And so my ice cream odyssey continues, as I seek out the next revelation, one dripping scoopful at a time.

ACKNOWLEDGMENTS

It takes a strong stomach and an adventurous attitude to research a book about ice cream. Thank you to my daughter, Julianna White, and my husband, Dan White, for always saying yes when I asked to stop for ice cream, no matter how far-flung the location. You were my tireless companions on this journey. You always encouraged me, and for that I am forever grateful.

Thanks to my mom, Sheila Ettinger, for showing me the ways of a culinary raconteur and for providing a fun, safe Grandma Camp so that I could get my work done. Mark and Steve Ettinger, thanks for occasionally allowing me to finish my own dessert as a kid. Thank you to my mother-in-law, Marilyn White, for providing a base for my Los Angeles explorations and to Edie and Doug Achterman for being so supportive of my literary endeavors.

A shout out to Heidi, Luke, and Symone for giving me a place to stay in Milwaukee and for taking me out to eat great frozen custard. I'll never forget your support and that visit to the *Bronze Fonz.*

Special thanks to Rose Newnham, who first told me about the frozen wonders of Penn State, and to Patrick, Henry, and Ellie for showing us such warm hospitality during our stay in New York City. I am graciously indebted to Bessie Weiss for many years of friendship and for pulling strings to set me up with a key interview for this book.

Thanks to my agent Tim Wojcik, who was supportive of this idea from the beginning. A very big thank-you to my editor Jess Renheim, who saw the narrative potential in an ice cream odyssey and gave me the creative freedom to make this book my own.

Thanks to my friends who spent hours discussing ice cream with me and encouraged me along the way: Robin Mejia, Jill Wolfson, Fidel Mejia, and Maria Harkleroad. Thank you, Elizabeth McKenzie, for helping with the subtitle for the book.

Thanks to Liza Warehouse and Peggy Townsend for their wonderful critiques, which helped get this manuscript to completion, and to my other Abbey writing cohorts for always providing a community to laugh, vent, brainstorm, and create.

NOTES

1: CONSUME MASS QUANTITIES

1 "Ice Cream Sales & Trends," International Dairy Foods Association, 2014.

2 According to the Food Channel, the United States currently occupies the number one spot in ice cream consumption.

3 Anne Cooper Funderburg, *Chocolate, Strawberry, and Vanilla: A History of American Ice Cream* (Bowling Green, OH: Bowling Green State University Popular Press, 1995), 7.

4 Anna Berkes, "Ice Cream," *Thomas Jefferson Encyclopedia,* Jefferson Library, https://www.monticello.org/site/research-and-collections/ice-cream.

5 Andrew Hough, "Ice Cream as 'Addictive as Drugs' Says New Study," *Telegraph,* March 5, 2012.

6 Denise Gellene, "East vs. West in Ice Cream Fight: Breyers' Attempt to Scoop Dreyer's Breeds Confusion," *Los Angeles Times,* June 19, 1986.

7 Laurence Vincent, *Brand Real: How Smart Companies Live Their Brand Promise and Inspire Fierce Customer Loyalty* (New York: American Management Association, 2012), 175.

8 Richard D. Lyons, "Obituaries: Reuben Mattus, 81, the Founder of Haagen-Dazs," *New York Times,* January 29, 1994.

9 Doron P. Levin, "Fat Times Are Over for Premium Ice Cream Makers," *New York Times,* July 31, 1994.

10 Lauren Hartill, "Frusen Gldj [*sic*] Ice Cream," *Christian Science Monitor,* September 28, 2000.

2: IT'S ALL ABOUT THE BASE

11 "A Thank You Letter from the Penny Ice Creamery," YouTube video, 2:22, posted by "thepennyice," October 27, 2010, https://www.youtube.com/watch?v=AmWjlA9FlAo&feature=player_embedded.

3: COOL SCHOOL

12 Elizabeth Zierah, "The Nose That Never Knows: The Miseries of Losing One's Sense of Smell," *Slate,* July 8, 2008.

13 George M. Gould, ed., *Medical News: A Weekly Medical Journal,* vol. 63 (Philadelphia: Lea Brothers and Co., September 2, 1893), 27.

14 It should be noted, however, that the concoction has also been described as "a large quantity of cherries and iced milk" on History.com, which lists cholera as a possible cause of his death. See "President Zachary Taylor Dies Unexpectedly," This Day in History, History.com, http://www.history.com/this-day-in-history/president-zachary-taylor-dies-unexpectedly.

15 Rachel Abrams, "Blue Bell Knew About Listeria Issues, F.D.A. Says," *New York Times,* May 7, 2015.

16 Bill Marler, "Everything You Never Wanted to Know About Listeria, but Need To," *Food Poison Journal,* July 4, 2013.

17 Tia Ghose, "Blue Bell's Listeria Scare: How It Grows in Ice Cream," Live Science, April 22, 2015, http://www.livescience.com/50573-what-is-listeria.html.

18 Karen Robinson-Jacobs, "Blue Bell–Deprived Houston Residents Line Up Early as Beloved Ice Cream Returns to Stores," *Dallas Morning News,* August 31, 2015.

19 Richard Newell Hart, *Leavening Agents* (Easton, PA: Chemical Publishing, 1914), 75–76.

20 Ibid., 76.

21 P.F. Fox and Paul L.H. McSweeney, eds., *Advanced Dairy Chemistry,* vol. 1, *Proteins,* 3rd ed. (New York: Springer Science + Business Media, 2003), 1027–1028.

22 Stacey Anderson, "When Keith Richards Wrote '(I Can't Get No) Satisfaction' in His Sleep," *Rolling Stone,* May 9, 2011.

23 Home ice cream makers may consult a free online ice cream butterfat calculator courtesy of *Ice Cream Geek: Explorations into Making and Eating the Food of the Gods,* http://www.icecreamgeek.com/?page_id=817.

4: WHAT MADE MILWAUKEE FAMOUS

24 Monica Davey and Rich Smith, "Murder Rates Rising Sharply in Many U.S. Cities," *New York Times,* August 31, 2015.

25 Kwame Opam, "Watch This 3D Printer Make Pizza Fit for Astronauts," *Verge,* January 24, 2014.

26 "Glendale Drive-in Served as Inspiration for Hangout in 'Happy Days,'" *Milwaukee Journal Sentinel,* August 19, 2008.

27 Lee E. Lawrence, "The Wisconsin Ice Trade," *Wisconsin Magazine of History* 48, no. 4 (Summer 1965): 257–267.

28 Ibid.

29 Ibid.

30 Peter Stott, "The Knickerbocker Ice Company and Inclined Railway at Rockland Lake, New York," *IA: The Journal of the Society for Industrial Archeology* 5, no. 1 (1979): 7–18.

31 "The Fattening Rooms of Calabar," BBC News, July 19, 2007.

32 Joseph C. Potter, "The Coin in Ice Cream," *Challenge* 2, no. 7 (April 1954): 53–55.

33 Patricia Burstein, "After Making His Millions in Ice Cream, Tom Carvel Can Still Dish Out a Few Hard Licks," *People,* July 31, 1978.

34 Glenn Fowler, "Tom Carvel, 84, Gravelly Voice of Soft Ice Cream Chain, Is Dead," *New York Times,* October 22, 1990.

35 Tom Carvel, as quoted in ibid.

36 Burstein, "After Making His Millions."

37 Amy Rabideau Silvers, "Founder of Kopp's, 92, Kept Customers Fed and Custard Flavored," *Milwaukee Journal Sentinel,* June 9, 2003.

38 Kopp's Frozen Custard Flavor Forecast, https://www.kopps.com/flavor-forecast.

39 Colleen Henry, "Prominent Milwaukee Couple Proposes Legalizing Marijuana," WISN 12 News, May 16, 2012.

40 Anne Cooper Funderburg, *Chocolate, Strawberry and Vanilla: A History of American Ice Cream* (Bowling Green, OH: Bowling Green State University Popular Press, 1995), 142.

41 James Joiner, "America's Drunkest States," *Daily Beast,* June 29, 2015.

5: BAD BLOOD, GOOD HUMOR!

42 Michael Daley, "How Brooklyn's First Ice Cream Girl Fought City Hall—and Won," *Daily Beast,* November 13, 2014.

43 Rich Calder and Natalie O'Neill, "Shut the Truck Up: City Bids to Curb Ice-Cream Jingles," *New York Post,* June 28, 2016.

44 Margalit Fox, "Les Waas, Adman, Dies at 94; Gave Mister Softee a Soundtrack," *New York Times,* April 27, 2016.

45 Smithsonian Snapshot Series, "Good Humor Ice Cream Truck," http://newsdesk.si.edu/snapshot/good-humor-ice-cream-truck.

46 Paul Dickson, *The Great American Ice Cream Book* (New York: Galahad Books, 1975), 34.

47 Daniel Neely, "Ding, Ding! The Commodity Aesthetic of Ice Cream Truck Music," in *The Oxford Handbook of Mobile Music Studies,* vol. 2, ed. Sumanth Gopinath and Jason Stanyek (New York: Oxford University Press, 2015), 150.

48 My paraphrase is derived from Daniel Neely's ("Ding, Ding! The Commodity Aesthetic") paraphrase of Anne Cooper Funderburg, *Chocolate, Strawberry, and Vanilla: A History of American Ice Cream* (Bowling Green, OH: Bowling Green State University Popular Press, 1995), 72, 74–75.

49 Funderburg, *Chocolate, Strawberry, and Vanilla,* 130.

50 "Good Humor Corp. Indicted in Brooklyn," *Pittsburgh Post-Gazette,* August 8, 1975.

51 "Good Humor Fined for False Records," *Pittsburgh Press,* April 2, 1976.

52 Mary Murphy, "Kool Man Takes On Mister Softee in Brooklyn Ice Cream Turf War," PIX 11 News, August 20, 2014.

53 Rita Delfiner, "Quiet Heroes Get Their Due. Mayor, Gov, and Regis Honor Winners. They're Making City 'A Better Place,'" *New York Post,* October 8, 2004.

54 Anonymous Captive Journo, "'Rihanna Is Keeping Us from Sleeping or Eating or Going Outside or Using a Bathroom': An Anonymous Rihanna Plane Captive Speaks Out," *Gawker,* November 19, 2012.

55 Ned Berke, "In List of City's Worst Housing Projects, Marlboro Houses Ranks 41st out of 349," *Bensonhurst Bean,* August 19, 2013.

56 "Two Brooklyn Cops Attacked in Marlboro Houses Stairwell; One Suffers Seizure," *Metro,* March 18, 2015.

57 Rose Dosti, "Mello Memories," *Los Angeles Times,* June 27, 1991.

58 "Food of the Eighties: Mello Roll Ice Cream Cone," http://www.inthe80s.com/food/mellorollicecreamconeø.shtml.

59 Matthew J. Perlman and Mark Morales, "Yogo Truck Driver Pulls Knife on Mister Softee Rival in Midtown Ice Cream Turf War," *Daily News,* August 15, 2013.

60 John Marzulli, "Mister Softee Silences Copycat Jingle Used by Rival Ice Cream Truck in Brooklyn Court," *Daily News,* June 27, 2016.

61 Jen Doll, "New York's Ice Cream Truck Turf Wars Get Ugly," *Wire,* July 25, 2012.

62 Ibid.

63 Ibid.

64 Phyllis Furman, "Food Truck Icon Van Leeuwen Artisan Ice Cream Hits Business Sweet Spot and Cooks Up Growth Plan," *Daily News,* August 27, 2012.

6: SHAKE IT OFF

65 Ron Winslow, "The Radium Water Worked Fine Until His Jaw Began to Fall Apart," *Wall Street Journal,* August 1, 1990.

66 N.T. Oliver, *Lee's Priceless Recipes* (Chicago: Laird and Lee, 1895), 37.

67 Anne Cooper Funderburg, *Sundae Best: A History of Soda Fountains* (Bowling Green, OH: Bowling Green State University Popular Press, 2002), 9.

68 Ibid.

69 Samuel Hanbury Smith, *Some Remarks on Medicinal Mineral Waters, Natural and Artificial: Their Efficacy in the Treatment of Chronic Diseases, and Rules for Their Employment, Especially Those of Carlsbad, Ems, Kissingen, Marienbad, Pyrmont, Pullna, Seidschutz, and Heilbrunn* (Hamilton, OH: D.W. Halsey, 1855), US National Library of Medicine Digital Collections.

70 Funderburg, *Sundae Best,* 12.

71 Ibid., 22.

72 Ibid., 22.

73 "Soda Water," *New-York Daily Times,* August 16, 1854.

74 Funderburg, *Sundae Best,* 73–74.

75 Ibid., 75.

76 Mark Pendergrast, *For God, Country & Coca-Cola: The Definitive History of the Great American Soft Drink and the Company That Makes It* (New York: Basic Books, 1993), 26.

77 Ibid.

78 Ibid., 27.

79 Ibid., 88.

80 Ibid., 8, 56.

81 David Musto, "America's First Cocaine Epidemic," *Wilson Quarterly* 13, no. 3 (Summer 1998): 62.

82 James Hamblin, "Why We Took Cocaine Out of Soda," *Atlantic Monthly,* January 31, 2013.

83 Tristan Donovan: *Fizz: How Soda Shook Up the World* (Chicago: Chicago Review Press, 2014), 33.

84 Geraldine M. Quinzio, *Of Sugar and Snow: A History of Ice Cream Making* (Berkeley: University of California Press, 2010), 127.

85 Funderburg, *Sundae Best,* 103.

86 Donovan, *Fizz,* 92.

87 Funderburg, *Sundae Best,* 124.

88 Frank J. Prial, "Takeover Target in 7-Up Fight: A Family-Controlled Company," May 11, 1978, *New York Times,* D1.

89 Anna Fels, "Should We All Take a Bit of Lithium?" *New York Times,* September 14, 2014.

90 Rupal Parekh, "Rewind: '50s Era 7Up Campaign Depicted Soda-Guzzling Babies," *Advertising Age,* August 27, 2012.

91 Jenny Chu, "I Quit Drinking, Then I Got Addicted to Food," *Salon,* June 8, 2014.

92 Ann MacDonald, "Why Eating Slowly May Help You Feel Full Faster," *Harvard Health Blog,* http://www.health.harvard.edu/blog/why-eating-slowly-may-help-you-feel-full-faster-20101019605.

93 Kareem Fahim, "Filling In a Few Blanks in an Old Brooklyn Real Estate Mystery," *New York Times,* July 22, 2008.

94 Ibid.

95 "Farmacy's Vague Reopening," *Brownstoner,* October 6, 2009.

96 Andrew Coe, "No Egg, No Cream, No Ethics," *New York Times,* August 24, 2003.

97 Ibid.

98 A. Emil Hiss, *The Standard Manual of Sodas and Other Beverages* (Chicago: G.P. Engelhard and Company, 1897).

99 Anne Cooper Funderburg, *Chocolate, Strawberry, and Vanilla: A History of American Ice Cream* (Bowling Green, OH: Bowling Green State University Popular Press, 1995), 66–67.

100 Ibid., 69.

101 Sally Shin, "Philadelphia Museum of Art—Edible Still Life," *Hungrysally* blog, November 18, 2015, https://hungrysallyblog.wordpress.com/2015/11/19/philadelphia-museum-of-art-edible-still-life/.

102 Charles Perry, "Raise a Mug to Root Beer's Craft-Brewed Comeback," *Los Angeles Times,* January 28, 2009, F1.

103 "Is Root Beer 'Insidious'?" *New York Times,* October 9, 1896.

104 "The Root Beer Habit," *Washington Post,* March 20, 1898, 22.

105 "Is Root Beer 'Insidious'?"

106 Alex Beggs, "Boozy Root Beer Is Taking the Country by Storm," *Bon Appétit,* December 21, 2015.

107 John Tierney, "What Is Nostalgia Good For? Quite a Bit, Research Shows," *New York Times,* July 8, 2013.

7: WILD COOKIE

108 Anne Cooper Funderburg, *Chocolate, Strawberry, and Vanilla: A History of American Ice Cream* (Bowling Green, OH: Bowling Green State University Popular Press, 1995), 117.

109 Ibid., 121.

110 "Hot Weather Enterprise," *New-York Tribune*, the Washington Post Company, July 25, 1900.

111 Nicola Twilley, "Accounting for Taste: How Packaging Can Make Food More Flavorful," *New Yorker*, November 2, 2015.

112 Antony Page and Robert A. Katz, "The Truth About Ben & Jerry's," *Stanford Social Innovation Review* (Fall 2012).

113 "Getting Your Licks," *Time*, August 10, 1981.

114 Page and Katz, "The Truth About Ben & Jerry's."

115 David Gelles, "How the Social Mission of Ben & Jerry's Survived Being Gobbled Up," *New York Times*, August 21, 2015.

116 Funderburg, *Chocolate, Strawberry, and Vanilla*, 34–35.

117 Nancy Gagliardi, "Female Entrepreneurs Are Redefining the Business of Ice Cream," *Forbes*, October 31, 2014.

118 Denise Restauri, "Meet the Woman Who's Using High Tech to Make Old Fashioned Ice Cream," *Forbes*, September 7, 2016.

119 Rebecca Riffkin, "Americans Still Prefer a Male Boss to a Female Boss," *Gallup*, October 14, 2014.

120 Matt Villano, "What's What with It's-It: Burlingame Institution Takes Frozen Assets to Another Level," *San Francisco Chronicle*, June 10, 2005.

8: BEASTS OF BURDEN

121 Dava Sobel, *Galileo's Daughter* (New York: Walker and Company, 1999), 318.

122 Carlos E. Medina, "Water Buffalo Living in Williston? A UF Professor Keeps a Herd of Water Buffalo on His Farm in Williston," *Gainesville Sun*, May 17, 2010.

123 Ibid.

124 Sam Anderson, "Go Ahead, Milk My Day," *New York Times,* October 11, 2012.

125 Sarah Maslin Nir, "Unwrapping the Mythos of Mast Brothers Chocolate in Brooklyn," *New York Times,* December 20, 2015.

126 "Heinz Carnival Cream (aka Ketchup Ice Cream)—A Mid-Century Recipe Test," *Mid-Century Menu,* http://www.midcenturymenu.com/2014/01/heinz-carnival-cream-aka-ketchup-ice-cream-a-mid-century-recipe-test/.

127 Tobi Elkin, "The 300 Flavors in Jon Snyder's Mind," *Narratively,* August 6, 2014, http://narrative.ly/the-300-flavors-in-jon-snyders-mind/.

128 Ibid.

9: THE CULTURE CLUB

129 Lily Leung, "Yogurtland Founder Returns, Trims Staff," *Orange County Register,* July 18, 2014.

130 Sharon Yang, "Harvard Students 'Devastated' About Yogurtland Closing," *Harvard Crimson,* September 15, 2015.

131 Jonathan Maze, "The Frozen Yogurt Shakeout Begins," *Nation's Restaurant News, On the Margin* blog, December 15, 2015.

132 Markham Heid, "Why Full-Fat Dairy May Be Healthier Than Low-Fat," *Time,* March 5, 2015.

133 "Ice Cream Calls for More Credit Than It Deserves," *Ottawa Citizen,* August 14, 1950.

134 Shane Snow, "What It's Like to Eat Nothing but This Magical, Healthy Ice Cream for 10 Days," *GQ,* January 28, 2016.

135 "Pinkberry in Decline," *NBC Los Angeles,* November 25, 2010.

136 Kate Mather, "Pinkberry Co-founder Gets 7 Years for Beating Homeless Man," *Los Angeles Times,* March 14, 2014.

137 Kimi Yoshino, "Pinkberry Settles Yogurt Suit," *Los Angeles Times,* April 11, 2008.

138 Jennifer Steinhauer, "Pinkberry Settles Suit Over Claims on Dessert," *New York Times,* April 12, 2008.

139 Yoshino, "Pinkberry Settles Yogurt Suit."

140 Tammy Kiter, "I Scream, You Scream, We All Scream for Ice Cream!" *From the Stacks,* New York Historical Society, Museum & Library, July 26, 2013; Dreyer's Grand Ice Cream Oral History Project, Regional Oral History Office, Bancroft Library at University of California, Berkeley, 2013.

141 Shelly Griffith, "George DeBaptiste," *Encyclopedia of Detroit,* Detroit Historical Society.

142 "Full Transcript of TIME's Conversation with President Obama and Misty Copeland," *Time,* March 14, 2016.

143 Dan Mitchell, "Probiotics Are 'A Waste of Money,' Study Finds," *Fortune,* May 10, 2016.

144 Ira Flatow, host, "Not Sweet Side Effects of Artificial Sweeteners," transcript of Science Friday discussion on National Public Radio, July 13, 2013.

145 Alice Park, "The Problem with Sugar-Free Kids," *Time,* n.d.

146 "This Can't Be Yogurt Inc. Can't Believe This Suit," *Wall Street Journal,* March 30, 1984, 1.

147 Karen Blumenthal, "Frozen-Yogurt War Turns Some Dealers Sour on the Business—Big Glut of Franchisees Leads to Charges of Swiping Names, Workers, Menus," *Wall Street Journal,* May 30, 1984, 1.

148 Ibid.

149 Amy Feldman, "How Canada's Serruya Family Made Some $300 Million off a Bunch of Faded Food-Service Brands," *Forbes,* June 19, 2016.

150 Grant Robertson, "Canada's First Family of Freeze Buys Cold Stone," *Globe and Mail,* August 20, 2013.

151 Derek Decloet, "As Sweet Stock Goes Sour, CoolBrands Has to Put Its Money Where Its Mouth Is," *Globe and Mail,* July 19, 2005.

10: ICE CREAM CRAZY

152 Danielle Garesh, "Animal Rights Activist Attacked Outside Palm Springs Restaurant," KESQ/CBS Local 2, March 16, 2015.

153 Marshall Sella, "Does a Duck Have a Soul? How Foie Gras Became the New Fur," *New York* magazine, June 18, 2005.

154 Carly Schwartz, "California Chefs Face Death Threats for Serving Foie Gras," *Huffington Post,* January 14, 2015.

155 A. Solomon et al., "Amyloidogenic Potential of Foie Gras," *Proceedings of the National Academy of Sciences* 104, no. 26 (2007).

156 "Amyloidosis," Mayo Clinic, http://www.mayoclinic.org/diseases-conditions/amyloidosis/basics/definition/con-20024354.

157 Lindsay Goldwert, "'Baby Gaga' Ice Cream Made of Human Breast Milk; Human Cheese Maker Talks Breast Milk Taboos," *Daily News,* February 25, 2011.

158 "Breast Milk Ice Cream Relaunched to 'Celebrate' Royal Baby," *Telegraph,* April 27, 2015.

159 "Making Oyster Ice Cream," YouTube video, 4:24, from KCRW's *Good Food* and *Deep End Dining,* posted by

"eddielinsanity," October 2, 2012. Watch it for yourself at https://www.youtube.com/watch?v=2gZ3AkJP6VM.

160 Sam Mason, "Ice Cream from the Garden," *Lucky Peach #15: Plant Kingdom,* May 19, 2015.

161 Lisa Bramen, "The Genetics of Taste," *Smithsonian,* May 21, 2010.

162 "Why We Love the Pain of Spicy Food," *Wall Street Journal,* December 31, 2014.

163 Eyder Peralta, "Making the Best out of Invasion, Missouri Shop Makes Cicada Ice Cream," NPR, June 7, 2011.

164 "Periodical Cicadas: Life Cycle and Behavior," Ohio State University College of Food, Agricultural and Environmental Science.

165 Kate Bratskeir, "It's Healthier to Eat a Bug Than It Is to Eat a Steak," *Huffington Post,* October 13, 2015.

166 Arnold van Huis, Joost Van Itterbeeck, Harmke Klunder, Esther Mertens, Afton Halloran, Giulia Muir, and Paul Vantomm, "Edible Insects: Future Prospects for Food and Feed Security," Food and Agriculture Organization of the United Nations, Rome, 2013.

167 Cordelia Hebblethwaite, "Eating Locusts: The Crunchy, Kosher Snack Taking Israel by Swarm," *BBC News Magazine,* March 21, 2013.

168 Silvia Killingsworth, "The Black Ant," *New Yorker,* August 24, 2015.

169 "List of Edible Insects," *Girl Meets Bug,* https://edibug.wordpress.com/list-of-edible-insects/; Mission statement, Insects Are Food, 2009, http://www.insectsarefood.com/about_mission.html.

170 Roy Greenslade, "The Economist Seeks Readers by Offering Them Insect-Laced Ice Cream," *Guardian,* July 3, 2015.

171 Peter Gerard, "Make Escamoles Ice Cream in 7 Easy Steps," *Bugsfeed: A Taste of Insects,* May 2, 2016.

EPILOGUE: JERSEY GIRL

172 Andrew Hough, "Ice Cream as 'Addictive as Drugs' Says New Study," *Telegraph,* March 5, 2012.

173 Josh Harkinson, "You're Drinking the Wrong Milk," *Mother Jones,* March 12, 2014.

174 Penelope Green, "Table-to-Farm Pioneer," *New York Times,* December 24, 2013.

175 Michael Wilson, "Stolen, Sold and Savored: Ice Cream Is a Hot Commodity in Manhattan," *New York Times,* September 4, 2016.

INDEX

Note: Page numbers in *italics* refer to illustrations.

Index

ABOUT THE AUTHOR

Amy Ettinger is an essayist, journalist, and editor. She has written for *The New York Times*, *New York* magazine, *The Washington Post*, *Salon*, and *The Huffington Post*. She lives in Santa Cruz, California, with her husband and daughter.